Sexual Harassment in Higher Education

Garland Studies in Higher Education
(Vol. 12)
Garland Reference Library of Social Science
(Vol. 1034)

Sexual Harassment
in Higher Education
Reflections and New Perspectives

Billie Wright Dziech
Michael W. Hawkins

GARLAND PUBLISHING, INC.
A MEMBER OF THE TAYLOR & FRANCIS GROUP
New York & London
1998

Library of Congress Cataloging-in-Publication Data

Dziech, Billie Wright, 1941–
      Sexual harassment in higher education : reflections and new
perspectives / Billie Wright Dziech, Michael W. Hawkins.
          p.   cm. — (Garland reference library of social science ;
vol. 1034. Garland studies in higher education ; vol. 12)
      Includes bibliographical references (p.) and index.
      ISBN 0-8153-2036-1 (hard : alk. paper)
      1. Sexual harassment in universities and colleges—United States.
2. Universities and colleges—United States—Sociological aspects.
I. Hawkins, Michael W.   II. Title.   III. Series: Garland reference library
of social science ; v. 1034.   IV. Series: Garland reference library of
social science. Garland studies in higher education ; vol. 12.
LC212.862.D957   1998
306.43—dc21   98–14229
                                                        CIP

The following have generously given permission to use quotations from these
copyrighted works: From "P.C. Follies: The Year in Review," Copyright, 1992,
U.S. News & World Report, by permission of *U.S. News & World Report.*
From the Antioch College Sexual Offense Prevention Policy, by permission
of Antioch College Office of Public Relations. From the University of Virginia
Sexual Harassment Policy documents and Dr. Ann J. Lane's comments, by
permission of Dr. Ann J. Lane.

Printed on acid-free, 250-year-life paper
Manufactured in the United States of America

Contents

Series Editor's Preface

Higher education is a multifaceted phenomenon in modern society, combining a variety of institutions and an increasing diversity of students, a range of purposes and functions, and different orientations. The series combines research-based monographs, analyses, and discussions of broader issues and reference books related to all aspects of higher education. It is concerned with policy as well as practice from a global perspective. The series is dedicated to illuminating the reality of higher and postsecondary education in contemporary society.

Philip G. Altbach
Boston College

Foreword

For the last few years, whenever I discuss sexual harassment in my undergraduate courses or during colloquia at colleges and universities, I typically begin with the following exercise: I ask students to identify the activities that would be summarized under the heading "campus violence." Students mention the following: hazing, rape, assault, battering, emotional abuse, and date rape, but the term "sexual harassment" is seldom, if ever, included. This omission still surprises me since current estimates of sexual harassment of college students by professors approximate 50 percent, ranging from sexual come-ons to sexual coercion (faculty threatening to lower students' grades for noncompliance with requests for sexual activity).

Students' responses reflect the silence that still surrounds sexual harassment on college campuses: sexual harassment remains a "hidden issue," as the Project on the Status and Education of Women referred to it in 1978. Since this 1978 report by the PSEW, much has been written about academic sexual harassment. One of the first books that addressed this issue is the classic *The Lecherous Professor* by Billie Dziech and Linda Weiner, which was published in 1984. In 1990, my edited volume *Ivory Power: Sexual Harassment on College Campuses* was published, with its second edition (*Sexual Harassment on College Campuses: Abusing the Ivory Power*) following in 1996. In addition to these texts, there are also the thousands of journal articles, book chapters, and conference presentations on academic sexual harassment that have appeared since 1978—in fields as diverse as psychology, English, business, women's studies, law, medicine, education, anthropology, and sociology.

In addition to the scholarly attention focused on academic sexual harassment are the many training programs on sexual harassment awareness provided to faculty, college administrators, nonfaculty campus employees, and students. Annual conferences on campus sexual victimization are common, many sponsored by organizations devoted to ending academic sexual harassment, including the Canadian Association Against Sexual Harassment and Sociologists Against Sexual Harassment.

In the intervening years, many campuses have revised their policy statements—some even including "consensual relationships" as part of sexual harassment—and have revised their investigatory procedures to deal with the psychology of the victimization process (such issues as powerlessness, anger, embarrassment, and fear of retaliation).

Why, then, in the years subsequent to all these programs and writings on sexual harassment do we still find college students in 1997 omitting the term "sexual harassment" from a list of campus violence?

In some of my own writings, I have offered the following explanation for why sexual harassment is the *hidden campus violence*. Sexual harassment confronts students with perceptions that are often invalidated by the campus. Students' experiences are relabeled as anything *but* sexual harassment, especially as "interpersonal problems" between two people rather than as an organizational issue in which the campus *must* intervene. Most students doubt their experiences; they are encouraged to conform to their professors' and campus administrators' relabeling of the experiences. Professors are seen as essential because they generate power: they give grades, write letters of recommendation, and speak to colleagues about students' performance in classes. Professors' greatest power lies in their capacity to motivate students to learn or convince them to end their college career. Consequently, students remain silent about their experiences with sexual harassment. And, the actual incidence of sexual harassment on college campuses remains hidden.

Through my work as a consultant to colleges and universities, I have learned that students are typically not informed about the incidence of sexual harassment in general or on their campus specifically. This information is kept hidden from them. A "null environment" is set up for them on campus where they are not provided with necessary information, especially concerning the sanctions for sexual harassment. They thus may be likely to reinterpret their experiences as not sexual harassment and remain silent about their victimization.

Furthermore, many research studies and training programs on sexual harassment still ask the question: "Does sexual harassment happen to college students?" If we continue to focus on this question and try to quantify sexual harassment, we perpetrate the belief that sexual harassment is not prevalent. Instead of asking "Does it exist?" let's instead ask, "What can we do about it?"

This latter question is one the current text addresses. This book is a handbook and guide for those who develop policies and procedures related to sexual harassment. It offers ways campus administrators, for example, can redefine power: not as "power over" students, but as "empowering" them. Through policies and procedures that take into account the psychology of the victimization process, institutions can encourage students to come forth with their concerns in a safe environment where they will not experience retaliation. These procedures can also make it very clear to faculty that sexual harassment is not tolerated at their college or university and that they will be sanctioned for it.

This text can assist professors who sexually harass students in labeling their behavior as sexual harassment—not as flirtation, paying compliment, or flattery. The text also helps faculty to admit to the inherent power differential between themselves and their students.

Finally, this text reminds all of us that an adequate program for dealing with sexual harassment on college campuses requires more than a general policy against the behavior. It requires the efforts and support of the campus administration, faculty, employees, and students, and the continual training of all members of the campus community, as well as a procedure that *encourages*, not merely allows, complaints. Once this campus-wide program is in place, the entire campus will benefit from an environment of cooperation, respect, and dignity. Such a program will increase the visibility of sexual harassment on college campuses, thereby keeping this form of victimization hidden no longer.

Michelle Paludi
Principal, Michelle Paludi & Associates
Consultants in Sexual Harassment
Schenectady, New York

Acknowledgments

We owe our deepest gratitude to the following who helped to make this work possible: Rob Dziech II, Lisa May Evans, Kimberlee S. Ullner, and Cheryl E. Bruner for legal research and writing assistance; Becky Gantz, Anne Mess, and Kelly Owens Dziech for manuscript preparation; Anne Abate, Mari Randolph, Jennifer Barnes, and Kelly Owens for library assistance at Dinsmore & Shohl; the University of Cincinnati and Dinsmore & Shohl LLP for their support; and, most of all, to Diane, Rob, and our children.

Acknowledgments

Introduction

As a lawyer primarily representing colleges and universities in the area of sexual harassment and other discrimination claims, I am very aware of the significance of the sexual harassment issue on campus. It impacts the entire organization from the student to the faculty member, to the Provost's office, and in some cases to the president and board. It may also significantly impact the entire community in which the institution is located.

Billie Dziech and I came to know each other while I was representing a university in a sexual harassment case. One thing we both realized was that in order for colleges and universities to avoid claims and liability and create an environment free of sexual harassment, more dialogue needed to exist on the subject. Also, having done a significant amount of in-house training to faculty and staff at colleges and universities on sexual harassment, we have learned that there is much confusion on this issue. One discussion led to another and thus this book.

While working on this book over the last two years, the law in this area has continued to develop and the media has covered some of the more sensational sexual harassment issues and incidents in the country. This process will continue after this book is in print and we will continue to learn. The key thing to learn from this book and the state of this issue in the United States is for colleges, universities, faculty, and students to be more proactive and preventative versus being engaged in damage control. In addition, they should all find ways to dialogue on this subject and reduce the problems associated with claims of sexual harassment and how to monitor it on campuses throughout the country.

I would also like to note that since the legal climate on this subject is continuously changing, anyone dealing with a sexual harassment issue should consult with counsel experienced with this area of the law. In conclusion, I'd like to note that this book and the discussions contained in it do not ignore the fact that there are claims that are without merit or certainly do not constitute sexual harassment under the law. Each incident must be evaluated on a case-by-case basis to determine whether it involves sexual harassment or conduct that may be viewed as inappropriate or without merit. Only through a proper review of each case will colleges, universities, faculty, and students recognize the rights and interests of all affected by the issue of sexual harassment.

Michael W. Hawkins

When Philip Altbach first approached me about writing a new book on sexual harassment, I agreed because I thought it would be a quick and easy task; but now that the manuscript is ready to be sent to the publisher, I know that second books are neither quick nor easy. *The Lecherous Professor* explored a familiar but newly labeled behavior in the unique setting of academe, and we were lucky in being the first with a work that was bound to be written sooner or later. This new book does not revisit old territory by surveying the research or attempting yet another definition of the term. *Sexual Harassment on Campus* instead explores some of the controversial and overlooked concerns that have emerged in educators' struggle to understand and cope with this elusive problem.

Writing about harassment is risky business because so many, on campus and off, construe it solely through a few high visibility cases and their own narrow interests and experiences. But to be able to reflect accurately on the individual and institutional costs of the behavior requires a shedding of preconceptions and biases and attentiveness to the conflicting voices heard on the American campus today. In the course of speaking at conferences, I have discovered there is no monolithic approach. Some institutions have devoted enormous time and resources to the issue, others almost none at all. In visiting colleges and universities across the country, I have talked with students who will be forever scarred by the behavior and with others who underwent almost identical experiences and emerged seemingly untouched. I have met faculty and administrators, both male and female, who were willing to risk their credibility and in some respects their careers on a highly controversial issue. They were a welcome antidote to those who made me less optimistic about my profession.

Sometimes a casual remark by a friend can bring these kinds of experiences into focus. Michelle Paludi was invited to speak at the same time as I at a prestigious university where one of the powerful professors who had married a student opposed adoption of a sexual harassment policy and boycotted our presentation. During the discussion period we both tried to keep our comments as moderate as possible to avoid exacerbating tensions on the already polarized campus. I remember being prepared to explain that while I strongly support bans on intimate relationships between faculty and students, I believe policies should contain provisions for unique circumstances in which "true love" occasionally occurs. Ironically, however, controversy erupted not over consensual relationships but when a radical feminist walked out after claiming that Michelle was being "too easy" on male perpetrators. After describing a similar bizarre experience of my own, I asked Michelle recently if she recalled that night, and she said something I won't forget: "Sure, I do. Why is it we remember the few who leave and not all the people who stay?"

In some respects, this book is an answer to that question. We remember the ones who leave because they shock us into recognition of the volatility and complexity of this issue. We remember the people who are uncivil or uncomprehending because we wish we had succeeded at convincing them to approach sexual harassment less simplistically, to see it through the pain of those who've been subjected to it and through the costs institutions have had to pay for it. The handful who deny the seriousness of harassment are, for me, as much a professional as a gender concern; and this book reflects that orientation. I began writing about harassment because I was a teacher who didn't like what she saw and heard about the behaviors of some of her colleagues. I believe there is nothing clever or articulate about faculty who depend on sex imagery to get people's attention. I'm embarrassed by the adolescent banality that characterizes the "true confessions" of professors who have slept with students, and I am stunned at some educators' pathetic need to believe, against all logic, that they're physically desirable to the typical student.

What worries me now is the public's changing attitude toward academe, because I suspect that it will have a significant impact on the sexual harassment issue. As taxpayers and contributors grow less tolerant of the enormous costs of higher education and less patient with educators' unique working conditions, academicians will need to cultivate sensitivity and pragmatism that do not come easily to those who are accustomed to having enormous control over others and over their own daily routines. Sexual harassment may emerge as a key issue on which educators will be required to demonstrate a good faith commitment to those who pay the bills, and that is the assumption upon which much of the following discussion is based.

Michael Hawkins and I begin by tracing the legal and regulatory evolution of the issue and by assessing the problems that confront higher education as it approaches a new century. Chapter Two challenges institutions to move beyond "cookie cutter" approaches to policy making and to confront harassment through analyses of their unique student and organizational characteristics and cultures. Chapter Three departs from conventional discussions by stressing the need for more specialized treatment of female harassees, for less reliance on the term "victim," and for greater investigation of women who appear unscathed by the behavior. The fourth chapter introduces a subject that has as yet captured little interest from researchers—the plight of the male on campus. Chapter Five attempts to define the most familiar myths about consensual relationships and argues that bans are the only safe course in dealing with them. The final section, certain to be controversial, contends that the sexual harassment issue has exposed higher education's excesses and contradictions and that its handling of the problem will be scrutinized carefully by an increasingly skeptical public.

The writing is deliberately non-academic because the issue demands "straight talk." The book will not win universal approval from academicians, but it's an honest work. After so many years of dealing with the topic, I am content to tell the truth as I see it, and I'm not bothered by being called a "prude" or a "Puritan." The academic life is a choice, and teaching is a responsibility, not an entitlement. When I accept other people's money to do my job, I contract with them to subordinate my needs and desires to the welfare of my students.

Anecdotal evidence, case law, and research prove indisputably that students suffer when professors engage them in intimate relationships and when they employ self-indulgent teaching methods that offend or intimidate. If it is prudish to ask people to do their work correctly, then I accept the label.

Second books are different from first, but I hope this one will be read with attention because I believe it poses even greater challenges to students, the public, and especially the academic profession. We have moved beyond the need for definitions and incidence statistics. Now that the foundations have been laid, educators will be increasingly called upon to establish priorities and make serious, sometimes painful choices. And that will not be an easy task.

Billie Wright Dziech

Sexual Harassment in Higher Education

Chapter One
Unfinished Business
The Evolution of an Issue

Will this never finish?
　　　　　　—Samuel Beckett, *Endgame*

We do what we can.
　　　　　　—Samuel Beckett, *Endgame*

As the twentieth century draws to a close, higher education has yet to resolve the confusion and complexity surrounding the issue of sexual harassment. To some extent, this is predictable because serious public discourse about the subject did not begin until two decades ago, and most Americans date their first genuine interest in the issue to 1991, when Clarence Thomas and Anita Hill confronted each other in a "he said/she said" media spectacle that perplexed and polarized the nation. But preoccupation with political theater and public morality plays can discourage recognition of the pervasiveness and longevity of the problem, which did not originate with people like Hill and Thomas or Paula Corbin Jones and Bill Clinton. As a matter of fact, two of the most interesting accounts of harassment appeared centuries before the United States Congress passed legislation making it illegal.

Given that many falsely assume sexual harassment to be a women's issue, it is perhaps ironic that one of the first recorded incidents of the behavior involved a male rather than a female. The book of Genesis tells the story of Joseph, who, after being sold by his brothers to the Ishmaelites, became a slave in the house of Potiphar, an officer of the Egyptian pharaoh. Having won favor in his master's eyes, Joseph was made overseer of the house and flourished there until Potiphar's wife attempted to seduce the "well favored"[1] young man. He successfully resisted her advances until one day she caught him by his clothing, and he fled, leaving his garment in her hand. The wife then accused Joseph of trying to seduce her, and Potiphar sent him to languish in prison.

Susanna, the heroine of another ancient tale of harassment, fared better than Joseph, although a male received more credit than she for her ordeal. In the tale of Susanna and the elders in the Apocrypha, the beautiful wife of Joachim aroused the passions of two judges or elders, who spied on her as she bathed in private in her garden. When they propositioned her and she refused their advances, they falsely accused her of being with a young man and sought to have her put to death. The Apocrypha notes, "The assembly believed them, because they were elders of the people and judges: and they condemned her to death."[2]

At this point a youth named Daniel intervened and exposed the plot. Referring to one of the elders as an "old relic of wicked days,"[3] Daniel admonished the two judges, "This is how you both have been dealing with the daughters of Israel, and they were intimate with you through fear."[4] The two were then put to death, "and from that day onward Daniel had a great reputation among the people."[5] Susanna, the classic victim, was thus saved, her most memorable words being those she uttered when trapped by the elders: "I am hemmed in on every side."[6]

Legal and Regulatory Evolution of the Issue

Sexual harassment is usually about "fear" and being "hemmed in on every side" by individuals whose power can make protest dangerous. For thousands of years the behavior was considered so normal, innocuous, or impossible to counter that it was not even given a name. Devoid of identifying terminology, it was dismissed by society and the legal system because, as Catherine MacKinnon, widely regarded as the legal architect of sexual harassment theory, observed, "It is not surprising . . . that women would not complain of an experience for which there has been no name. Until 1976, lacking a term to express it, sexual harassment was literally unspeakable, which made generalized, shared and social definition of it inaccessible."[7]

Awareness and understanding grew as women began entering the workforce in larger numbers and the women's movement and sexual revolution of the 1970s gradually altered society's perceptions of the genders. Before cases dealing with the issue were actually adjudicated, the term appeared in a 1976 *Redbook*[8] article and in the writing of the Working Women United Institute[9] and the Alliance Against Sexual Coercion.[10] As discussion increased, the courts began to hear from women who sought redress for physical and emotional injuries resulting from what the law would eventually describe as "sexual harassment." During this period, federal statutes such as the Civil Rights Act of 1964, the Equal Employment Opportunity Act of 1972, and the Education Act Amendment of 1972 contained provisions prohibiting sex discrimination. Because sexual harassment affects both institutional employees and students, all of these were relevant to campuses. It was not until 1975, however, that a federal court actually heard a case in which sexual harassment was the primary cause of action.

In *Corne v. Bausch and Lomb, Inc.*,[11] two female employees resigned after their supervisor repeatedly made verbal and physical advances. They argued that the company was liable for the supervisor's behavior. The Arizona court that had the case, like others which had reviewed sexual harassment claims, regarded the harasser's conduct as a personal matter relating to the relationship between the parties, as opposed to an issue affecting women as a group.

There is nothing in [Title VII] which could reasonably be construed to have it apply to "verbal and physical advances" by another employee, even though he be in a supervisory capacity where such complained of acts or conduct had no relationship to the nature of employment.

It would be ludicrous to hold that the sort of activity involved here was contemplated by the Act. . . . Also, an outgrowth of holding such activity to be actionable under Title VII would be a potential federal lawsuit every time any employee made amorous or sexually oriented advances toward another. The only sure way an employer could avoid such charges would be to have employees who were asexual.[12]

Thus the court held that the employer could not be liable for the harasser's conduct under any of the federal anti-discrimination statutes.

MacKinnon made history in the 1976 case of *Williams v. Saxbe* when she observed that courts' viewing of sexual harassment as a personal matter ignored the intent behind Title VII of the 1964 Civil Rights Act. She reasoned that because "sexual harassment does occur to a large and diverse population of women, [this] supports an analysis that it occurs *because* of their group characteristics, that is, sex."[13] Therefore, she maintained, the victim should have a remedy under Title VII. A federal district court subsequently held that such liability could be found where the conduct at issue creates an "artificial barrier to employment that was placed before one gender and not the other, despite the fact that both genders were similarly situated."[14] The ruling established the foundation of what would become known as "quid pro quo" sexual harassment, a form of discrimination in which the employer conditions job benefits or privileges on the employee's willingness to submit to sexual favors.[15]

Although sexual harassment law began evolving in the employment arena under Title VII, students remained immune to federal legislation until 1980, when the first charge of sexual harassment was brought in federal court under Title IX of the 1972 Education Act Amendments. In *Alexander v. Yale University,*[16] five Yale students and one professor filed an action involving a range of claims. Only one student, who claimed that her professor offered to give her an A in exchange for sexual favors and then gave her a C when she refused, was allowed to proceed in the action.[17]

In holding that the student could maintain an action under Title IX, the *Alexander* court was the first to analogize Title IX actions for sexual harassment to Title VII.[18] It stated that "it is perfectly reasonable to maintain that academic advancement conditioned upon submission to sexual demands constitutes sex discrimination in education, just as questions of job retention or promotion tied to sexual demands from supervisors have become increasingly recognized as potential violations of Title VII's ban against sex discrimination in employment."[19] Even though the district court found that the student stated a valid claim for sexual harassment under Title IX, the suit was dismissed in 1980 because she had graduated from Yale, and the university had established a grievance procedure for dealing with complaints, which was the relief she sought in the action. As in other early cases under Title VII, the *Alexander* court recognized a cause of action for quid pro quo sexual harassment only if the plaintiff could show that a refusal to submit to sexual demands had resulted in denial of some "tangible benefit." Without showing a direct causal connection between these factors, courts would not, at that point, allow relief under federal anti-discrimination statutes.

The Equal Employment Opportunity Commission's 1980 Guidelines on Discrimination Because of Sex included a definition of sexual harassment that reflected developing trends in the courts. The Guidelines defined sexual harassment to include not only what has become known as quid pro quo sexual harassment—requests for sexual favors where submission to or rejection of such conduct affects the terms or conditions of employment—but also "hostile environment" sexual harassment—"conduct [which] has the purpose or effect of substantially interfering with an individual's work performance or creating an intimidating, hostile or offensive work environment."[20]

In 1980 and 1981, two federal court decisions, *Brown v. City of Guthrie*[21] and *Bundy v. Jackson*,[22] became the first cases in which courts allowed plaintiffs to succeed in sexual harassment claims under Title VII without showing the loss of a "tangible job benefit." These cases were the first to recognize that even when there is no overt demand for sexual favors, another category of behavior can create covert barriers to equality and be equally damaging physically and psychologically. Ultimately, this would become known as "hostile environment" sexual harassment, the most controversial and highly litigated area of the issue.

Six years elapsed between the date of the first federal hostile environment sexual harassment victory and the date on which the United States Supreme Court finally provided federal courts with a consistent framework within which to analyze the growing number of sexual harassment claims. In *Meritor Savings Bank, FSB. v. Vinson*,[23] the Supreme Court affirmed that the prohibition against sex discrimination under Title VII provided a basis for relief for hostile environment sexual harassment. The Court's decision established several key points.

Title VII protects employees from sexual harassment caused by sexually based words or conduct that results in a pervasive, unwelcome, hostile and offensive work environment. The actions must be severe and perva-

sive enough to alter the employee's conditions of employment, but no economic job related threat is necessary.

An employee's "voluntary" participation is not significant, so long as the environment is "unwelcome."

Evidence of matters such as an employee's dress and personal fantasies may be relevant to whether or not the sexual actions created an unwelcome hostile environment.

An employer's liability for the actions of its supervisors is to be determined on a case by case basis. Relevant evidence will include the scope of the supervisor's authority, the knowledge of other managers of the events in question, the employer's policies concerning sexual harassment, and the existence of a complaint procedure which is known and available to employees.[24]

While the *Meritor* decision provided a framework within which courts could begin to decide whether an individual's conduct was actionable, it did little to sort out confusion among and within federal court systems about the extent of an employer's liability for actions of offending employees or about the standard to be used in deciding whether conduct is severe and pervasive enough to alter terms and conditions of employment. As a result, there is currently no consensus, and each federal circuit must attempt to fashion appropriate criteria for evaluating these issues.

Despite the similarities between the prohibition against sex discrimination under Titles VII and IX, federal courts expanded liability for sexual harassment in the workplace but resisted such expansion in Title IX cases. For example, they refused to find liability for quid pro quo sexual harassment where the harassee could not demonstrate an associated loss of a tangible benefit and would not, until very recently, recognize a cause of action under Title IX for hostile environment sexual harassment. As late as 1989, in *Bougher v. University of Pittsburgh*,[25] a federal district court refused to find that Title IX provided such relief. Ironically, only three years earlier in *Moire v. Temple University School of Nursing*,[26] the same district court had inferred that Title IX could prohibit hostile environment sexual harassment and suggested that the EEOC Guidelines on Discrimination Because of Sex could apply to Title IX.

Unlike the EEOC, which has established and revised its guidelines to reflect recent court decisions, the Department of Education, which enforces the anti-discrimination provisions of Title IX of the Education Act Amendments of 1972, has not adopted a formal definition of sexual harassment. Instead, in 1981, the Office for Civil Rights (OCR) of the Department of Education promulgated a definition in a policy memorandum which states simply that "sexual harassment consists of verbal or physical conduct of a sexual nature imposed on the basis of sex by an employer or agent of a recipient [of federal funds] that denies, limits, provides different, or conditions the provision of aid, benefits, services or treatment protected under Title IX."[27] However, because this definition is not included in the agency's regulations, it is usually not referred to by courts in sexual harassment cases brought under Title IX.

In 1992, when it appeared that the scope of recovery for hostile environment sexual harassment under Title IX would not develop, the Supreme Court heard a case involving a high school student who alleged she had been sexually harassed by an individual who was both her athletic coach and a faculty member. In *Franklin v. Gwinnett County Public Schools*,[28] Christina Franklin alleged that her coach had engaged her in sexually oriented conversation, solicited sexual favors, forcibly kissed her on the mouth, and harassed her at home. Claiming that school officials were aware of the conduct and took no action, she sought equitable relief as well as monetary damages, which many courts prior to the time had held were unavailable to plaintiffs under Title IX.

In addressing liability and the availability of monetary damages under Title IX, the *Franklin* Court stated:

[W]hen a supervisor sexually harasses a subordinate because of the subordinate's sex, that supervisor "discriminates" on the basis of sex [citations omitted]. . . . We believe the same rule applies when a teacher sexually harasses and abuses a student. Congress surely did not intend for federal monies to be expended to support the intentional actions it sought by statute to proscribe.[29]

The *Franklin* ruling established a new cause of action and broadened the remedies available under Title IX. In rendering its decision, the Supreme Court borrowed language which it had employed in its 1986 ruling in *Meritor Savings Bank, FSB. v. Vinson,* a Title VII sexual harassment claim. It stated that in the future, federal courts analyzing Title IX sexual harassment claims should look to Title VII as a guide for determining liability.

Despite the growing number of sexual harassment claims litigated in the federal court system within the last ten years, the Supreme Court has been cautious in providing more definite boundaries for determining liability under Titles VII and IX, leaving federal courts to ascertain details on a case-by-case basis. As lower courts continue to struggle with the arduous task of evaluating sexual harassment under both Titles VII and IX, the Supreme Court occasionally adds a piece to the puzzle—never really providing a clear portrait of the full extent of the law, but implying that in time a complete picture may emerge.

In its most recent decision, *Harris v. Forklift Systems, Inc.,*[30] the Supreme Court broadened the scope of sexual harassment liability for employers by holding that the victim of hostile or abusive work environment sexual harassment need not show that the improper conduct seriously affected his/her psychological well-being or led to an injury. The Court held that such proof was not required since the standard established under Title VII "takes a middle path between making actionable any conduct that is merely offensive and requiring the conduct to cause a tangible psychological injury."[31] *Harris* also reaffirmed the dual standard established in *Meritor,* which requires plaintiffs to prove both that a "reasonable person" would have found the environment to be hostile or abusive.[32] Although this decision reduced the burden on plaintiffs pursuing claims under Title VII, it did little to assist in establishing a bright-line standard for separating conduct that is merely offensive from that which creates a hostile environment.

In addition to the Supreme Court, another source of relief for plaintiffs came from the United States Congress in the form of the Civil Rights Act of 1991. Prior to the 1991 Act, remedies available to plaintiffs in sexual harassment cases were limited to equitable relief in the form of back pay, front pay, or reinstatement. Under the new legislation, compensatory and punitive damages are available under certain circumstances, and a trial by jury is also an option.

The availability of such remedies can be expected to prompt greater numbers of both valid and frivolous claims.

In sorting out the valid from the frivolous, the federal court system has attempted to establish some degree of uniformity and predictability. While the Supreme Court's decision in *Harris* helped to clarify whether an alleged harassee must prove psychological injury, the Court overlooked the opportunity to address another inconsistency, that of applying an objective test to identify illegal behavior. Some federal circuits have concluded such decisions should be based on a "reasonable woman" standard.[33] In 1991, the Ninth Circuit Court of Appeals adopted this approach in maintaining that "a sex-blind reasonable person standard tends to be male-biased and tends to systematically ignore the experiences of women."[34] Although opponents argue that the reasonable woman standard is unworkable because a man cannot suppose what a reasonable woman would think without relying on stereotypes, in its proposed Guidelines on Harassment, the EEOC, nevertheless, embraced the standard; and the problem now confronting litigators is that the Supreme Court's decision to apply the reasonable person test may imply rejection of the reasonable woman standard employed by the EEOC.

Further inconsistency exists within the federal judicial system with respect to assessing liability under Title VII. In *Meritor*, the Court stated that liability for sexual harassment claims is to be determined under traditional common law agency principles.[35] However, because agency law principles vary from state to state, there is not, and can never be, a uniform legal basis for assessing liability between circuits or within federal circuits, since most circuit courts exercise jurisdiction over federal cases in more than one state. In addition, further conflict over liability has arisen since at least one federal circuit has held that individuals can be held personally liable under Title VII.[36]

Meanwhile, as the United States Congress and the federal judicial system struggle with the issue, administrative agencies, state judicial systems, and state legislators face similar battles. Unlike the Department of Education's OCR, which issued a policy statement in 1981 and has since remained silent, the EEOC has attempted to clarify its rules. In 1990, it issued Policy Guidance on Current Issues of Sexual Harassment. This document set forth its position on developing aspects of sexual harassment law. Then in 1993, the EEOC issued proposed Guidelines on Harassment, but these were not finalized because of negative public comment and have not been reissued.

With the exception of Alabama, Georgia, and Mississippi, all states have enacted Fair Employment Practices statutes which prohibit discrimination on the basis of sex in both private and public employment. (Georgia and Mississippi have statutes which prohibit discrimination only in the public sector.) While the remedies available under these statutes vary from state to state, the courts in various jurisdictions have taken the lead in interpreting statutes to prohibit both quid pro quo and hostile environment sexual harassment. Some state courts have gone a step further and have recognized new "sexual harassment tort," or have expanded liability under existing tort law in order to provide relief to plaintiffs.[37]

Problems Confronting Academe

Overview

As various components of the legal system gave shape and form to sexual harassment law under Title VII, collegiate institutions recognized responsibility for discouraging and controlling sexual harassment. Many assumed that once people understood the pervasiveness of the problem and its often devastating effects, that once policies, procedures, and laws were in place, the behavior would cease to trouble the American campus. Great strides were made as a result of this initial optimism. Increasingly, people on and off campus do appear to "get" the problem. Even the most obstreperous now acknowledge the existence of harassment, reportage is higher than ever before, and though too often sensationalized, the issue continues to capture media and public attention.

But if the last decades have taught anything, it is that sexual harassment is far more complex and enigmatic than anyone originally assumed; and taken collectively, the uncertainties and controversies that have marked progress have also tempered idealism. Yesterday acceptable and unacceptable gender behaviors seemed easily identifiable; and while most distinctions are generally apparent, the confusion about definition remains. It is exacerbated by the existence of ambiguous or "gray" behaviors and situations about which even reasonable women and men disagree, by confusion about distinctions between illegal as opposed to inappropriate behavior. Once it seemed possible to generalize policies and procedures to varied institutions; now there is a need for these, like education and training programs, to be adapted to unique cultural and organizational environments.

Yesterday those concerned about harassment assumed that a "victim was a victim" and that paramount responsibility should be directed toward protecting people from the indignity and possible damage of sexual harassment. While this must remain the primary imperative, experience has demonstrated that reactions to the behavior vary and that there are, in some instances, serious hazards in overstating the victimization theme. Today the need is to discover when and how to stress strength as well as helplessness, and self-help as well as protection.

Because sexual harassment was initially defined as a women's issue, little attention was paid to its effects on males who were subjected to or who witnessed the behavior. Two decades ago few foresaw that male alienation and battles over political correctness would eventually color discussion of harassment and create acrimony and division. Few foresaw that as women moved into positions of power and authority, sexual harassment complaints would be brought by males against females.[38] Nor was it possible to predict that at the turn of the century there would be debate over consensual relationships between faculty and students and, most enigmatic and perhaps most peculiar of all, that a small number of feminists would eventually argue that sexual harassment policy is an attempt to infanticize and desexualize women.

In the 1980s, works like *The Lecherous Professor* and *Ivory Power* seemed adventurous in their attempts to provoke understanding of a relatively obscure campus issue. Today there are thousands of publications on sexual harassment. Research and surveys are an ongoing national activity, and conferences regularly include programs on the topic. The current challenge is much different. It is not so much to encourage people to "get" harassment, but rather "to get it right," not to continue arguing the credibility of the issue, but rather to focus on the oversimplified, neglected, and unresolved areas of concern.

What the public, law makers, and educators need now is not more horrific statistics and salacious anecdotes, but attempts to place stories and numbers within meaningful contexts. What is needed is pragmatism and balance in discussion, recognition that sexual harassment evolves from the inappropriate behaviors of an aberrant few and is exacerbated by misunderstandings, hostilities, and ignorance that have characterized gender relations for centuries. What is most essential is recognizing that dialogue and debate about sexual harassment have moved almost imperceptibly into a new era in which people must be prepared to confront the complexity, ambiguity, and unpredictability that will continue to characterize an enduring human concern.

Definitional Ambiguity

While the legal dimensions of the issue have become increasingly secure and clear, definitional ambiguity remains a problem. Quid pro quo sexual harassment is widely understood and censured because the wrong of an authority figure threatening or attempting to bribe a student or employee for sex is obvious. In various analogue studies at academic institutions, respondents of both genders were consistently able to recognize severe cases of harassment and clear absence of the behavior.[39] Hostile environment harassment was another matter. Milder forms of harassment elicited differing levels of recognition,[40] and extensive field research needs to be done to clarify whether these findings can be replicated in the "real world" of the campus. There, as elsewhere, regulatory and legal terms like "intimidating," "hostile," and "offensive" seem fraught with ambiguity for those who argue that what intimidates, offends, or creates hostility in one person may have no or a completely opposite effect on another. Inherent in the EEOC's definition, which is the most widely used on campus as well as in other organizations, is an undeniable subjectivity that disturbs many, especially academicians, who are traditionally concerned about assaults on academic freedom, and constitutional rights.

The national debate over political correctness exacerbated controversy over the definitional problem. In 1992, *U. S. News and World Report*'s John Leo offered a tongue-in-cheek catalogue of "P.C. Follies: The Year in Review."

P.C. Follies: The Year in Review

Political correctness had a banner year in 1991. A batch of new "isms" was announced, many new oppressions were discovered and opponents were soundly thwacked and occasionally gagged so that a kinder, gentler campus might emerge.

Dead Painter Harasses Prof

Nancy Stumhofer, English instructor at Penn State's Schuykill campus, has been sexually harassed by Goya's famous painting, "Naked Maja." Any picture of a nude female, she argued, "encourages males to make remarks about body parts." The offending picture had hung on the same classroom wall for 10 years before it began harassing Stumhofer. It has been exiled to a student center, where it is presumably on probation.

Exciting Year at Binghamton

The little-known State University of New York at Binghamton had a big-league PC year:

A student was charged with lewd and indecent behavior for posting two Penthouse centerfolds on his dormitory door. (A student panel found him guilty, but the administration later dropped the charges). . . .

Pipe Dream

The University newspaper reported one example of alleged sexual harassment in the economics department as this compliment: "She's so smart and pretty, too. . . ."

A Milestone in Sexual Harassment

Richard Hummell, professor of chemical engineering at the University of Toronto, said his sexual-harassment case cost him and his university more than $200,000 in costs and fees. Hummell was convicted in 1989 of "prolonged and intense staring" while swimming in a university pool. Barbara Amiel, a columnist for Maclean's, *described the case as "the utter debasement of the genuinely serious nature of sexual harassment."*[41]

Whatever one's response to Leo's satire, there is genuine need on campus and in the research community for more objective and uniform definitions of sexual harassment. Efforts to bring understanding have resulted in several studies that label specific behaviors by type and severity along a continuum. The behaviors thus identified range in number from three to eleven, but the instrument constructed with greatest attention to psychometric criteria was developed by Louise Fitzgerald and her colleagues, who used the very early work of Frank Till[42] to create an inventory known as the Sexual Experiences Questionnaire. Fitzgerald and her colleagues defined harassment on five levels: (1) gender harassment (generalized sexist remarks and behavior), (2) seductive behavior (inappropriate and offensive, but essentially sanction-free sexual advances), (3) sexual bribery (solicitation of sexual activity or other sex-linked behavior by promise of rewards), (4) sexual coercion (coercion of sexual activity by threat of punishment), and (5) sexual imposition (gross sexual imposition or assault).[43]

Despite efforts like Fitzgerald's, there is still no universally accepted definition of sexual harassment, and the resulting ambiguity has been used by some as justification for denying the reality of certain types of harassment, especially that of hostile environment. Nevertheless, hostile environment sexual harassment is here to stay. It has been repeatedly recognized in case law and rulings by the Supreme Court, and no amount of wailing and gnashing of teeth by opponents will cause it to disappear. What individuals and institutions can do is to prevent it from occurring and to discourage excessive reactions to the issue. If some academicians need to reflect more seriously on the kinds of jokes they tell in class and department offices, others must realize that hyperbolizing sexual harassment damages its credibility.

With the exception of the research community, which needs a coherent, preestablished definition from which to work, it may be unrealistic to expect absolutely precise definitions. Sexual harassment is too multifaceted and surreptitious and its victims too diverse to hope that some future act of rhetorical or legal wizardry will produce definitive insight upon which everyone will agree. But this does not mean that the behavior itself or that false allegations are unmanageable. Courts at all levels have emphasized a reassuringly consistent theme with respect to defining sexual harassment: determinations will be made on a case-by-case basis. In *Harris*, the most recent case to be heard by the Supreme Court, this point was reaffirmed.

Justice O'Connor, writing for the Court, stated that while Title VII clearly bans conduct that would affect a reasonable person's psychological well-being, the test for whether conduct can be perceived as creating a hostile or abuse environment "is not, and by its nature cannot be, a mathematically precise test."[44] She contended that "whether an environment is 'hostile' or 'abusive' can be determined only by looking at all the circumstances."[45] Even though mathematical precision is not possible, the Court did set forth a number of factors for evaluating whether circumstances justify a conclusion that sexual harassment has occurred. These include "the frequency of the discriminatory conduct; its severity; whether it is physically threatening or humiliating, or a mere offensive utterance; and whether it unreasonably interferes with the employee's work performance."[46] Thus, while the verbiage is necessarily imprecise, the elements to be reviewed to determine the existence of actionable conduct are relatively clear.

The result is that frivolous claims of sexual harassment are difficult to maintain. Since the legal standard of actionable conduct under developing law discourages complainants from bringing actions based on purely subjective feelings about being "harassed," contemporary institutions must assume responsibility for educating students and employees about the differences between illegal and ignorant or insensitive conduct. This is crucial because false or tenuous claims affect the credibility of those that are genuine and because federal courts are beginning to force complainants to bear the burden of costs when claims are determined to be without sufficient factual or legal basis.

Generally, federal courts tend to be reluctant to impose sanctions against plaintiffs who bring what are held to be frivolous suits because they view "massive fee awards against plaintiffs . . . [as] contrary to Congress' goals of 'promoting vigorous prosecution of civil rights violations under Title VII.'"[47] But increasing numbers of claims based on facts that do not approach the established standard of actionable conduct have influenced courts to discourage such suits under both Titles VII and IX. Each court has the authority to exercise discretion in awarding such sanctions under either the Federal Rules of Civil Procedure or under provisions of the statutes themselves.

The Free Speech/Academic Freedom Debate

Beyond concerns about definitional ambiguity lies the even more imposing issue of whether sexual harassment prohibitions limit academic freedom and freedom of speech. Many fear that continued attempts by employers and institutions to limit liability and isolate themselves from claims will result in overenforcement of political correctness that infringes on these fundamental freedoms. Others argue that attempts to regulate speech in the classroom will have a "chilling effect" on faculty who may be confused about the types of speech prohibited by the regulation.

In an affidavit submitted in a highly publicized case involving allegations of hostile environment sexual harassment under Title IX, William Van Alstyne, former general counsel, former national president, and former chair of Committee A of the National Committee on Academic Freedom and Tenure of the American Association of University Professors (AAUP), defined academic freedom.

Academic freedom, as it is generally understood in the University community, encompasses rights of faculty to speak freely outside of the classroom, to pursue research and to publish freely outside of the classroom, and to teach in the classroom without unreasonable interference. . . . At a minimum, this concept of academic freedom permits faculty members to choose pedagogical techniques or examples to convey the lesson they are trying to impart to their students.[48]

On the other hand, the right of students to academic freedom—the right to pursue educational objectives without harassment, fear, or intimidation—must also be given paramount consideration. Therein lies the conflict and paradox as institutions struggle with discrimination and harassment.

The Constitution's free-speech clause provides another seemingly irreconcilable obstacle to those who argue for university policies proscribing verbal conduct of a sexual nature. The Supreme Court has ruled that "educators do not offend the First Amendment by exercising editorial control over the style and content of student speech in school-sponsored expressive activities so long as their actions are reasonably related to legitimate pedagogical concerns."[49] Nevertheless, this right to control speech is qualified by well-established Supreme Court precedent recognizing the need to protect free speech in the classroom for the sake of academic freedom. In *Keyishian v. Board of Regents of the University of the State of New York*, the Supreme Court stated:

Our Nation is deeply committed to safeguarding academic freedom, which is of transcendent value to all of us and not merely to the teachers concerned. That freedom is therefore a special concern of the First Amendment which does not tolerate laws that cast a pall of orthodoxy over the classroom. . . . The classroom is peculiarly the "marketplace of ideas." The Nation's future depends upon leaders trained through wide exposure to that robust exchange of ideas which discovers truth "out of a multitude of tongues, [rather] than through any kind of authoritative selection." In Sweezy v. New Hampshire, *354 U.S. [234,] 250 [(1957)], we said:*

> *The essentiality of freedom in the community of American universities is almost self-evident. No one should underestimate the vital role in a democracy that is played by those who guide and train our youth. To impose any strait jacket upon the intellectual leaders in our colleges and universities would imperil the future of our Nation. . . . Scholarship cannot flourish in an atmosphere of suspicion and distrust. Teachers and students must always remain free to inquire, to study, and to evaluate, to gain new maturity and understanding; otherwise our civilization will stagnate and die.*[50]

This "freedom" is not, however, absolute.[51] Discriminatory conduct, including sexual harassment, is not shielded by the Constitution. In order to be protected, speech must address a matter of public concern.[52] Whether it is a matter of public concern is determined by the content, form, and context of the speech.[53] In addition, an individual's interest in speaking freely must outweigh the government's interest in promoting the efficient provision of public services. Because of the Supreme Court's deference to pedagogical issues, a very high standard thus exists when harassing conduct is presented in the context of education.

Amid these competing rights and interests institutions struggle to determine the best means of striking a balance between protecting themselves from sexual harassment claims by students and defending against actions by faculty who are disciplined for violating institutional policies proscribing certain conduct. Predictably, professional associations have attempted to assist in this process. The AAUP recently updated its Sexual Harassment Suggested Policy and Procedures for Handling Complaints. The policy begins with the statement "The [AAUP] has traditionally opposed every kind of practice that interferes with academic freedom."[54] Nevertheless, in setting forth justification for the implementation of sexual harassment policy, the organization cited its Statement on Professional Ethics, which reiterates the ethical responsibility of faculty members to avoid "any exploitation of students for . . . private advantage."[55] It also noted that this general norm is applicable to a "faculty member's use of institutional position to seek unwanted sexual relations with students or anyone else vulnerable to the faculty member's authority."[56]

In its Statement on Freedom and Responsibility, the AAUP also acknowledged that intimidation and harassment conflict with the tenets of academic freedom and that "the unprofessional treatment of students and colleagues assuredly extends to sex discrimination and sexual harassment, as well as to other forms of intimidation."[57] Thus the AAUP addressed sexual harassment policy as a balance between the academic freedom of both the faculty member and the student with neither having a right to infringe upon the similar right of the other.

Following the Supreme Court's 1992 decision in *Franklin v. Gwinnett County Public Schools*, which allowed monetary damages in cases brought under Title IX, the American Council on Education (ACE) also revised its sexual harassment policy "in light of legal developments which have occurred"[58] and defined sexual harassment to include not only physical conduct, but also "verbal abuse of a sexual nature."[59] Its policy statement also expressed concern that

[t]he educational mission of a college or university is to foster an open learning and working environment. The ethical obligation to provide an environment that is free from sexual harassment and from the fear that it may occur is implicit. The entire collegiate community suffers when sexual harassment is allowed to pervade the academic atmosphere through neglect, the lack of a policy prohibiting it, or the lack of educational programs designed to clarify appropriate professional behavior on

campus and to promote understanding of what constitutes sexual harassment.[60]

Both the AAUP and the ACE thus recognize the responsibility of institutions to address the issue of sexual harassment by developing policies which identify prohibited behavior of both a physical and verbal nature. They also recommend the implementation of sanctions against the faculty who violate prohibitions. Yet universities and colleges have had limited success garnering support for enforcement of these policies and procedures. A case in point involved a tenured college professor who challenged the constitutionality of his college's policy against harassment after he was subjected to a sexual harassment proceeding and disciplined as a result of a complaint filed against him by a student.[61] Holding in favor of the professor, the Court in *Cohen v. San Bernardino Valley College* stated the policy was unconstitutional as applied to the professor since he was not on notice that his "longstanding teaching style" was violative of the policy. The case demonstrates an issue being raised increasingly in university settings and challenges university counsel to evaluate their own policies as the courts clarify the demarcations between academic freedom and academic responsibility.

Statistical Ambiguity

Part of the difficulty lies in the confusion and controversy over measurement of the prevalence of the problem nationwide and on individual campuses. Statistics appear, as one disgruntled college president observed, "all over the place," and some survey results have appeared so hyperbolic as to ignite controversy and backlash. This was the case, for instance, when an American Association of University Women survey found that 85 percent of females in grades eight through eleven claimed to have experienced harassment.[62] There have been efforts to synthesize information from research studies, most of which are isolated, and to examine the conceptual and methodological problems associated with sexual harassment research.[63] R.D. Arvey's and M.A. Cavanaugh's "Using Surveys to Assess the Prevalence of Sexual Harassment: Some Methodological Problems" addressed the issue of statistical ambiguity in an attempt "to summarize some of the problems and issues associated with using survey methodologies to develop estimates of the percentages of individuals who are being or who have been sexually harassed, to look critically at a variety of methodologies that have been employed in developing estimates of sexual harassment and suggest some ways in which survey instruments and research methods might be improved."[64]

Arvey and Cavanaugh identified several areas of concern. The first, definitional and categorization problems, had several components. They noted that surveys differ significantly in their basic definitions of harassment, that items may not have equivalent meanings for all respondents, and that few differentiations are made between trivial as opposed to severe examples of the offense. They expressed concern about questionnaire formatting and methods, noting that "some researchers develop survey items that assess incidence of behaviors that they themselves have defined as constituting sexual harassment. . . . However, not all individuals will necessarily consider these behaviors sexual harassment."[65] An equally significant difficulty is the array of limitations that arise when researchers use retrospective self-reports. The researchers observed that widespread use of convenience samples and low response rates may result in sample selection bias, that not enough attention is paid to reliability and validity concerns, and that having respondents report simultaneously on the existence of harassment and its impact also invites scientific problems. They concluded by noting that caution must be used in generalizing across populations findings from sexual harassment surveys. Institutions that contemplate surveying their constituents would do well to consider Arvey and Cavanaugh's recommendations: develop precise definitions, establish reasonable constraints on the time period during which an individual may describe having been harassed, establish psychometric integrity for survey instruments, beware of both sample and researcher bias, and refrain from using the label "sexual harassment" in seeking information about or assessments of events and behaviors.

Despite limitations in survey methodology, an overview of contemporary research generates several "safe" and probably conservative statistics. In a detailed review of research studies since 1980, J. Rubin and S.B. Borgers asserted that "when examining the incidence of sexual harassment in universities a pattern emerges—it exists as a common occurrence in our universities. While reported frequencies vary, it is suggested that 30 percent may be a reliable estimate."[66] This statistic is most frequently used when defining sexual harassment as a continuum ranging from sexist remarks to assault and when the respondents are females, particularly students. It is difficult to draw conclusions about female staff since research is so limited. The most highly regarded data for females in the workplace is 42 percent, the finding of a random-sample survey of 24,000 U.S. government employees. This survey by the U. S. Merit Systems Protection Board was conducted in 1981 and updated in 1988.[67] It also found that 15 percent of men reported having been targets of harassment in the preceding two years. That figure has not been readily generalizable to academe where research on male students, faculty, staff, and administrators has been extremely limited. Studies have yielded results for different behaviors as widely varying as 2 percent to 22 percent.[68] All surveys report the overwhelming majority of harassers of both genders to be men, but there are no reliable studies providing insight into the percentage of academicians who engage in sexual harassment. It is not, after all, a behavior about which educators or institutions routinely boast. The unfortunate result is that while prevalence numbers are high and perpetrator statistics unknown, the two are often equated to give the impression that large percentages of male academicians harass.

Low Reporting and Institutional Stonewalling

Despite high prevalence rates and counter to early predictions that academe and the workplace were doomed to suffer widespread capricious complaints, only an inordinately small percentage of harassment is ever reported. In the U.S. Merit System Protection Board Study, 11 percent of targets reported the offense, and only 2.5 percent initiated formal grievances. The most often cited reporting range for the workplace is 1 percent to 7 percent[69], and for academe, 4.3 formal complaints per year.[70] A study by C. Robertson, C.E. Dyer, and D. Campbell found false complaints to be negligible.

In the survey we asked respondents how many false complaints they had ever received. . . . Of the 256 respondents who answered, 82 percent said none. In all, sixty-four false complaints were reported from the other

18 percent of the schools . . . 12 percent reporting one only and 6 per-
cent two to four. . . . A rough extrapolation from the numbers given
would make the false complaints less than 1 percent of the annual com-
plaints. This is a maximum estimate that does not take into account
that some complaints listed as false by administrators actually may have
been genuine according to our definition.[71]

Low reportage has been attributed to numerous factors—fear of retaliation, reluctance to engage in conflict or threaten a relationship with an authority figure, belief that the behavior will disappear if ignored, concern that institutional remedies are inadequate and powerless to affect change, and conviction that the complaint will be disbelieved. S. Riger suggested in "Gender Dilemmas in Sexual Harassment Policies and Procedures" that yet another reason for few grievances may be women's perception of gender bias in construction of policies that "are not compatible with the way that many women view conflict resolution. Gender bias in policies, rather than an absence of harassment or lack of assertiveness on the part of victims produces low numbers of complaints."[72] As in the case of other ambiguous issues surrounding sexual harassment, institutions have done little to further knowledge of this phenomenon of low reportage on their own campuses, and "no news" has too often been regarded as "good news."

Infatuated with image and threatened by competition, colleges and universities share little practical information about prevalence, number and types of formal and informal complaints, grievance resolution, and sanctions on campus. They may engage in theoretical exchange, but, as Dziech noted in a *Chronicle of Higher Education* article, "We work in isolation, treating each situation on each campus as if it were unique. Our passion for privacy has outweighed our common sense."[73] Fitzgerald echoed the need for a more comprehensive view of the issue when she called for "collection of nationally representative data on prevalence rates in both work-related and educational contexts on an ongoing basis. Standardized questions concerning experiences of sexual harassment should be routinely included in governmentally sponsored surveys of both educational and work-related settings."[74]

Noting that most of the research is dominated by analogue rather than field studies, her observations reinforce the need for "hands on" knowledge of the problem and greater cooperation among institutions serious about curtailing it. There is no way of knowing the number of institutions that have succeeded in winning gag orders from courts to protect their images, but it is clear that failure to disclose information about sexual harassment can have serious repercussions. The most obvious is that lack of disclosure encourages denial and acts as a deterrent to reportage.

Many colleges and universities attempt to fulfill students' demands for thorough investigations and for definitive responses to sexual harassment, but their efforts go unrecognized because their obsessions with preserving privacy and maintaining their images lead them to behave surreptitiously when grievances arise. The results are devastating. In the absence of awareness and candid discussion of sexual harassment, people can be lulled into the complacent assumption that it is nonexistent. Victims erroneously assume that theirs are isolated circumstances and that their complaints will be unwelcome. Institutions that discipline professors for inappropriate behaviors and do not bother to inform victims create skepticism and mistrust among students.[75]

In recent years another serious repercussion of institutional "stonewalling" has become apparent. Lack of information encourages anxiety and/or hyperbole on both sides of the issue. Maintaining that he could be "railroaded out tomorrow if [he] pat[ted] a student on the shoulder or [told] a joke in class," a tenured professor of twenty years told a training session audience:

You have no idea what these people have planned. It sends chills up my spine. They'll shackle you in the classroom and follow you to your office to watch everything you do and say. Everything we do will be watched by the harassment police, and the administration will be happy to help because it's just one more way of getting rid of us if we don't toe the party line. What I'd like to know is if there's so much of this stuff really going on, how come no one has ever introduced me to a student who's made a complaint? How come if my salary is posted in the library, there's no data on people complaining about harassment?

Two weeks later a student in a large state university system expressed a diametrically opposed perspective on the clandestine way in which sexual harassment is treated in her state. She contended that she and several others had brought grievances to their institution and were generally ill treated. As a result, she claimed, they approached members of the legislature who were considering an investigation of the state university system but were deterred from doing so when the governor and a politician who had accepted an appointment with the federal government "squelched the investigation" because it would be "politically embarrassing."

Both anecdotes demonstrate the bind in which institutions have been placed—or place themselves—when information about sexual harassment is concealed. Institutions must be cautious about public disclosure because a sexual harassment claim, particularly if false or distorted, can cause great damage to the accused, the accuser, and the institution, but they must recognize that, appropriately framed, disclosure is preferable to secrecy.

Such information does not have to be distributed in a manner that encourages identification of victims or perpetrators or that creates an impression that sexual harassment is rampant on campus. It can instead be a conscientious documentation of the institution's attempt to recognize, resist, and eradicate unacceptable behavior by academicians. Students are far more secure in an environment that admits its problems than in one that cloaks them in secrecy, and institutions that reduce sexual harassment to a professional discipline issue rather than allowing the media to magnify it into titillating scandal maintain control over their public images.[76]

The Future

Though "out of the closet" in terms of theory and policy, sexual harassment remains an elusive and evolving concern for higher education. Too often it is defined by isolated, worst-possible scenario cases that allow zealots to exaggerate the situation on campus. Some complainants have alleged nervous breakdowns over failed affairs with academicians; some institutions have been overzealous, and others extraordinarily negligent in dealing with perpetrators, but these are partial glimpses of a reality that seldom reaches courtroom or Hollywood proportions. Most college professors bear little resemblance to the "liberal-chic-academic look"[77] of the assassinated professor, Thomas Callahan, in *The Pelican Brief*; and, unlike Darby, his lover, most students are not brilliant, gorgeous women who qualify "for law school and arrive there liberated . . . loose"[78] and capable of solving the murder of a Supreme Court Justice.

On campus, as well as off, valid claims of sexual harassment are more pathetic than tragic, more banal and vulgar than interesting and exciting. There is a dynamic peculiar to academic harassment that replicates the languid pace at which academe moves and the simultaneously idealistic and sanctimonious manner in which it behaves. Most institutions have mastered the basics of the issue by implementing policies and procedures that are in compliance with the letter of the law, but appearances can deceive; and often higher education fails to comprehend the total sexual harassment dynamic because its knowledge of itself and its mission may be limited and conflicted.

In a sense, the issue has become a litmus test for a profession that is very adept at advising business, industry, and government, but is still working to put its own house in order. Since the 1970s, priorities on the American campus have increased in number and complexity, while students and taxpayers have grown weary of exorbitant fees, ineffective instruction, and institutional excesses. Once regarded as a bastion of reason, moderation, and dignity, academe at this point in history is too often characterized by the conflicting ideologies of intemperate and self-indulgent personalities who are given excessive attention and latitude. Control of sexual harassment requires individual and organizational self-knowledge, self-discipline, and self-sacrifice; and these are not easy goals to achieve.

Notes

1. Genesis 39:6. *Life Application Bible*, King James Version. Wheaton, Ill.: Tyndale House, 1989.
2. Susanna 41. *Oxford Annotated Apocrypha*, Revised Standard Version, ed. B. M. Metzger. (New York: Oxford University Press, 1965)
3. *Id.*, 52.
4. *Id.*, 57.
5. *Id.*, 64.
6. *Id.*, 22.
7. C.A. MacKinnon, *Sexual Harassment of Working Women: A Case of Sex Discrimination* (New Haven: Yale University Press, 1979), p. 27.
8. See C. Safran (1976), "What Men Do to Women on the Job: A Shocking Look at Sexual Harassment," *Redbook* (November), 217–24.

9.   See P. Crull (1983), "The Impact of Sexual Harassment on the Job: A Profile of the Experiences of 92 Women," *Working Women's Research Series*, Report No. 3.
10. See "Alliance against Sexual Coercion," *University Grievance Procedures, Title IX and Sexual Harassment on Campus* (Boston: Alliance Against Sexual Coercion, 1980).
11. *Corne v. Bausch and Lomb, Inc.*, 390 F. Supp. 161 (D. Ariz. 1975).
12. *Id.* at 163–64.
13. MacKinnon, p. 27.
14. *Williams v. Saxbe*, 413 F. Supp. 654, 657–58 (D.D.C. 1976).
15. *Id.*
16. *Alexander v. Yale University*, 459 F. Supp. 1 (D. Conn. 1977).
17. *Id.* at 3–4.
18. *Id.*
19. *Id.* at 4.
20. EEOC Policy Guidance, N–915.050, March 19, 1990.
21. *Brown v. City of Guthrie*, 22 Fair Empl. Prac. Cas. (BNA) 1627, 30 Empl. Prac. Dec. (CCH) P33, 031 (W.D. Okla. 5/30/80).
22. *Bundy v. Jackson*, 641 F.2d 934 (D.C. Cir. 1981).
23. *Meritor Savings Bank, FSB. v. Vinson*, 477 U.S. 57 (1986).
24. *Id.*
25. *Bougher v. University of Pittsburgh*, 713 F. Supp. 139 (W.D. Pa. 1989) *aff'd*, 882 F.2d 74 (3d Cir. 1989).
26. *Moire v. Temple University School of Nursing*, 613 F. Supp. 1360 (E.D. Pa. 1985).
27. A.J. Califa, Director for Litigation, Enforcement, Policy Service, "Title IX and Sexual Harassment Complaints," *Memorandum to Regional Civil Rights Directors*, August 31, 1981.
28. *Franklin v. Gwinnett County Public Schools*, 112 S. Ct. 1028, 1031 (1992).
29. *Id.* at 1037.
30. *Harris v. Forklift Systems, Inc.*, 114 S. Ct. 367 (1993).
31. *Id.* at 369.
32. *Id.*
33. See *Yates v. Avco*, 819 F.2d 630, 637 (6th Cir. 1987); *Andres v. City of Philadelphia*, 895 F.2d 1469, 1482 (3d Cir. 1990); *Ellison v. Brady*, 924 F.2d 872 (9th Cir. 1991); *Burns v. McGregory Electronic Industries, Inc.*, 989 F.2d 959, 962 (8th Cir. 1993).
34. *Ellison v. Brady*, 924 F.2d 872 (9th Cir. 1991).
35. *Meritor Savings Bank, FSB. v. Vinson*, 477 U.S. 57 (1986).
36. *Parolene v. Unisys Corp.*, 879 F.2d 100, 104 (9th Cir. 1990).
37. See *Kerans v. Porter Paint Company*, 575 N.E.2d 428 (Ohio 1991) (creating new common law sexual harassment tort).
38. See *Huebshen v. Department of Health and Social Services*, 547 F. Supp. 1168 (W.D. Wis. 1982), *rev'd on other grnds*, 716 F.2d 1167 (7th Cir. 1983); *Wright v. Methodist Youth Services, Inc.*, 511 F. Supp. 307 (N.D. Ill. 1981).
39. See T. Reilly, S. Carpenter, V. Dull, and K. Bartlett (1982), "The Factorial Survey: An Approach to Defining Sexual Harassment on Campus," *Journal of Social Issues*, 38, 99–110; E. Weber-Burden and P.H. Rossi (1982), "Defining Sexual Harassment on Campus: A Replication and Extension," *Journal of Social Issues*, 38, 111–120; M. Sullivan and D.I. Bybee (1987), "Female Students and Sexual Harassment: What Factors Predict Reporting Behavior," *Journal of the National Association for Women Deans, Administrators, and Counselors*, 50, 11–16; J. W. Adams, J.L. Kottke, and J.S. Padgitt (1983), "Sexual Harassment of University Students," *Journal of College Student Personnel*, 24, 484–90; L.J. Rubin and S.B. Borgers (1990), "Sexual Harassment in Universities During the 1980's," *Sex Roles*, 23, 397–411.
40. See T. Reilly et al.; Weber-Burden and Rossi; Sullivan and Bybee; Rubin and Borgers; L.F. Fitzgerald and A.J. Omerod (1991), "Perceptions of Sexual Harass-

ment: The Influence of Gender and Academic Context," *Psychology of Women Quarterly*, 15, 281–94; S. Kenig and J. Ryan (1986) "Sex Differences in Levels of Tolerance and Attribution of Blame for Sexual Harassment on a University Campus," *Sex Roles*, 15, 535–49; G.N. Powell (1986), "Effects of Sex Role Identity and Sex on Definitions of Sexual Harassment," *Sex Roles*, 14, 9–19.

41. J. Leo, "P.C. Follies: The Year in Review" (1992), *U.S. News and World Report*, 112, 3, p. 22.

42. F. Till (1980), *Sexual Harassment: A Report on the Sexual Harassment of Students*, Washington, D.C., National Advisory Council on Women's Education Programs.

43. L.F. Fitzgerald, S.K. Shullman, N. Bailey, M. Richards, J. Swecker, Y. Gold, M. Ormerod, and L. Weitzman (1988), "The Incidence of Sexual Harassment in Acadamia and the Workplace," *Journal of Vocational Behavior*, 32, 152–75.

44. *Harris v. Forklift Systems, Inc.*, 114 S. Ct. 367, 371 (1993).

45. *Id.*

46. *Id.*

47. *Miller v. Los Angeles County Board of Education*, 827 F.2d 617, 619 (9th Cir. 1987).

48. *Silva v. University of New Hampshire*, 888 F. Supp. 293 (D.N.H. 1994).

49. *Hazelwood School District v. Kuhlmeier*, 484 U.S. 260, 276 (1988).

50. *Keyishian v. Board of Regents of the University of the State of New York*, 385 U.S. 589, 603 (1967).

51. *Parducci v. Rutland*, 316 F. Supp. 352, 355 (M.D. Ala. 1970).

52. *Connick v. Myers*, 461 U.S. 138 (1983).

53. *Id.*

54. "Sexual Harassment: Suggested Policy and Procedures for Handling Complaints" (1995), *Academe*, 81, p. 62.

55. *Id.*

56. *Id.*

57. *Id.*

58. American Council on Education, *Sexual Harassment on Campus: A Policy and Program of Deterrence* (Washington, D.C.: American Council on Education, 1992), p. 1.

59. *Id.*

60. *Id.*

61. *Cohen v. San Bernardino Valley College*, 92 F.3d 968 (9th Cir. 1996), *cert. denied*, 1997 U.S. Lexis 1918 (1997).

62. American Association of University Women (1993), *Hostile Hallways: The AAUW Survey on Sexual Harassment in America's Schools*. Washington, D.C.: American Council on Education.

63. See Rubin and Borgers and P.A. Charney and R.C. Russell (1994), "An Overview of Sexual Harassment," *American Journal of Psychiatry*, 151(1), 10–17; D. Gillespie and A. Leffer, (1987), "The Politics of Research Methodology in Claims-Making Activities. Social Science and Sexual Harassment," *Social Problems*, 34, 490–508; J.E. Gruber (1990), "Methodological Problems and Policy Implications in Sexual Harassment Research," *Population Research and Policy Review*, 9, 235–54; J.E. Gruber (1992), "A Typology of Personal and Environmental Sexual Harassment: Research and Policy Implications for the 1990's," *Sex Roles*, 26, 447–63; K. McKinney (1990), "Sexual Harassment of University Faculty by Colleagues and Students," *Sex Roles*, 23, 421–38; R.D. Arvey and M.A. Cavanaugh (1995), "Using Surveys to Assess the Prevalence of Sexual Harassment: Some Methodological Problems," *Journal of Social Issues*, 51, 39–52.

64. Arvey and Cavanaugh, p. 40.

65. *Id.*, p. 43.

66. Rubin and Borgers, p. 405. See also Charney and Russell and B.W. Dziech and L. Weiner, *The Lecherous Professor: Sexual Harassment on Campus* (Boston: Beacon Press, 1984).

67. See "U.S. Merit System Protection Board: Sexual Harassment in the Federal Workplace: Is It a Problem," Washington, D.C.: U.S. Government Printing Office, 1981, and "U.S. Merit System Protection Board: Sexual Harassment in the Federal Workplace: An Update," Washington, D.C.: U.S. Government Printing Office, 1988.

68. See McKinney; J.R. Richman, J.A. Flaherty, K.M. Rospenda, and M.L. Christensen (1993), "Mental Health Consequences and Correlates of Reported Medical Student Abuse," *JAMA*, 267, 692–94; A. Metha and J. Nigg (1982), "Sexual Harassment: Implications of a Study at Arizona State University," *Women's Studies Quarterly*, 10, 24–26; B. Lott, M.E. Reilly, and D.R. Howard (1982), "Sexual Assault and Harassment: A Campus Community Case Study," *Signs: Journal of Women in Culture and Society*, 8, 296–319; M. Komarony, A.B. Bindman, R.J. Maber, and M.A. Sande (1993), "Sexual Harassment in Medical Training," *New England Journal of Medicine*, 328, 322–26; M.P. Goodwin, B. Roscoe, M. Rose, and S.E. Repp (1989), "Sexual Harassment: Experiences of University Employees," *Initiatives*, 52(3), 25–33; E.L. Dey, J.S. Korn, and L.J. Sax (1996) "Betrayed by the Academy: Sexual Harassment of Women College Faculty," *Journal of Higher Education*, 67, 149–73.

69. See Charney and Russell and J.A. Livingston (1982) "Responses to Sexual Harassment on the Job: Legal, Organizational and Individual Actions," *Journal of Social Issues*, 38, 5–22.

70. See Charney and Russell and C. Robertson, C.E. Dyer, and D. Campbell (1988), "Campus Harassment: Sexual Harassment Policies and Procedures at Institutions of Higher Learning," *Signs: Journal of Women in Culture and Society*, 13, 792–812.

71. C. Robertson et al., p. 800.

72. S. Riger (1991), "Gender Dilemmas in Sexual Harassment Policies and Procedures," *American Psychologist*, 46, p. 498.

73. B.W. Dziech (1991), "Colleges Must Help to Unravel the Bewildering Complexities of Sexual Harassment," *Chronicle of Higher Education*, 38(12), B3.

74. L.F. Fitzgerald (1993), "Sexual Harassment: Violence Against Women in the Workplace," *American Psychologist*, 48, 1073.

75. B.W. Dziech, "Author's Note" in *The Lecherous Professor: Sexual Harassment on Campus*, 2nd ed., B.W. Dziech and L. Weiner (Boston: Beacon Press, 1990), p. xxii.

76. *Id.*, pp. xxii–xxiii.

77. J. Grisham, *The Pelican Brief* (New York: Doubleday, 1992), p. 11.

78. *Id.*, p. 17.

Chapter Two
Making Shelter
Institutional Responsibility

Someone has to be responsible. Someone has to pick up the pieces.
Someone has to make shelter.

—May Sarton

Values are like tides, invisible but mighty.

—George Keller

Whenever faculty or administrators engage in destructive or indiscreet behavior with students or other employees, the institution automatically becomes responsible, but the task of "pick[ing] up the pieces [and] mak[ing] shelter" assumed particular urgency with the enactment of laws prohibiting discrimination. Suddenly colleges and universities had not only traditional custodial and collegial responsibilities, but were also thrust into active and often conflicting roles in sexual harassment cases. Called upon to protect the interests of both targets and perpetrators, institutions were forced to serve as quasi-prosecutors, defense attorneys, and judges during grievances and, given the attention and resources demanded of them, became, in an ironic sense, victims of sexual harassment themselves.

Some responded rapidly, others reluctantly, to the demands made upon them, and by now most can claim to meet the basic standards of good policy and practice: (1) provide the campus community with a coherent and comprehensive definition of sexual harassment (most use the EEOC definition as a base), (2) issue a strong policy statement expressing disapproval of the behavior, (3) establish an accessible grievance procedure that allows for both formal and informal complaints, (4) conduct student, faculty, and staff programs that educate all constituencies about the problem, and (5) employ multiple sources (catalogues, posters, campus newspaper and radio and television presentations) to communicate policies and procedures.[1] Yet somehow even the most diligent efforts have not been adequate. In the 1980s, it appeared possible to curtail and even eliminate harassment simply by enacting laws and developing policies. Few foresaw that laws could be "bent," if not broken; that rigorous legal and grievance processes might be cited as deterrents to reportage; that approaches that worked well in some organizational settings would fail in others; that perceptions of what constitutes harassing behavior could be influenced by individual, cultural, and generational, as well as gender, variables—in short, that understanding and preventing sexual harassment would be an ongoing, never-quite-final endeavor.

Today research efforts, while informative, seem sometimes too pedantic, too suspended in time and rooted in earnest but redundant efforts to discover the precise definition or the exact prevalence figure that will legitimize the already obvious: sexual harassment, though difficult to recognize in its less severe forms, is a destructive force that poses serious threat to individuals and institutions. The literature on the issue clearly establishes that the sexual harassment dynamic in an organization is affected by gender composition, power differentials, and individuals' perceptions of the organization's receptivity or resistance to harassment,[2] but this information alone is not sufficient to guide campus efforts at control. The generic, "cookie cutter" approaches to policy and prevention that some institutions have adopted possess equally limited possibilities. While there is benefit to be gained from recognition of harassment as an historical and national phenomenon, it is also crucial for academicians to realize that there is another dimension to the issue. On the campus, harassment must be seen as a local issue, a manifestation of a professional problem as encompassing as that of gender. Sexual harassment is inarguably about power and gender, but it is also about academics' need to understand their students, the institutions in which they work, and their own professional priorities and responsibilities.

Not one or two, but all of these concerns must be taken into account if a college or university is to answer the compelling questions with which it should be concerned: (1) Given that sexual harassment is a firmly established legal concept with an ever expand-ing body of case law, how knowledgeable and current are we about legal requirements? (2) How effective and up-to-date are our poli-cies, procedures, and educational and counseling efforts? (3) What factors in our institution pose potential risk or actually foster sexual harassment? (4) What conditions discourage harassees from using procedures and support systems? (5) How can we move beyond sim-ply complying with the law to affect genuine attitudinal and behav-ioral change on the campus? In short, institutions must discover ways to ensure effective handling of complaints and to demonstrate commitment to eradicating sexual harassment while simultaneously reducing potential liability for both the accused and accusers.

The first inquiry (What is required by the law?) is crucial. If an institution deals with sexual harassment without clear understand-ing of the law and the expectations that it creates, its good faith efforts may prove ineffective. Since this legal area continues to evolve, institutions must consistently monitor their level of compliance and educate their employees about their responsibilities to students and colleagues. Painstaking compliance and continuously updated legal education is crucial if an institution is to avoid complaints and to create hospitable environments in which men and women can work and learn together.

The second inquiry (How effective are policies and prevention efforts?) is perhaps the most compatible for academicians because it involves collection and analysis of data. Periodic review of policies and procedures is necessary because institutions' experiences with harassment change from year to year. Educational efforts must be ongoing because new employees and freshmen who arrive on cam-pus in the fall will not have had the opportunity to hear speakers who lectured on coping strategies or legal remedies in previous years. The posters that enthusiastic committees displayed two years earlier may have been discarded or grown discolored and thus ignored as other material accumulates on bulletin boards.

"How well are we doing?" is a question that must be constantly addressed, and the research upon which the answer is based must be analyzed with the utmost objectivity. If an institution of 30,000 has one or two sexual harassment complaints per year, it may not be "doing well," as many would suppose. The truth may be rather that the small number of complaints indicates something amiss, perhaps that the university's students are too naive to recognize harassment or too frightened to come forward. Educational programs and counseling must be more than routine procedures. Participants should be encouraged to express opinions about their effectiveness, and the institution must give those who seek help the opportunity to evaluate anonymously the quality of support they receive. Curtailing sexual harassment involves more than creating complex processes and idealistic services. It demands constant reassessment, willingness to admit failure, and ability to cope with the ever-changing needs of diverse individuals and groups.

The final three concerns (determining institutional risk factors, identifying conditions that discourage harassees from using procedures and support systems, and encouraging attitudinal and behavioral change) demand considerable resources, knowledge, and commitment. Addressing them requires that educators approach sexual harassment from a less simplistic perspective and view it as part of a larger institutional need. In other words, to discourage harassment, create better support for harassees, and develop active rather than reactive approaches to the problem, individual academicians and institutions must know more about the collective demographics and cultures of student bodies and the seemingly objective but unique characteristics that define and differentiate each campus's academic and work climate.

Sexual Harassment and Student Characteristics and Culture

On any campus the sexual harassment dynamic operates within a context that necessitates understanding of its students' collective as well as individual characteristics and cultures. In an article on college administration, Alexander Astin, director of a thirty-one-year-old survey of freshmen that reaches 350,000 students annually, made an observation relevant to the sexual harassment issue:

A high-quality institution is one that knows about its students. . . . Further, the high-quality institution has a method for gathering and disseminating this information, enabling it to make appropriate adjustments in programs or policies when the student data indicate that change or improvement is needed. In other words, quality is equated here not

*with physical facilities or faculty credentials but rather with a continu-
ing process of critical self-examination that focuses on the institution's
contribution to the student's intellectual and personal development.*[3]

Sexual harassment challenges colleges and universities to reexamine their commitments. On too many campuses the lures of research, publication, and media attention have overshadowed institutions' primary responsibility, which is to provide education,
advising, and inspiration to students. The voracious appetite for research dollars and reputation often forces educators to trivialize their
relations with students, and much of the professional denial of harassment is a predictable by-product of unfamiliarity with the needs
and concerns of those whose presence on campus makes higher education possible. Sexual harassment reminds educators that attention
should be focused not only on laboratories and libraries, but also on
the human beings for whom those facilities were created.

The more knowledge an institution has about its student body,
the better it will be at predicting and preventing harassment. Obviously, anticipating individual students' vulnerabilities is impossible,
but there are identifiable characteristics that may place some more
at risk than others of falling prey to perpetrators, and there are cultural indicators which can alert institutions to students' collective
attitudes and susceptibilities. This is one of the most fertile areas for
future research within institutions because such information can be
used to tailor educational programming and policies to individual
student bodies. A consultant addressing a very homogeneous, traditional student body has to employ an entirely different tenor and
emphasis from those he or she would use in discussing harassment
with a predominantly liberal student audience. The latter may require procedures and policies that might be totally inhospitable to
the former.

Sexual harassment is an issue that involves human perceptions
and interactions, so people and their individual needs and characteristics must always be the focal point. By now it is clear that on the
campus, as well as in the workplace, gender and attitudes toward
women influence individuals' perceptions of appropriate gender behaviors.[4] This being the case, it is apparent that while the basic message and intent must be the same, educational programming and

consultants for students at VMI would have to differ radically from those at Barnard. Beyond these more apparent factors lies an enormous range of possibilities that might affect not only assessment of policies and programming on individual campuses but might also predict student responses and vulnerabilities to varying types of behavior. These are what T.C. Fain and D.L. Anderton label "diffuse status characteristics, in that individuals bring status grouping and stereotypical responses with them into the organization from the larger social community."[5] The limited number of field and analogue studies of academe and the workplace suggests that such characteristics are interesting not simply for further research but for consideration by those responsible for harassment concerns on the campus.

For example, studies have examined the effects that traditional sex-role orientation and self-esteem have on perception of and willingness to tolerate harassment. N.J. Malovich and J.E. Stake found that women with high self-esteem and traditional sex-role attitudes were most tolerant of the behavior and least likely to recognize its potential for harm.[6] An earlier study by G.N. Powell, based upon the presumption that androgynous individuals are high in self-esteem, reported no effect for masculinity and only a weak link to femininity.[7] D. Lester and colleagues did not find a highly significant correlation between self-confidence and perceptions of sexual harassment.[8] Several studies have postulated that religion may influence gender behaviors and attitudes;[9] thus D.D. Baker, D.E. Terpstra, and K. Larntz postulated that "those with high levels of religiosity will expect women to react more passively to social-sexual behaviors than will those with low levels of religiosity."[10] Nevertheless, they discovered only a "limited"[11] effect. Fain and Anderton reported that unmarried, minority, and young women are the most likely targets of harassment in the workplace,[12] a conclusion that has been strongly replicated elsewhere.[13] A. McCormack[14] and K.R. Wilson and L.A. Kraus[15] found that family background characteristics and feminist beliefs were not linked to harassment.

Considering the limitations in research methods discussed in Chapter 1, what do the sporadic and frequently flawed studies such as these have to offer? If nothing else, they suggest that sexual harassment involves more than definitions and statistics and that be-

cause this is the case, institutions would do well to identify characteristics that may influence their students' vulnerabilities and responses to various forms of harassment. For example, economic con-
straint is obviously a potent influence on those pursuing degrees.
Financial dependence on the institution tends to discourage complaints about it; people who lack the freedom to move from campus
to campus may feel compelled to tolerate or submit to inappropriate
behavior and may hesitate to protest because they perceive the costs
of doing so to be too high. "I listened to his dirty jokes every day for
a whole year because there wasn't anywhere else I could go," one
scholarship student said of a professor. While campus administrators may argue that she did indeed have intake offices to receive her
complaint, her reasons for rejecting them deserve consideration.

Academic status can also create vulnerabilities. Like those with
economic problems, weak students feel as though they cannot move
freely between academic majors or institutions, so many assume it is
easier to keep quiet and "take" harassment rather than complain.
They may suspect, probably justifiably, that grievances against perpetrators will be evaluated in relation to their grades, so they avoid
grievances. Sometimes the reverse occurs. Anecdotal evidence suggests that at a few institutions serving the intellectually gifted, demarcations between teachers and students can be so blurred that
improper relations become the norm. Ironically, this possibility was
indirectly supported in a study that concluded, "Students at selective institutions are relatively more likely to be harassers [of faculty
women] than are students at other institutions. It may be that both
faculty and students at such institutions are more likely to push the
limits of appropriate behavior and less likely to fear sanction than at
other types of institutions."[16] If it is true that the higher a student's
academic and career ambitions, the more likely he or she will be to
"push the limits," then it is also true that such a student will be more
susceptible to those who can curtail those ambitions. The reverse
may also occur.

Research on correlations between self-esteem and assertive reactions to sexual harassment suggests that those with lower self-
confidence probably perceive fewer possibilities of success in altering their situations and so are less likely to engage in strong
responses.[17] Thus first-generation or returning collegians are at

greater risk than those who are sophisticated about academics and campus life, since they are more likely to be awed by and thus feel subordinate to or dependent on their professors. Those who feel out of place and humbled by the collegiate experience may judge academicians less harshly than their more confident peers, and their very responsiveness to academic authority may act as an invitation to abuse of such authority or may discourage reporting of inappropriate behavior.

The point is that institutional demographics contain messages that demand attention. The legal definition of sexual harassment does not vary from institution to institution, but student bodies do. An urban community college with a large percentage of women who drop in and out needs to be aware that its students are different from the postadolescents attending the expensive, elite, coeducational institution up the road. Unless each takes responsibility for educating itself about its students, it can make only superficial attempts to teach them about harassment and to protect them from its dangers. Colleges and universities cannot directly alter the personal vulnerabilities or response tendencies of individual students, but with education and energy, many can tailor programs and procedures to the needs of their constituents; and in some cases even very large institutions can particularize their efforts by working closely with disparate units.

Knowledge of student culture is an equally urgent concern. It can guide efforts to teach students about appropriate behavior and encourage them to use institutional resources when standards are violated. It can provide faculty with insights that will help them avoid questionable actions and threatening situations. The problem is that on many campuses information about students' values, interests, and extracurricular behaviors is in short supply. How many colleges and universities make a point of assessing their students' ethical standards, religious beliefs, and sexual mores? What do they know about how they spend time out of class? About their knowledge of contemporary social issues like sexual harassment? Are they familiar with the books and magazines they read, the television programs and movies they see, the music they prefer? Most educators would probably argue that such information has little relevance to the work for which they are paid, but the truth is that knowledge about student culture would not only provide insight into the dynamics of sexual harassment, but would also transform the teaching-learning process in many classrooms.

If the prototypal student on a campus is a postadolescent who routinely watches MTV, listens exclusively to rock and rap music, reads primarily *Sports Illustrated* or *People* magazine, never attends church, and interacts with adults only out of necessity, his or her perceptions of appropriate male-female behaviors will differ enormously from those of another institution's typical collegian who has more eclectic tastes, greater familiarity with societal issues and organized religion, and more diverse generational ties. The variations among three well-known midwestern institutions offer useful illustrations of this point. Ohio State University, Wittenberg University, and Antioch College in Ohio are between fifteen and forty minutes from one another, but differences in student populations alone render them light-years apart.

One of the largest public institutions in the nation, Ohio State serves a clientele of more than 54,000 students and is too diverse to classify accurately. Associated with the Lutheran Church, Wittenberg's approximately 3,000 academically select students are educated in a moderate or mixed environment where they are encouraged to develop social awareness within the context of traditional values. Their overall character and collegiate experience is very different from that of Antioch's 630 students, most of whom are attracted to the institution because of its tradition of liberalism and social activism. While laws apply identically to each environment, efforts to educate about and protect students from sex offenses must vary.

Recently Antioch students encouraged the formation of a Sexual Offense Policy that can be used to reinforce the point about the need for heterogeneous approaches to regulating sexual behavior. Such a policy would never have been conceived, let alone implemented, amid the enormous heterogeneity of an Ohio State or the moderation of a Wittenberg. Antioch's guidelines have been widely lampooned in the media and by traditional collegians to whom its approach to sexual relations appears artificial and even absurd. The portion of the policy entitled "Consent" contains seven points.

1. For the purpose of this policy, "consent" shall be defined as follows: the act of willingly and verbally agreeing to engage in specific sexual contact or conduct.

2. If sexual contact and/or conduct is not mutually and simultaneously initiated, then the person who initiates sexual contact/conduct is responsible for getting the verbal consent of the other individual(s) involved.

3. Obtaining consent is an ongoing process in any sexual interaction. Verbal consent should be obtained with each new level of physical and/or sexual contact/conduct in any given interaction, regardless of who initiates it. Asking "Do you want to have sex with me?" is not enough. The request for consent must be specific to each act.

4. The person with whom sexual contact/conduct is initiated is responsible to express verbally and/or physically her/his willingness or lack of willingness when reasonably possible.

5. If someone has initially consented but then stops consenting during a sexual interaction, she/he should communicate withdrawal verbally and/or through physical resistance. The other individual(s) must stop immediately.

6. To knowingly take advantage of someone who is under the influence of alcohol, drugs, and/or prescribed medication is not acceptable behavior in the Antioch community.

7. If someone verbally agrees to engage in specific contact or conduct, but it is not of her/his own free will due to any of the circumstances stated in (a) through (d) below, then the person initiating shall be considered in violation of this policy if:

    a) the person submitting is under the influence of alcohol or other substances supplied to her/him by the person initiating;

    b) the person submitting is incapacitated by alcohol, drugs, and/or prescribed medication;

    c) the person submitting is asleep or unconscious;

    d) the person initiating has forced, threatened, coerced, or intimidated the other individual(s) into engaging in sexual contact and/or sexual conduct.[18]

Although Antioch's Sexual Offense Policy is not specifically relevant to sexual harassment, it does underscore the point about the need for individually tailored policies. While most people cannot envision pausing at every interval of sexual contact and negotiating an agreement to proceed, the majority of the Antioch community, including students, clearly can conceive itself doing so, and that is what matters. Antioch's policy was written for Antioch and exists to serve students who apparently agree with its premises and are willing to subscribe to its demands. Effective policymaking evolves from knowledge and understanding of student constituencies, as well as familiarity with the law and popular harassment policy models; and while such information can provide only limited insight into the minds of heterogeneous individuals who comprise student bodies, it is nevertheless invaluable. Ultimately there is much to be gained from such knowledge—it can provide insight into harassment, but it can also serve as an impetus for greater commitment to the teaching vocation, as a reminder to academicians that they are responsible for preparing students to behave with greater sensitivity and civility in the world that lies beyond the campus.

Sexual Harassment and Institutional Characteristics and Culture

As has been noted earlier, most of the research on sexual harassment and organizational climates has focused on gender ratios and power disparities, which are indisputably the most significant concerns, but colleges' and universities' experiences with harassment are also affected by other factors that initially seem irrelevant to the problem. In order to understand fully how harassment works on their campuses and how to defend themselves against it, institutions need to engage in the kinds of self-analysis they employ in strategic planning. They must see themselves as if for the first time, as if they were strangers to their own organizations, and then they must ask themselves how their unique characteristics and cultures influence the dynamics of the harassment issue. Some organizational theorists would probably differentiate the objective characteristics (e.g., size, location, type) by which institutions are defined from the more subtle and complex elements of organizational climate and culture, but the three are so closely intertwined in academic institutions that they are discussed simultaneously here.

The topics of sexual harassment and organizational culture became popular at roughly the same time; this is why it is surprising that so few have attempted to examine the former through analysis of the latter. Every organization has a culture, however fragmented or dysfunctional, and that culture affects everything and everyone in the organization. A.M. Pettigrew noted that

> *there has been a history of confusion about the concept [of organizational culture] from its origins in social anthropology. . . . However, some progress has been made, and most scholars would now agree that organizational culture is a phenomenon that involves beliefs and behavior; exists at a variety of different levels in organizations; and manifests itself in a wide range of features of organizational life such as structures, control and reward systems, symbols, myths, and human resource practices.*[19]

T. Deal and A. Kennedy defined the five elements of culture as the environment in which the organization operates, the values or basic concepts and beliefs of the organization, the heroes or role models who personify its values, the rites and rituals that demonstrate what the organization stands for and respects, and the cultural network or informal means of communication by which primary interaction occurs.[20]

G. Morgan observed that the cultural metaphor is only one of several by which to explain and theorize about organizations. He defined it as "shared meaning, shared understanding . . . shared sense making. . . . [I]n talking about culture we are really talking about a process of reality construction that allows people to see and understand particular events, actions, objects, utterances, or situations in distinctive ways."[21] Morgan argued that while the culture metaphor and several others are accurate descriptors of organizations, they are also only partial because organizations are so complex and paradoxical that there is no "single authoritative position"[22] from which to view them. Even so, the culture metaphor appears most enlightening for the purpose of analyzing the sexual harassment issue in order to produce effective change on campus.

Pettigrew's observation about corporate change is especially relevant to academic institutions' attempts to combat harassment:

"We still know relatively little about the what, why, and how of climate and culture change. This is especially worrying in the culture area, since academic consultants and major consulting firms have rushed into producing culture change packages and programs before we even have a critical mass of high-quality case studies about how culture change processes occur."[23] Although there was originally no choice but to "rush in" and attempt to deal with sexual harassment by writing generic policies where none had previously existed and by providing basic education about the issue, institutions that have completed those phases should now be concentrating on producing more intrinsic changes. This will require review of not simply existing policies and programs but sweeping self-analysis that probes the roles of institutional history, mission, methodology, and governance/power in the dynamics of harassment.

History

Whether it is an extension of or a reaction against its history, an institution's present always reflects its past, and that past influences the harassment issue profoundly. A college that served male students for more than a century before it admitted women must educate its faculty about harassment in different ways from a traditionally co-educational university. A female college with few male faculty or administrators should provide special orientation for a male professor who has taught only in coeducational or exclusively male settings. An institution where presidents are historically figureheads with little power must reassess the conventional wisdom that heads of organizations, using the "top-down" approach, should lead movements to eliminate harassment. A university that has endured a very public sexual harassment suit will have tensions and a sense of urgency in constructing policy that a less unfortunate institution will not experience. To state the point simplistically, an institution cannot move from where it is to where it wants to be unless it has a clear understanding of where it has been. It may create procedures and policies that look impressive on paper, and it may provide elaborate training and support services, but these will be largely exercises unless they reflect the historical context within which students and employees function.

Mission

Collective agreement about institutional mission is another crucial step to eliminating sexual harassment. The clearer an institution's sense of mission and the more consistently it adheres to its goals, the more coherent will be its approach to harassment. Unfortunately, many, if not most, colleges and universities have very indeterminate concepts of mission, and their sense of ambiguity has grown worse over the last quarter of a century. M.D. Cohen and J.G. March contended:

Almost any educated person can deliver a lecture entitled "the Goals of the University." Almost no one will listen to the lecture voluntarily. For the most part, such lecturers and their companion essays are well-intentioned exercises in social rhetoric, with little operational content. . . .

    College presidents live within a normative context that presumes purpose and within an organizational context that denies it. They serve on commissions to define and redefine the objectives of higher education. They organize convocations to examine the goals of the college. They write introductory statements to the college catalog. They accept the presumption that intelligent leadership presupposes the pursuit of rational goals. Simultaneously, they are aware that the process of choice in the college depends little on statements of shared direction. They recognize the flow of actions as an ecology of games . . . each with its own rules. They accept the observation that the world is not like the model.[24]

An institution that is unclear about its priorities, that substitutes hollow rhetoric for action is ill-equipped to assume the responsibilities necessary to curtail harassment. It cannot ask, let alone answer, the hard questions that arise when a difficult grievance occurs. If, for instance, Shady Lawn College, which describes itself as "student-centered," employs a Pulitzer Prize–winning scientist who also happens to proposition several students each year, if his research earns millions of dollars for the institution, how will it go about dealing with grievances against the professor? The institutional hierarchy may read secrecy and successful containment of his behavior as survival, while the affected students will view these as betrayal of the college's commitment to them.

    If a university defines one of its major goals as providing a nurturing environment and does not offer its faculty guidance about establishing appropriate parameters in relating to students, no one should be surprised when some cross behavioral lines that have not been clearly articulated. If the institutional climate appears extremely authoritarian and faculty highly insular, it should come as no shock that students avoid institutional grievance mechanisms. If a university declares preparation of a responsible and civil citizenry a priority and yet tolerates rampant sexism in its classrooms, students will suspect that its sexual harassment policy, like its mission statement, consists merely of words.

When a college or university sets out to reexamine its mission statement or to compose or review harassment policies, it needs to acknowledge the relation between sexual harassment and ambiguity about or failure to live up to its mission. It needs to ask itself not only, "What do we hope to do here?" but also, "How well are we succeeding? What part does harassment play in our inability or refusal to live up to our goals and priorities? How does it interfere with our attempts to fulfill the mission we have recorded on paper?" This technique draws the harassment issue into the center of academic discourse rather than relegating it to the periphery where narrow, specialized concerns can languish indefinitely. When discussion of sexual harassment is framed within a larger context, when it is intentionally linked to the intrinsic rather than the marginal concerns of the institution, people tend to take the issue seriously and to believe that the institution regards it with earnestness.

Instructional Methodology

Methodology is associated and overlaps with mission. Organizations must be aware not only of what they wish to accomplish but how they go about fulfilling their goals. To conduct an exhaustive analysis of methodology or what could even be called "technology" on the contemporary American campus would be a forbidding task. Nevertheless, institutions should consider the role that methodology plays in the sexual harassment dynamic because it is more intricate than has been assumed to date. Ambiguity of methodology is as much a problem as ambiguity of mission on many campuses. In the case of instruction, for example, many educators know what they want to teach, but determining how best to teach it can be problematic and sometimes, as in the case of sexual harassment, hazardous because there are so many models and so few parameters.

Instructional methods vary not only from professor to professor, but from discipline to discipline, department to department, and college to college. Because the academic tradition of professional autonomy discourages critical analysis of pedagogical methods and supervision of classrooms and offices, educators may be deterred from recognizing danger signals for students and themselves. Nevertheless, even though the principle of professional autonomy will be preserved as long as there are college professors to exercise it, there are ways institutions and individuals can become more cognizant of problems that might arise in particular instructional settings. Professors can, for example, be educated about the basics of sexual harassment and then separated into subcultures or smaller units determined by similarities of function. Each of these groups can analyze the environment in which its members work and the ways in which they perform their tasks. This is not an especially time-consuming endeavor and can provide insight not only into sexual harassment but other crucial teaching concerns as well.

An illustration may clarify the point. A university includes several colleges, each with a variety of departments that may house more than one discipline. When that institution decides to comply with the law and train its faculty and staff about sexual harassment, it may hire a speaker or produce a memo to familiarize people with essential information about the issue. Once that is accomplished, the university, like most organizations, will assume it has fulfilled its obligation, and except for an occasional article in the student paper or the posting of signs on campus to discourage the behavior, the "educational" effort will be over. But if it is serious about protecting its students and personnel, the university must recognize that this is only the beginning, that sexual harassment assumes very different forms in its disparate subcultures, and that faculty and staff can protect themselves from misunderstanding if they are encouraged to be more aware of their assumptions and behaviors.

Students majoring in communications, media, and the arts, for instance, are accustomed to class content and interactions with professors that might deeply offend a classics or mathematics major. K.M. Galvin addressed this issue in "Preventing the Problem: Preparing Faculty Members for the Issues of Sexual Harassment."[25] Galvin noted that in such settings, professors routinely establish close physical contact with students (e.g., hold their rib cages to demonstrate breathing techniques), initiate intense discussions about erotic themes, analyze student performers' sexual appeal, and travel off campus with interns. Clearly such behaviors could be misunderstood by a student unfamiliar with them, just as the instructional techniques could easily be misused by an educator whose intentions were inappropriate. The art and performance disciplines are not the only areas subject to misinterpretation and misapplication. Any of the medical fields or academic disciplines using hands-on equipment could, for instance, suffer the same problems.

The atmosphere maintained in classrooms is likely to pervade other offices in a unit, making concern about sexual harassment an even more complex issue. If the teaching of a particular subject is characterized by informality, faculty are likely to maintain casualness in other campus interactions. Where there is great heterogeneity of disciplines and/or limited communication among academic units, misunderstandings are inevitable. Thus, to cope effectively with harassment, institutions need to examine prevailing teaching methods and departmental climates, establish clear behavioral parameters, educate everyone associated with the unit about its individual environment, and provide resources for those who believe boundaries have been violated.

Size

Institutional size undoubtedly affects efforts to understand and prevent harassment. It does not take a genius to recognize that the University of Michigan and Berea College in Kentucky are very different places and that any considerations of sexual harassment must acknowledge their diversities. On small campuses faculty members, administrators, staff, and students are generally so well acquainted that inappropriate behaviors and indiscretions are rapidly detected. At the nation's huge universities, some of which are almost the size of small towns, facilities are open around the clock, and faculty are unknown to one another as well as students. The difficulties of supervising permanent faculty operating on main campuses are magnified a thousandfold if one considers the problems posed by coping with adjunct faculty and satellite campuses. Sociologist Burton Clarke addressed this point in an article on academic governance: "A faculty member does not interact with most members of the faculty. In larger places, he may know less than a fifth, less than a tenth. Paths do not cross. . . . The campus is a holding company for professional groups rather than a single association of professionals . . . more like the United Nations and less like a small town."[26]

The dilemma of large institutions may extend well beyond their difficulties with detection. The larger the student body and staff, the more difficult it is to educate people effectively, to ensure that policies and procedures are understood and observed, and to encourage use of support services. On the other hand, universities have enormous financial and political interests at stake, so many have devoted considerable attention and resources to policymaking, educational programming, and support services. Magnitude is a weak excuse for ignoring the sexual harassment problem, and large institutions can ensure that it is properly addressed in subunits, where education and perhaps even counseling can be tailored to individual cultures and constituencies.

Whether an institution is large or small, size presents difficulties, none of which are insurmountable. A young woman who transferred from a small private liberal arts college to a state university recalled, "I couldn't breathe there [the small institution] after I got upset over Dr. S. Everyone knew and everyone in the school took a side. I just had to get out." At this same state university, another woman complained, "I hate this place. They've got their fancy roles and offices and say they're helping you but no one does anything about this guy. He just stays lost in the crowd year after year." The responsibility of the institution in both cases is to ask itself how size influences perpetrators, harassees, and efforts to contain the behavior and then to create mechanisms to offset the problems.

External Support and Governance Systems

Another reason that "cookie-cutter" approaches to harassment will not work is that varying external and tangential governance and support systems influence organizational culture and affect its perceptions of acceptable as opposed to unacceptable behavior. This was Warren Bennis's point in observing that "an organization must interact not only with its primary environments . . . but also with many technological, legal, social, economic, and institutional structures that constrain the activities of the organization and over which it has very little direct control."[27] Imprudent institutions wait until grievances occur to consider how legislators, governing boards, alumni, and donors will respond to an issue like consensual faculty-student relationships. Smart colleges and universities write mission statements, develop instructional technologies, conduct research, hire, and create all policies and programs, not just those pertaining to sexual harassment, with their support constituencies in mind.

Even routine procedures like hiring, though seldom perceived as such, are directly relevant to the sexual harassment issue. Faculty generally control selection of colleagues; defining themselves largely in terms of discipline expertise, they hire in their own images and focus on applicants' education, research, and publications. They rarely pay attention to the larger institutional perspective. In many colleges and universities no attempts are made to investigate whether candidates' styles and values are compatible with external constituencies whose support is essential to institutional survival. Most academics balk at observations like this because it seems to imply disregard for academic freedom and intolerance of diversity and eccentricity. On the contrary, it simply asserts a reality of life for contemporary colleges and universities: when institutions are struggling to survive and to avoid unnecessary controversy, they must be astute enough to employ faculty with consideration of philosophy and style rather than reputation alone.

There are indeterminate or gray areas in sexual harassment theory, and common sense necessitates recognition that behavior which may succeed or go unchallenged at a state-funded research university in one section of the country could result in disaster at a small private college in another location. When a grievance does arise, the reputations and financial support systems of the two institutions may be threatened in different ways, so both must anticipate how their external constituencies will react and have rapid and effective response mechanisms in place before trouble occurs.

Concern for Public Image

As noted in Chapter 1, when complaints do occur, most organizational cultures encourage the ineffective responses of secrecy and stonewalling. This is especially true in higher education because of its service mission and its preoccupation with public image. But organizational reality is often at odds with the temptation to conceal, and the unusually loose or diffuse organizational structure of academe discourages and even prohibits the total concealment colleges and universities seek in stressful circumstances. Every organization has what Deal and Kennedy defined as a "cultural network [which is] the primary means of communication within the organization [that] ties together all [of its] parts . . . without respect to positions or titles. The network is important because it not only transmits information but also interprets the significance of the information for employees."[28] In academe, this network is usually enormous.

Much of the business of an institution, including proceedings concerning sexual harassment, is carried out by committees that require secretarial staff; faculty, support personnel, and students are more often than not cognizant of situations involving complaints. Any or all of these could activate the network that conveys not only information about a particular case, but also sends a message about the institution's priorities in dealing with harassment. If the message is that institutional image and self-protection are primary, the negative repercussions for employees and students can be devastating.

This is not to suggest that confidentiality should not be a concern. Confidentiality about identities and specific details of grievances is almost always in the best interest of everyone concerned. Institutions have a responsibility to provide training in maintaining confidentiality and to develop sanctions for those who violate it and thus abrogate their responsibility to the institution, but they must also recognize that "confidentiality" and "disclosure" are not antithetical terms. One of the most effective ways to discourage harassment is to admit its existence not as a theoretical but an actual campus problem. This means that colleges and universities must be committed to responsible disclosure that provides a very general overview of institutional efforts to curtail harassment.

In an annual report sexual harassment might be defined as one category of concern. Then the institution might indicate the number of reports of the behavior and the number of formal and informal grievances that have occurred within a designated period; it could conclude its report by indicating how many complaints were found to be valid and resulted in sanctions against offending parties. The academic mind resists this approach because it subscribes to the myth of pastorality that envisions academe as a contemporary Eden miraculously removed from the crude realities of the "outside" world; but since its inhabitants are now and always have been subject to the same temptations and human frailties as others, and since higher education does not enjoy a reputation for candor, it would improve its image by demonstrating straightforwardness about the campus environment. Far more important, limited disclosure would send an essential message to the campus community.

Many colleges and universities attempt to fulfill students' demands for thorough investigations and for definitive responses to sexual harassment, but their efforts go unrecognized because their obsessions with preserving privacy and maintaining their images lead them to behave surreptitiously when grievances arise. The results are devastating. In the absence of awareness and candid discussion of sexual harassment, people can be lulled into the complacent assumption that it is nonexistent. Victims erroneously assume that theirs are isolated circumstances and that their complaints will be unwelcome. Institutions that discipline professors for inappropriate behaviors and do not bother to inform victims create skepticism and mistrust among students.

The argument for disclosure does not require that institutions publish names and details of grievances, nor that they jeopardize recruitment and public image. It suggests simply that faculty, administrators, staff, and, most of all, students would benefit from straightforward communication about sexual harassment on their campuses. As they have designed individualized policies and procedures, institutions can and should establish disclosure mechanisms fitted to their particular needs and circumstances. Grievants whose complaints are judged credible deserve information about the discipline administered; otherwise, supposition and rumor triumph and the victim's risk appears worthless. The entire campus community has the right and the obligation to be notified about the number and types of grievances heard and penalties allocated.[29]

Internal Governance
The sexual harassment dynamic may also be influenced by the extent to which institutional units do or do not share responsibility and decision making. When the issue first attracted attention, there

was little proof for claims that perpetrators' actions and harassees' responses might be affected by diffused authority systems and perceptions about professorial collegiality, but years of experience have demonstrated that this is precisely the case. Possibly the single most troubling situation that faces policymakers today is that despite their efforts, the number of individuals filing complaints is shockingly small compared to that of those reporting experience with harassment. The discrepancy is too large to explain away without considering harassees' anxiety about retaliation and institutional paralysis.

The most frequently cited deterrent to reporting in any organization is fear of retaliation; such concern is especially pronounced on college campuses where collegiality is perceived to be a strong force. A parent attending an orientation lecture that included discussion of harassment voiced what is probably a widely held impression: "In my day teachers stuck together, and it only got worse in college. I wouldn't tell my daughters to put up with anything, but I'm not letting them get cut up by a bunch of professors either. If [harassment] happens to one of them, they're out of here, not staying and getting ganged up on by a bunch of people protecting their own."

When they are not expressing concern about retaliation, the subjects of harassment explain their reluctance to come forward by citing uncertainty about the effectiveness of support personnel and by expressing doubt that anyone has power to handle a complaint decisively. Such responses derive from perceptions that authority is so diffused in higher education that no one is ultimately accessible enough or powerful enough to effect real change. Tenure and staggering layers of bureaucracy and rules appear to protect professors who would be summarily dismissed in other organizations. Support personnel typically lack the clout of faculty, so students, staff, and colleagues of perpetrators are frequently moved to inaction and silence.

Another result of academe's curious culture of shared governance is that subcultures with equal power may be characterized by so many diverse and conflicting interests and values that it becomes impossible to focus attention on an issue like sexual harassment, let alone to reach consensus about it. Much of the literature describes higher education as a fragmented, weak, or dysfunctional culture. Cohen and March referred to it as "prototypic organized anarchy,"[30] as a "garbage can model"[31] of organization, and while such descriptions do not necessarily apply to all colleges and universities, Deal and Kennedy's warning is worth considering: "The problem with fragmented cultures is that they do not mesh well when they need to. When people from the different cultures come together, each listens to different drummers, and confusion and frustration result from their inability to see eye to eye on matters that need to be discussed and resolved."[32]

How does a college president pressured by legal constraints convey a sense of urgency about the harassment issue to a non-tenure-track English instructor whose professional future depends on gaining recognition from the Modern Language Association? How does a faculty member who wishes to avoid false accusations successfully argue for a training program when budget cuts have limited support services for harassees? How does a university professor who year after year hears complaints against a colleague in another college of the institution navigate the professional maze to meet his/her obligations to students? How do people in engineering and theater departments agree upon standards of conduct and conversation between professors, students, and staff?

Sex Ratios, Power Distribution, and Unionization

The answer to all of these is "not very easily," and the organizational mosaic becomes even more intricate when subcultures with disparate gender compositions and power inequalities enter the mix. There are few institutions where males do not dominate females in both number and status, and this fact has great influence on the campus environment. The supposition that men and women would respond uniformly to the harassment issue was never valid, but as numerous studies have established,[33] gender does influence experiences and attitudes so that even when males and females agree on points relevant to harassment, they are approaching it from different perspectives that must take gender into account. A female and male professor who argue that sexual harassment is a nonissue undeserving of attention on campus may have two entirely separate agendas; he, to avoid criticism of his own questionable behavior, and she, to win approval from male colleagues hostile to the issue. Males and females who define harassment as an exclusively female problem and exaggerate its effects may also be driven by different responses: he by gender guilt, she by gender anger.

While it is important to recognize that male and female perceptions differ and interesting to explore response variations within genders, a more crucial practical concern is determining how consensus about policies and procedures can be reached amid such diversity and sex ratio imbalance. It is a formidable task, but it must be taken seriously because in situations where gender warfare dominates a campus culture or subculture, eliminating sexual harassment becomes secondary to gaining turf in the battle to prove gender supremacy. One way to decrease contentiousness during educational training is to begin with consciousness raising about differences in male and female perceptions of specific behaviors and then proceed to issues such as definition, liability, incidence, and costs of sexual harassment. Consensus occurs most readily when the perceptions and opinions of both genders are acknowledged, and policies, procedures, and sanctions gain widest acceptance when they are conceived by individuals committed to allowing objective information rather than personal agendas to dominate decisions about the issue.

Power inequalities between the genders are but one characteristic of academe's organizational maze. The literature on sexual harassment emphasizes the power discrepancy between professors and students, so few consider that despite the status they demand and receive, faculty are actually a subculture of the enormous operation that higher education has become. On most campuses they are outnumbered many times over by administrative, secretarial, maintenance, and other support personnel who must also cope with the harassment issue. Yet an infrequently discussed but increasingly controversial problem is the discrepancy in the treatment of complaints against faculty as opposed to those against employees in less influential positions. In many institutions there is a perception among staff that a caste system protects the professoriate and more readily indicts the less powerful. When employee status affects handling of accusations and imposition of sanctions, morale suffers and acrimony develops among the subcultures. Thus one of the urgent but overlooked challenges on the modern campus is composing policies that avoid unfair status distinctions.

To increase the complexity even further, contemporary administrators must struggle with the restrictions imposed by campus unions. A sexual harassment suit filed by a secretary against a maintenance worker could bring her union into conflict with his, which might argue that his case is being handled differently from that of an AAUP member found guilty of a worse offense. Conflicting approaches to sexual harassment among different campus unions can cause dissension, just as discord may arise within the ranks as unions struggle to determine proper positions on the issue. The professoriate is particularly vulnerable in this respect since the traditions of autonomy and diffused governance combine with educators' power in the insular world of academe.

George Keller, author of *Academic Strategy: The Management Revolution in Higher Education*, was perceptive in observing:

[T]he academic profession is not a self-policing profession. The American Association of University Professors has, since its founding in 1915, been principally a narrow protective league that guards faculty rights such as academic freedom and tenure rather than an encompassing professional association that insures professional standards, behavior, and obligations and censures or expels culpable members for fraud, abuse of intellectual freedom, incompetence and gross violations of ethics.[34]

On some campuses, the AAUP has demonstrated strong commitment to helping eradicate sexual harassment, but since this is not uniformly the case, Keller's assertion should serve as a caveat to members and leaders of faculty unions. They must be vigilant in remembering that their duties differ from those of workers in factories and businesses. The primary "products" of higher education are knowledge and people, so both employees and students, the largest interest group and the real "work" of an institution, suffer when members of academic unions violate ethical standards and are excused by colleagues whose first priority is faculty rights.

If there were ways to alter the culture of the academy, to reinvent some of its most cherished traditions and unify fragmented and conflicting subcultures, sexual harassment would be a less serious problem; but while academicians are always eager to create processes and policies, they are no more and perhaps less enthusiastic than others about introspection. Their characteristic approach to a problem is to appoint or elect a committee that conducts research, argues over details, and devises a new procedure and often another layer of bureaucracy. To a large extent, this system has worked with sexual harassment. There is a sense of control where chaos and ignorance about the issue formerly reigned. If that was the primary goal of policymakers, most have succeeded, but if the ultimate hope was to create environments or cultures that actively mitigate against harassment, much remains to be done.

In an ironic sense, colleges and universities have themselves become victims of perpetrators. The potential costs to institutions now that harassment is a recognized legal and social concern are incalculable, and the dangers the behavior poses to the organizational climate are enormous.

Sexual harassment is a serious organizational problem that not only dehumanizes those who are harassed, but inevitably negatively influences the effectiveness of organizing activities and diminishes the quality of work life for organization members. It clearly causes personal and professional harm to the targets of harassment. It promotes distrust and hostility between those individuals who are the initiators and targets of sexual harassment, between those who are accused of harassment and their co-workers [and/or students] who level accusations, as well as between those who side with these different parties to sexual harassment. . . . Such distrust and hostility ultimately lead to the creation of defensive organizational climates in which working relationships (and levels of cooperation) between organization members deteriorate. . . . Sexual harassment also distracts organization members from the accomplishment of important organizational goals, irrevocably decreasing both the quality of organizational life and the productivity of organization activities.[35]

This view was echoed by a college president whose institution suffered through a lengthy sexual harassment grievance: "We lost a lot of money and a lot of public respect, but these were nothing compared to all we lost as professionals and a community. We have wounds now that will never heal. Everyone is paying for what one person did." The message is that harassment can impose enormous personal, professional, financial, organizational, and social burdens that no amount of rhetoric about the spuriousness of the issue can erase. Sexual harassment has become and will remain a legitimate concern for institutions not only because it creates hazards for targets of the behavior, but because it costs too much in too many ways educational institutions cannot afford.

Notes

1.   See E.L. Dey, J.S. Korn, and L.J. Sax (1996), "Betrayed by the Academy: The Sexual Harassment of Women College Faculty," *Journal of Higher Education*, 67, 149–73 and R.O. Riggs, P.H. Murrell, and J.C. Cutting (1993). *Sexual Harassment in Higher Education: From Conflict to Community* (ASME-ERIC Higher Education Report No. 2). Washington, D.C., George Washington University, School of Education and Human Development.

2.   See B. Gutek, *Sex and the Workplace* (San Francisco: Jossey-Bass, 1985); R.M. Kanter (1977), "Some Effects of Proportions on Group Life: Skewed Sex Ratios and Responses to Token Women," *American Journal of Sociology*, 965–90; D.N. Israeli (1983), "Sex Effects or Structural Effects? An Empirical Test of Kanter's Theory of Proportions," *Social Forces*, 153–65; T.C. Fain and D.L. Anderton (1987), "Sexual Harassment: Organizational Context and Diffuse Status," *Sex Roles*, 17, 291–311.

3.   A. Astin, "Proposals for Change in College Administration," in *Maximizing Leadership Effectiveness*, ed. A. Astin and R. Scherrei (San Francisco: Jossey-Bass, 1981), p. 62.

4.   See J. Adams, J.L. Kottke, and J.S. Padgitt (1983), "Sexual Harassment of University Students," *Journal of College Student Personnel*, 24, 484–90; S. Kenig and J. Ryan (1986), "Sex Differences in Levels of Tolerance and Attribution of Blame for Sexual Harassment on a University Campus," *Sex Roles*, 5, 535–49; B. Lott, M.E. Reilly, and D.R. Howard (1982), "Sexual Assault and Harassment: A Campus Community Case Study" *Signs: Journal of Women in Culture and Society*, 8, 296–319; N. Maihoff and L. Forest (1983), "Sexual Harassment in Higher Education: An Assessment Study, "*Journal of the National Association for Women Deans, Administrators, and Counselors*, 46, 3–8; S.C. Padgitt and J.S. Padgitt (1986) "Cognitive Structure of Sexual Harassment: Implications for University Policy," *Journal of College Student Personnel*, 34, 34–39; M.E. Reilly, B. Lott, and S.M. Gallogly (1986), "Sexual Harassment of University Students," *Sex Roles*, 15, 333–58.

5.   Fain and Anderton, p. 294.

6.   N.J. Malovich and J.E. Stake (1990), "Sexual Harassment on Campus: Individual Differences in Attitudes and Beliefs," *Psychology of Women Quarterly*, 14, 63–81.

7.   G.N. Powell (1986) "Effects of Sex Role Identity and Sex on Definitions of Sexual Harassment," *Sex Roles*, 14, 9–19.

8.   D. Lester, B. Banta, J. Barton, N. Elian, L. Mackiewicz, and J. Winkelried (1986), "Is Personality Related to Judgments about Sexual Harassment?" *Psychological Reports*, 59, 1114.

9.   See D.D. Baker and D.E. Terpstra (1986), "Locus of Control and Self-esteem Versus Demographic Factors as Predictors of Attitudes toward Women, "*Basic and Applied Social Psychology*, 7, 163–72; A.L. Rhodes (1983), "Effects of Religious Denomination of Sex Differences in Occupational Expectations," *Sex Roles*, 9, 93–108; A. Thornton, D.F. Alwin, and D. Camburn (1983), "Causes and Consequences of Sex-Role Attitudes and Attitude Change," *American Sociologi-*

cal Review, 48, 211–27; D.D. Baker, D.E. Terpstra, and K. Larntz (1990), "The Influence of Individual Characteristics and Severity of Harassing Behavior on Reactions to Sexual Harassment," *Sex Roles*, 22, 305–25.

10. Baker, Terpstra, and Larntz, p. 308.

11. *Id.*, p. 319.

12. Fain and Anderton, p. 309.

13. See D.C. DeFour, "The Interface of Racism and Sexism on College Campuses" in M. Paludi, ed., *Sexual Harassment on College Campuses: Abusing the Ivory Power* (Albany: State University of New York Press, 1996).

14. A. McCormack (1985), "The Sexual Harassment of Students by Teachers: The Case of Students in Science," *Sex Roles*, 13, 21–32.

15. K.R. Wilson and L.A. Kraus (1983), "Sexual Harassment in the University," *Journal of College Student Personnel*, 24, 219–24.

16. See Dey.

17. See Malovich and Stake.

18. The Antioch College Sexual Offense Policy, Approved by the Board of Trustees, June 8, 1996.

19. A.M. Pettigrew, "Organizational Climate and Culture: Two Constructs in Search of a Role," in *Organizational Climate and Culture*, ed. B. Snyder (San Francisco: Jossey-Bass, 1990), pp. 414–15.

20. See T.E. Deal and A.A. Kennedy, *Corporate Cultures: The Rites and Rituals of Corporate Life* (Reading, Mass.: Addison-Wesley, 1983).

21. G. Morgan, *Images of Organization* (Newbury Park, Calif.: Sage, 1986), p. 128.

22. *Id.*, p. 341.

23. Pettigrew, p. 415.

24. M.D. Cohen and J.G. March, *Leadership and Ambiguity: The American College President*, 2nd ed. (Boston: Harvard Business School Press, 1974), pp. 195, 197.

25. See K.M. Galvin, "Preventing the Problem: Preparing Faculty Members for the Issues of Sexual Harassment," in *Sexual Harassment: Communication Implications*, ed. Gary L. Kreps (Cresskill, N.J.: Hampton Press, 1993).

26. B. Clarke, quoted in George Keller, *Academic Strategy: The Management Revolution in Higher Education* (Baltimore: Johns Hopkins University Press, 1983), p. 36.

27. W. Bennis and Burt Nanus, *Leaders: The Strategies for Taking Charge* (New York: Harper & Row, 1985), pp. 137–8.

28. Deal and Kennedy, p. 85.

29. B.W. Dziech, "Author's Note" in *The Lecherous Professor: Sexual Harassment on Campus*, 2nd ed., by B.W. Dziech and L. Weiner (Boston: Beacon Press, 1990), p. xxii.

30. Cohen and March, p. 3.

31. Cohen and March, p. 211.

32. Deal and Kennedy, p. 137.

33. See Baker, Terpstra, and Larntz; Malovich and Stake; Rubin and Borgers.

34. G. Keller, *Academic Strategy: The Management Revolution in Higher Education* (Baltimore: Johns Hopkins University Press, 1983), p. 29.

35. G.L. Kreps, "Promoting a Sociocultural Evolutionary Approach to Preventing Sexual Harassment: Metacommunication and Cultural Adaptation" in *Sexual Harassment: Communication Implications* (Cresskill, N.J.: Hampton Press, 1993), pp. 310–11.

Chapter Three
Of Butterflies and Birds
Helping Women Deal with Sexual Harassment

Pain can make a whole winter bright,
Like fever, force us to live deep and hard,
Betrayal focus in a peculiar light
All we have ever dreamed or known or heard
And from great shocks we do recover.
—May Sarton, "Humpty Dumpty"

When authors and researchers first named and began to study sexual harassment, major obstacles and goals confronted them. They needed credible definitions of the behavior and proof that this obscure issue was more than a figment of capricious or hostile imaginations. They had to demonstrate that it was not an innocent, innocuous, normal, or amusing activity; that it could cause psychological, physical, academic, and career damage. Once laws became involved, they wanted not simply to encourage concern for the legal ramifications of the problem, but also to convince people that sexual harassment was, first and foremost, a moral and professional concern, an offense that harmed not only individuals, but institutions and organizations as well, and that created profound gender division.

In the beginning, information about the effects of the behavior was largely anecdotal and probably suspect to those who had never heard of, much less witnessed, the more outrageous and offensive actions of perpetrators. Some collected the ugly accounts and, in retelling them, assumed that others would be equally enraged at incidents of academicians humiliating, threatening, and propositioning students and colleagues. But this assumption often proved false. Few harassees were willing to come forward publicly, so much of the discussion relied on secondhand information. Those who had some frame of reference that predisposed them to understand the problem recognized its significance. Others, unwilling to relinquish confidence in the benevolent nature of higher education and unable to comprehend unsubstantiated stories of trauma they could not see, disbelieved what they heard and read about sexual harassment.

In time researchers, particularly those in the social sciences, created greater clarity and credibility by collecting data on individuals subjected to the behavior. The statistics were shocking; they confirmed *Redbook* magazine's conclusion in its 1976 survey of workplace harassment: "The problem is not epidemic; it is pandemic—an everyday everywhere occurrence."[1] Even more compelling, however, were the words of those willing to describe their interactions with perpetrators. The vast majority were females, and it was difficult to remain untouched by their experiences and reactions. Logically, albeit unconsciously, their voices led them to be called "victims," and the name persisted.

It endured because case law, legislative efforts, and research revealed so much about the prevalence and the costs of harassment, and after two decades, attorneys, legislators, and researchers are still providing crucial insight into the sexual harassment dynamic as it affects women. An impressive amount of information has accumulated to explain prevalence, perceptions, negative consequences, and coping strategies among females, but far less is known about differential responses to the behavior and about counseling harassees so that ultimately women, who are the primary targets of the behavior, can emerge as something other than "victims" in their own and society's eyes.

Women and Sexual Harassment: The Known

Despite definitional and statistical ambiguities and limitations in research methodology, it is possible to present a fairly definitive overview of women and sexual harassment. As previously noted, the "safe" prevalence statistic is 30 percent, and there is general agreement that for a variety of reasons the offense is underreported. Although Fitzgerald and her associates maintained that female graduate students are more likely to experience harassment than undergraduates,[2] some studies report that younger women are the most frequent targets and that they are more tolerant of the behavior than older females.[3] Using data from the 1981 Merit System Review and Studies, Fain and Anderton observed that in the workplace, both minority and marital status increase females' vulnerability.

Relationships between minority status and pressure for sexual favors, gestures, and dates are statistically significant. For these behaviors, minority individuals are more likely to be sexually harassed. . . . The relationship between marital status and all types of sexual harassment is clearly significant. Percentage differences in harassment between marital groups are greater than differences between racial . . . groups. For all types of harassment, divorced, separated, and widowed women are most likely to be harassed. . . . Previously married and single women may be viewed as better targets by harassers for sexual pursuit.[4]

It is also clear that there are significant gender differences in perceptions about harassing behavior. Women are far more likely than men to define specific behaviors as harassment[5] and to find them less acceptable.[6] They are also more willing than males to blame themselves when it occurs, to view it as inevitable, and to endure it without significant protest.[7]

Coping strategies vary across a continuum from passive to assertive. A minority of women submit to harassment, but the vast majority attempt to cope by denying, ignoring, or trivializing the behavior. When this does not work, they turn to indirect mechanisms; they avoid harassers, take friends with them if interaction is necessary, discuss their boyfriends or spouses in perpetrators' hearing. Some deliberately appear unattractive in the presence of offenders; many drop classes, change majors, or leave school rather than risk confrontation.[8] Women are more likely to report severe incidences of harassment, but research in this area is ambiguous, since at least one study found that what students believe they will do in a given situation is quite different from their actual responses when confronted with harassment.[9] As indicated previously, reporting is extraordinarily low, given high prevalence rates, and one study found that when female students do report harassment, they are most likely to do so to a woman not in the perpetrator's department.[10]

Riger hypothesized that females are negatively influenced by gender bias in grievance procedures which incorrectly assume that males and females are identical in their perceptions of sexual harassment and their orientations to dispute resolution.[11] She noted that women students prefer informal attempts to resolve harassment disputes, probably because females are less comfortable with the adversarial character of formal proceedings and more so with informal approaches that attempt "to restore harmony or at least peaceful coexistence among the parties involved [as opposed to] formal procedures that attempt to judge guilt or innocence of the offender."[12] Informal mechanisms are, nevertheless, problematic for women because, as Riger pointed out, informal grievances are even less likely than formal to result in appropriate and adequate sanctions. In addition, the confidentiality surrounding informal approaches prevents other harassees from knowing about complaints and thus may deprive the complainant of support. Perhaps even more significant is that it protects perpetrators' identities and allows institutions to underestimate the seriousness of the problem because informal grievances are seldom included in reports of prevalence rates.

In most respects, then, college women are the "ideal" targets for sexual harassers. The majority are young; many, if not most, are unmarried; and they are, above all, relegated not only by gender but also by student status to positions of subordinance in institutions of higher education. There are indisputably exceptions, but in general, B.R. Snyder's observations about "the hidden curriculum" remain true a quarter century after he stated them.

The college system is such that the professor can work out his own philosophy, as well as his aggressions, on students. He can chop them down because they seem too independent, arrogant, creative; or because they are too casual, careless, condescending. Obviously only a few professors are looking to make scapegoats and victims out of their students, but many other members of the faculty seem to get caught up by the contest. A professor may inadvertently adopt the role assigned to him by students and fellow faculty members, and increasingly become a cynic, wit, detached man, or watchdog at the gate.

The fact is that, while most professors do want their students to explore ideas, generate new questions, and engage in intellectual risktaking, they find themselves caught in a trap that militates against these goals. Large classes, rigid testing methods, overextended schol-

ars who derive their principal rewards from research all reinforce the system.[13]

And, as Chapter 2 argues, the system, by its very nature, sometimes may act as a haven for perpetrators and deter harassees' protests. In a 1967 essay, Farber described the predicament of the typical student.

Students don't ask that orders make sense. They give up expecting things to make sense long before leaving elementary school. Things are true because the teachers say they're true. . . . Outside of class, things are true to your tongue, your fingers, your stomach, your heart. And that's just fine anyway. Miss Wiedemeyer tells you a noun is a person, place, or thing. So let it be. You don't give a rat's ass; she doesn't give a rat's ass. The important thing is to please her. Back in kindergarten, you found out that teachers only love children who stand in nice straight lines. And that's where it's been ever since.[14]

People who have been taught to "stand in nice straight lines" do not protest easily. This is especially true if those individuals happen to be female. After all the jubilation about the last decades' emancipation of women from stereotypes, the truth is that many females are still socialized to greater passivity, nonassertiveness, and acquiescence to authority than males. Females are consistently recognized and rewarded by teachers for their cooperation and obedience. When gender socialization combines with student domestication, and sexual harassment occurs, the combination can be devastating.

The complex and troubling responses sexual harassment evokes in women have been titled the "sexual harassment syndrome" and are described in detail in M.A. Paludi's and R.B. Barickman's *Academic and Workplace Sexual Harassment: A Resource Manual.*

Sexual Harassment Trauma Syndrome

Emotional Reactions
        Anxiety, shock, denial
        Anger, fear, frustration

> Insecurity, betrayal, embarrassment
> Confusion, self-consciousness
> Shame, powerlessness
> Guilt, isolation

Physical Reactions
> Headaches
> Sleep disturbances
> Lethargy
> Gastrointestinal distress
> Hypervigilance
> Dermatological reactions
> Weight fluctuations
> Nightmares
> Phobias, panic reactions
> Genitourinary distress
> Respiratory problems
> Substance abuse

Changes in Self-Perception
> Negative self-concept/self-esteem
> Lack of competency
> Lack of control
> Isolation
> Hopelessness
> Powerlessness

Social, Interpersonal Relatedness, and Sexual Effects
> Withdrawal
> Fear of new people, situations
> Lack of trust
> Lack of focus
> Self-preoccupation
> Changes in social network patterns
> Negative attitudes and behavior in sexual relationships
> Potential sexual disorders associated with stress and trauma
> Changes in dress or physical appearance

Career Effects

      Changes in study and work habits

      Loss of job or promotion

      Unfavorable performance evaluations

      Drop in academic or work performance because of stress

      Lower grades as punishment for reporting sexual harass-
      ment or for noncompliance with sexual advances

      Absenteeism

      Withdrawal from work and school

      Changes in career goals[15]

Counseling Harassees: Ambiguity and Caution

Close examination of these responses, which have been validated in study after study, indicates these reactions would not be readily observable to casual and even sometimes intimate acquaintances. Embarrassment and shame do not, for example, lead one to make public proclamations about one's state of mind, not even to the individual causing the embarrassment and shame. Thus many of the extreme acts of harassment, performed in private, are borne in silence and escape attention. Because the effects are largely invisible or attributable to or even the result of other causes, it is easy to assume that sexual harassment is a myth and even easier to believe that it is an exaggerated concern. As experience with harassees has grown, it has become increasingly apparent that it is, in many cases, a life-changing event. The authors of an article in the *American Journal of Psychiatry* asserted that "sexual harassment [is] a life event that engenders loss. . . . [It] should be recognized as a psychosocial stressor warranting a rating of 4 (severe) to 5 (extreme)"[16] according to health professionals' *Diagnostic and Statistical Manual of Mental Disorders.* While not all sexual harassment results in extreme trauma, much of it does, and colleges and universities are seldom equipped to cope with severe victimization.

    Although she did not deal directly with harassment, R. Janoff-Bulman, author of *Shattered Assumptions: Towards a New Psychology of Trauma,*[17] provided a model for understanding such trauma. She asserted that the majority of people possess what C.M. Parkes described as an "assumptive world,"[18] a core set of assumptions about the self and the external world that comprises their theories of reality and enables them to comprehend events and act in the present, as well as plan for the future. Janoff-Bulman proposed that most people approach life with the fundamental assumption that the world is benevolent, that it is meaningful, and that they are worthy and capable of control.

These three assumptions can be more narrowly defined to describe the expectations that students bring to the educational experience. From the earliest stages, children are taught that teachers are kind, caring, and beneficent; that they have students' best interests at heart; that the classroom is a benevolent, safe world designed to lead to positive outcomes. The very images used to describe higher education imply peace and separation from the harried "real" world; thus people refer to the "groves of academe," the "contemplative life," the "ivory tower." Children are told that behaviors have consequences and that they will be rewarded or punished in class for what they do or do not do; if school is identified as an orderly and meaningful place, then what happens to students in it is in their minds logically the result of their own choices and actions. Enlightened educators and parents encourage development of self-esteem in children; thus they attempt to inculcate perceptions of the learner as moral, capable, and able to shape the outcomes of his or her educational experience.

When such assumptions are "shattered," as Janoff-Bulman described the process, many individuals are never the same.

Overwhelming life events force victims to confront their own fragility at a deep experiential level. Their vulnerability is glaringly exposed. Psychologically, they are unprepared, for at the very core of their being they believed in their own security and protection. . . . Nothing seems to be as they had thought, their inner world is in turmoil. Suddenly the self- and worldviews they had taken for granted are unreliable. They can no longer assume that the world [academe] is a good place or that [the people in it] are kind and trustworthy. They can no longer assume that the world [academe] is meaningful or what happens [there] makes sense. They can no longer assume that they have control over negative outcomes or will reap benefits because they are good people. The very nature of the world [academe] and self seems to have changed; neither can be trusted, neither guarantees security. . . .

Traumatic life events [like sexual harassment] provide powerful evidence that the world is a frightening place in which they are not protected. Suddenly the victim's inner world is pervaded by thoughts and images representing malevolence, meaninglessness, and self-abasement. They are face to face with a dangerous universe, made all the more frightening by their total lack of psychological preparation.[19]

Few are aware of the total costs of severe harassment; they fail to realize that not only the victims of perpetrators but others on and off campus may eventually become caught in the dynamic. If others are supportive, the woman being harassed may regain her sense of control, but if her predicament so threatens others' assumptions about educators, they may revictimize her. Nonvictims are poorly prepared psychologically for the complexities sexual harassment raises. If one's roommate can be assaulted by a professor, then that individual may herself be at risk. If instructors violate students' trust, the professoriate may be less high-minded than its members choose to believe. If sexual harassment is epidemic on campus, parents may have to think twice about sending their daughters miles away to face very real perils in unfamiliar environments. The experiences of those who have been harassed disconcert those who have not because they threaten basic assumptions about higher education and people's ability to affect it.

Thus their responses to harassees are not as universally sympathetic and supportive as might be expected. In "Changed Lives: The Psychological Impact of Sexual Harassment," M.P. Koss used recent research to provide an overview of nonvictims' typical responses to victims: "The victimization is either denied or trivialized. . . . [V]ictims are seen as responsible for their fate . . . ignored . . . seen as losers . . . feared . . . or avoided because they are depressed."[20] To deny or trivialize sexual harassment, to stigmatize or blame a peer, student, or daughter for her predicament allows one to maintain simplistic assumptions about academe and minimizes responsibility for intervening on behalf of the harassee. Noting that 33 percent of workers in the Merit System Review survey felt the grievance process exacerbated their dilemmas by forcing them to relive the original harm and to experience revictimization, Charney and Russell declared:

If there is retaliation by the perpetrator, a disappointing institutional response, lack of support from co-workers or peers, insensitivity or blame at home, or a lengthy, unsatisfactory grievance procedure, then the victim is said to suffer a "second injury." Revictimization, or second injury, further diminishes an individual's trust in other people and in society in general. The individual may be left with a sense of isolation and vulnerability in a world that may seem unpredictable and unjust.[21]

Those who acknowledge the existence of harassment but nevertheless argue that females (or males) should invariably be able to withstand it know little about human beings. It is naive to assume that everyone is psychologically prepared to cope with threatening experiences or trauma. People respond to sexual harassment in an infinite variety of ways because they have vastly dissimilar backgrounds, value systems, and psychological strengths and weaknesses. A professor may proposition a homecoming queen or a feminist activist, and both may promptly file grievances. On the other hand, a former rape victim might be completely traumatized by a seemingly innocuous advance. Such dissimilarity in people's responses to similar incidents accounts for the courts' establishment of the reasonable-person standard in sexual harassment litigation.

Harassees' reactions are never totally predictable, which is why sexual harassment is so dangerous. In theory, contemporary women should have no inordinate need for protection. But in reality, students and institutional employees possess individual histories and unique personalities that prevent them from acting or reacting in ideal ways. When harassment occurs, people cannot be forced to be stronger or more sophisticated than they are. Institutions can only take them as they present themselves and try to provide them with the support that fits their individual situations.

Given the hue and cry about how the subjects of harassment should act, it is worthwhile to recall the insight offered by Carl G. Jung in *The Undiscovered Self.* His instruction to psychologists can be applied not only to academic support personnel, but to everyone who harbors the simplistic notion that it is possible to control other people's responses to sexual harassment.

People think you have only to "tell" a person that he "ought" to do something in order to put himself on the right track. The psychologist has come to see that nothing is achieved by telling, persuading, admonishing, giving good advice. He must also get acquainted with the details and have an authentic knowledge of the psychic inventory of his patient. He has therefore to relate to the individuality of the sufferer and feel his way into all the nooks and crannies of his mind.[22]

Janoff-Bulman reinforced this point when she observed:

At the outset it is imperative to recognize that the response to any particular life event must be understood in terms of the particular victim or victims. . . . Any traumatic reaction reflects both the individual victim and the particular victimizing event. This may appear to be a simplistic point, but it is an important one, for there is considerable evidence that we typically underestimate the power of situations and overestimate the power of the individual in understanding any given behavior.[23]

So much has been written and said about sexual harassment as a power and gender issue in education that sometimes the most crucial terminology is neglected. Sexual harassment of students by professors is, above all, betrayal. It is the betrayal of a weighty trust; and directed at certain types of students, it can alter, perhaps irrevocably, their perceptions of one of the few "safe havens" in a world of complexity and unpredictability. It confounds every assumption many students hold about schools, teachers, the world, and themselves; and the force of such betrayal can affect vulnerable individuals in totally unforeseeable ways.

This is the reason it is unwise to generalize about how women should react to harassment. Jung's approach is perceptive.

The distinctive thing about real facts . . . is their individuality. Not to put too fine a point on it, one could say that the real picture consists of nothing but exceptions to the rule, and that, in consequence, absolute reality has predominately the character of irregularity. . . . Hence it is not the universal and the regular that characterize the individual, but rather the unique. He is not to be understood as a recurrent unit but as something unique and singular which in the last analysis can neither be known nor compared with anything else.[24]

Because responses to the behavior are so unique, higher education is ill prepared to deal with them. Colleges and universities exhibit not only diffusion of authority, but also diffusion of responsibility and uneven levels of knowledge. This exacerbates harassees' difficulties. Unlike a business where there is usually one designated source to which complainants turn, academic institutions have several. In even the smallest college a student might seek support from a faculty member, a department head, a dean, student services personnel, or a high-level administrator. Although this allows for choice, it also invites problems. The individual working with the subject of the abuse has opinions, interests, and associations which inevitably color the interaction. Consequently, objectivity, the most crucial characteristic of any counseling arrangement, may be forfeited. Even more significant is that few of the array of individuals who may conceivably become involved with harassees have the expertise and experience to act in counseling capacities; and for all their good will, inexperienced counselors may ultimately do more harm than good.

Janoff-Bulman noted that dealing with victims of trauma is no easy matter: "Survivors of traumatic events seek to arrive at a new non-threatening assumptive world, one that acknowledges and integrates their negative experience and prior illusions. . . . [They seek] benevolence, meaning, and self-worth, while having been forced to confront malevolence, meaninglessness, and helplessness."[25] She suggested that frequently victims employ one or more cognitive strategies or reappraisal processes to regain control and recover a more positive view of themselves and the world.

The first of these involves the victim making "downward"[26] comparisons between herself and her situation, as opposed to those who have fared more poorly or are in more dire straits. Such comparisons enable the survivor to recognize that her problems could be worse, and that she is, after all, coping well. Stressing that she did not in any way blame victims for their lot, Janoff-Bulman risked "rais[ing] people's hackles"[27] by asserting that even self-blame can act as a strategy for overcoming trauma. She argued that if it occurs early in the recovery process and involves the victim's blaming herself for a specific behavior rather than a character defect, self-blame may help to "minimize the threatening, meaningless nature of the [traumatic] event"[28] by allowing the victim to assert, "This might not have happened if I had acted differently." Finally, she suggested that survivors cope by transforming their victimization and finding purpose in their suffering, by discovering that pain has taught them something that will benefit themselves or others. This brief overview is somewhat oversimplified and is only one of numerous approaches to victimization and trauma survival. Nevertheless, if one uses it as a model, it provides crucial insight into the difficulties confronting institutions that engage in counseling of harassees.

Janoff-Bulman cautioned that treatment of trauma is complex: "Although therapists often have their preferred therapies, it is nevertheless the case that the particular client . . . should determine the optimal therapeutic approach. Work with trauma survivors may call for particularly eclectic therapists."[29] Herein lies the challenge to academicians. Counseling of harassment victims must be on their terms. When the abusiveness of perpetrators and the innocence of those who suffer because of them is apparent, one's strongest instincts are to propel harassees forward to a point at which they too will feel righteous anger at their plights. The desire to empower harassees is enormous because this is the primary and perhaps the most effective way to curtail sexual harassment.

But excessive zeal may impede rather than speed progress for some. Two anecdotes from students illustrate this point.

Student A: *No question I was spaced out by what he did. You don't think a college teacher is going to reach down your blouse in his office. It shook me up, so my roommate said maybe I should see a counselor. But, geez, this lady made me feel worse. Here I was telling myself that it wasn't the end of the world and that I'd get over it, but she's telling me that it's like terminal cancer or something. After two times I quit going because I didn't want to end up depressed once a week.*

Student B: *I know I could have discouraged Dr. X if I had been smarter about the time of day I went to his office. He has a big reputation, and I should have listened about that, but Dr. Y upset me because she insisted there was no way to avoid him. That only made me feel worse because now I have to face knowing it could happen again with somebody else no matter how smart I try to be or what I do.*

With the best intentions, two counselors or quasi-counselors attempted to sympathize with students. The first attempted to acknowledge the gravity of sexual harassment, as well she should. Nevertheless, in this case such recognition would best be accomplished at a later time when the harassee was prepared emotionally to deal with it. If the student's perception was accurate, the counselor allowed her own justified anger over the issue to interfere with treatment and subsequently increased the harassee's sense of disorientation and impotence in a hostile world. Similarly, the female in the second situation was denied what was for her a necessary step in the healing process. In order to regain a sense of control over her life, she needed at this point to believe that her actions could have altered a negative outcome, but the counselor's insistence that "there was no way to avoid" the incident exacerbated her feeling of being at risk in a world she could not control.

In dealing with subjects of sexual harassment, institutions must ensure that faculty and staff recognize their limitations and avoid assuming roles for which they are unprepared. Few faculty members or administrators possess the expertise to work with seriously traumatized victims, and even academic personnel who are trained to provide therapy must exercise vigilance. Because sexual harassment is viewed as a specialized area, the tasks of counseling often fall to those who serve dual functions in an institution. They work with harassees, but may also teach, conduct research, and consult in the field. Most probably perform impeccably in all these roles, but they must be on constant guard to avoid allowing their fervor over the issue to affect their interactions with harassees, whose basic interests are almost always personal. Learning to cope with sexual harassment is the primary task for targets of the behavior. Ultimately, issues of gender and student and female empowerment may become significant, but the first concern must be survival.

V.C. Rabinowitz offered a detailed prescription to be used in counseling harassees. What is most evident in reviewing her advice is that very few people on campus are equipped to deal with seriously traumatized victims of harassment.

• Acknowledge [the harassee's] courage by citing how difficult it is to label, report, and discuss harassment.

- Encourage the ventilation of her feelings and perceptions, and validate them. . . .

- Provide information to [the] student about the incidence of harassment to assure her that she is not alone. . . .

- Counteract her tendencies to blame herself for the harassment by explaining its origins in power relations. Assure her that she is in no way responsible for her professor's sexual interest in her. [Note that this approach is different from that described earlier by Student B.] Tendencies to self-blame are likely to be strongest in women who . . . have complied with harassers in any way. . . . These women need to know that their past behavior may well have been constrained, and in any case that past activities do not control future choices.

- Aid the student in her search for meaning in victimization. She will need to rebuild shattered assumptions. . . .

- Monitor the physical, emotional, academic, and interpersonal toll of harassment. . . .

- Offer a safe forum for the expression of anger and resentment. . . .

- Offer skills training. . . . The student may need training in one of the following areas: assertiveness, problem solving, decision making, self-efficacy, or stress management.

- Teach the student to validate herself.[30]

Education and expertise are clearly essential in counseling those who are seriously damaged by first-time harassment, but they are even more crucial in situations in which the harassee has formerly suffered sexual abuse. In an article in *The Counseling Psychologist*, P.A. Frazier and B.B. Cohen noted that among college women, estimates of child sex abuse have ranged from 4 percent to 49 percent; the authors' concern was that since this is the case, "special training in the area of sexual victimization seems imperative in order for counseling psychologists (and other mental health professionals) to avoid contributing to the secondary victimization of those seeking help."[31] The recommendations for counselor training they offer, like the counseling "prescriptions" presented by Rabinowitz, demand expertise and a time commitment unavailable to the typical educator or advocate, and contemporary institutions must make informed decisions about their responsibilities with respect to providing psychological and even legal support for complainants.

Sooner or later institutions must report harassment and determine whether those who pursue formal grievances deserve institutional support as they cope with the alleged abuse and the hearing process. Many contend that because higher education is heavily reliant on tuition and public funding, it owes complainants support while grievances are being considered. If an institution does acknowledge its obligation, it must decide if counseling should come from within or outside. When the agents of the institution do become responsible for treatment, they are placed in precarious positions and could be accused of divided loyalties. The basic argument against provision for support until a grievance is settled is, of course, financial. Therapy, even that conducted within the institution, is costly, and colleges and universities are not eager to assume such a burden when there is no guarantee that it is justified. Simply having a complaint filed does not mean harassment has occurred, so an institution may owe the accuser nothing. In fact, if the accusation is false, action may need to be taken against the complainant. There are no easy answers to the dilemma. Given the diversity of charges and varying needs of complainants, perhaps the best course institutions can take is to establish mechanisms that allow them to consider requests for psychological support by analyzing the unique circumstances of individual cases.

In any case, an emerging problem facing colleges and universities is determining how to deal with those who are unusually sensitive to sexual harassment because of past experience. A well-established tenet of the law of torts holds that a perpetrator takes the injured party as he/she is found. As a consequence, courts typically hold those responsible for tort offenses liable for any and all damages which flow from an injurious act, even when the injured party is a "hypersensitive" or "eggshell" plaintiff. Nevertheless, the law of sexual harassment, though generally viewed as a tort, has created a different standard that effectively disposes of claims based on abnormal sensitivities, even those caused by mental illness. The Supreme Court's *Meritor* and *Harris* decisions created a dual standard for sexual harassment claims. It demands that the allegedly improper conduct must not only offend the harassee, but must also be proven to be offensive to a reasonable person.[32] A Missouri federal district court clarified that Title VII was not intended to provide protection for the hypersensitivities of all workers, but to force "[e]mployers [to] police the environment for the benefit of the average person or 'reasonable person.'"[33] When generalized to Title IX, this approach reinforces the need for education and counseling that encourage the most vulnerable harassees and their strongest advocates to understand the legal parameters governing sexual harassment and to recognize the importance of discovering how to rise above its damages.

Beyond Victimization

Today, as never before, public discussion of sexual harassment must center on coping, self-validation, and empowerment. In the 1970s and 1980s, the urgency to make people understand the problem led to emphasis on its indignities and irrevocable damage. People who had seen the serious casualties were, like witnesses of most injustices, driven to ensure that if they could help it, no one would ever again be deprived of a job, change a career, leave school, or become ill because of harassment. "Never again" is a commitment that must be kept, but contemporary sexual harassment has to be understood in terms of alterations in the educational, legal, and social landscapes over time. With two decades of intense scrutiny, sexual harassment now requires a more sophisticated approach. Overzealous attempts to validate the issue in terms of quantity and severity can lead to incredulity and backlash. As has been noted, the public has been skeptical about research that has found enormous percentages of female harassees. More important is that concentration on numbers and "horror stories" may divert attention from the most intrinsic point. Sexual harassment is wrong. It is not only illegal and unprofessional; it is immoral behavior. One victim is enough. One time is enough. One small injury is enough. Hundreds of harassees and extraordinary trauma are not required to certify its abuse.

Perhaps it is time to reconsider even the nomenclature surrounding the issue. Without question, sexual harassment creates victims. Their numbers are legion, and often their injuries are enormous. But not everyone who endures harassment emerges as a victim, and one has only to turn on a television set to be persuaded of the negative effects that excessive claims of victimization have had on American culture. Some females, regardless of age or power differentials, can handle perpetrators. These women are not "victims," and to describe them as such is inappropriate and probably demeaning, given the term's connotations of weakness or irresoluteness. Hindsight is always easier than foresight, as the cliché suggests; and this being the case, now is the time to reconsider use of the term "victim" to describe those who are subjected to harassment. "Subject," "object," "target," "harassee," are more appropriate descriptors for the total population, and such an approach to labeling does not exclude use of "victim" to describe particularly traumatized subjects.

Decreased use of the term "victim" would allow research and discussion to move forward with more precision, less controversy, and less misunderstanding. One of the clearest examples of this point is a book titled *The Morning After: Sex, Fear and Feminism on Campus*. Written in 1993, by twenty-four-year-old Katie Roiphe, a Princeton graduate student, the work enjoyed widespread attention from those who tend to regard harassment as a myth or an insignificant issue. Roiphe's general argument was that sexual harassment is a highly exaggerated problem, that concern about hostile environments encourages paranoia and hyperbole, and that attention to the issue creates a victim mentality which discourages females from assuming responsibility.

She argued that feminist obsession with rape and sexual harassment is dangerous and antithetical to earlier feminist aspirations.

The image that emerges from feminist preoccupation with rape and sexual harassment is that of women as victims, offended by a professor's dirty joke, verbally pressured into sex by peers. The image of a delicate woman bears a striking resemblance to that fifties ideal my mother and the other women of her generation fought so hard to get away from. They didn't like passivity, her wide-eyed innocence. They didn't like the fact that she was perpetually offended by sexual innuendo. They didn't like her excessive need for protection.[34]

Assuming her and her mother's worldviews to be superior and inclusive, Roiphe failed to separate her disagreement with certain types of feminists from sexual harassment's realities. The most compelling of such realities is that some women (and some men) are indeed made uncomfortable or are offended by dirty jokes and sexual innuendo. Not all the women of her generation agreed with Roiphe's mother's ideals, and even today many of the females inhabiting academe are very traditional women who would not be impressed with Roiphe's references to her own sexual liberalism. And many students, employees, or parents would not share the generosity she expressed toward lecherous professors when she asserted, "Rules about sexual harassment . . . should target serious offenses and abuses of power rather than environments that are 'uncomfortable,' rather than a stray professor looking down a shirt."[35]

Those who counsel harassees are confronted with the frustrating realization that females of a variety of ages and backgrounds often do exhibit passivity and need for protection. Given the power inequalities that exist in academe, even the most assertive at times require intervention and defense. Thus some of Roiphe's observations appear naive: "Feminists drafting sexual harassment guidelines [most institutional guidelines are composed by heterogeneous institutional groups, not feminists alone] seem to have forgotten childhood's words of wisdom: sticks and stones may break my bones, but names will never harm me."[36] Contrary to Roiphe's optimistic view of women's invulnerability, any law or medical school student, as well as any typical college freshman, could easily explain just how much "harm" receiving a "name" from a professor can do.

Even more disassociated from the realities of campus life was the author's inclusion of a remark she attributed to Veronique Neiertz, Secretary of State for Women's Rights in France. Cited as admirable was Neiertz's ministry's "common sense advice to women who feel harassed by coworkers; [it is] to respond with 'a good slap in the face.'"[37] While Neiertz may be excused for not knowing the basics of American civil procedures, most citizens of the United States recognize that even though in this country "feeling harassed" does not automatically create liability for sexual harassment, it also does not constitute legal provocation for assaulting a co-worker or a college professor.

Equally troubling was Roiphe's assertion "The clarity of the definition of sexual harassment as a 'hostile work environment' depends on a universal code of conduct, a shared idea of acceptable behavior that we just don't have. Something that makes one person feel uncomfortable may make another person feel great."[38] This is, of course, precisely the point. People must be attentive to their behaviors and must consider the likelihood of creating hostile work and academic environments because what makes one person feel "great" may create anxiety and trauma in another. Indeed individuals and institutions do not possess "a universal code of conduct, a shared idea of acceptable behavior," and for this very reason many have learned through bitter trial and error that it is best to err on the side of caution.

Still there is truth in Roiphe's concern about the threat that victim mentalities pose for women. From the beginning, experts and the media have focused attention on those who fit the classic victim stereotype. This was appropriate since their concerns were the most immediate and their experiences best reinforced contentions about the damage inflicted by harassment. The credibility of the issue needed to be established, laws passed, and policies written, and examples drawn from the most egregious circumstances helped to speed the process. Unfortunately, however, emphasis on the severely injured has resulted in limited knowledge about individuals who experience harassment, recognize and admit it, and rise immediately and often unaided above its indignities. Some would contend that so few fit this category that they are not worthy of analysis. Others might argue that no one undergoes harassment without being negatively affected; and while there may be some truth in these views, it is also true that there is a vast difference between victimization and discomfort. That distinction needs to be made. Doing so will not diminish the wrong of sexual harassment. It will provide a more accurate portrait of the individuals subjected to the behavior.

This group of women, who might be labeled "the unscathed" are often classified in the same category as those who are in denial, or they may even be negatively described as "male identified."[39] This is a term used by D. Silverman over two decades ago to designate females who were successful, skilled, and unlikely to recognize the seriousness of harassment. Malovich and Stake discussed a subgroup of women students who might fit the unscathed category. In their study, participants' self-esteem and sex-role attitudes were measured on two different instruments; then they were asked to complete a survey of their personal experiences with harassment and were also required to respond to scenarios which probed their attitudes toward the behaviors. The researchers found that high self-esteem women were more likely than low self-esteem females to report harassment. An especially relevant discovery was the following.

[H]igh self-esteem women gave little indication that the harassment had hurt them personally or caused them to doubt themselves. Rather than becoming more fearful and avoidant, [they] . . . tended to write about their changed opinions of their teachers. For example: 'I had less respect for the instructor' and 'I felt shame for him not me.'

In contrast, the low self-esteem women tended to describe the experience as painful or frightening, and they indicated that they tended to avoid the teacher as a result of the harassment. For example, one student wrote about her experience: 'I just felt uneasy and I think it affected my learning because I hated going to his desk and asking questions.'

The reports the high self-esteem women gave of their harassment experiences were consistent with their reactions to the scenarios. They expected that the events depicted in the scenarios would lead to fewer negative emotional effects and more positive educational effects than did the low confidence women. Presumably because they felt capable of handling such situations, they were less likely to endorse the option of accepting the teacher's offer for more personal contact.

From the standpoint of the high self-esteem women, these findings are a positive indication that harassment has not been, and probably will not be a serious problem for them.[40]

Future research needs to focus on such women. Beyond self-esteem, they may possess similar personality traits, backgrounds, and values that predispose them to being able to withstand harassment and that will predict their responses to others affected by the behavior. Those who can rise unscathed above sexual harassment may have something to offer those who are more vulnerable, and to search for their message is not to diminish the severity of the offense.

Women who feel themselves to be victims, to be profoundly damaged by unwanted sexual attention or discrimination deserve reassurance, support, and validation; but they must also, in appropriate order, be warned against passivity and dependence and encouraged to seek empowerment. Although taken out of context, Joseph Conrad's description of the Roman invaders of Britain provides an analogy targets of harassment must be led to ponder when considering perpetrators: "They were conquerors, and for that you want only brute force—nothing to boast of, when you have it, since your strength is just an accident arising from the weakness of others. They grabbed what they could get for the sake of what was to be got."[41] When the time is right, the lesson to be learned from having survived even the most devastating abuse is that no one is destined to remain a victim. Everyone is, as Jean-Paul Sartre pointed out, free to choose his or her fate: "Therefore everything takes place as if I were compelled to be responsible. . . . To make myself passive in the world, to refuse to act upon things and others is still to choose myself."[42]

When the time is right, the most compelling lesson victims can learn is the power of choice, action, and thus survival. It is a lesson that must come in its own way and its own time. Those who assume that people are naturally endowed with the capacity to resist boorishness or abuse are irrational, yet it is equally unwise to dwell so much on the abuse and the abuser that one encourages weakness where strength should be learned. *Zorba the Greek* contains a simple story that teaches a lesson applicable to harassees and those who counsel them.

I remember one morning when I discovered a cocoon in the bark of a tree, just as the butterfly was making a hole in its case and preparing to come out. I waited a while, but it was too long appearing and I was impatient. I bent over it and breathed on it to warm it. I warmed it as quickly as I could and the miracle began to happen before my eyes, faster than life. The case opened, the butterfly started slowly crawling out and I shall never forget my horror when I saw how its wings were folded back and crumpled; the wretched butterfly tried with its whole trembling body to unfold them. Bending over it, I tried to help it with my breath. In vain. It needed to be hatched out patiently and unfolding of the wings would be a gradual process in the sun. Now it was too late. My breath had forced the butterfly to appear, all crumpled, before its time. It struggled desperately and, a few seconds later, died in the palm of my hand.[43]

The analogy emphasizes the risk of pressuring people to respond to harassment in ways that are uncharacteristic or premature. Just as creatures in nature cannot be expected to survive in hostile environments or forced too early from their natural habitats, so humans cannot be made to accomplish tasks for which they are psychologically unprepared. Those who cavalierly ascribe to women innate capacities they acquire only through experience should realize that it is as foolish to demand that an eighteen-year-old incest survivor confront a harassing professor as it is to expect flight from a day-old bird.

On the other hand, the *Zorba* analogy can remind harassees that while they may not have chosen or deserved their fates, there are positive lessons to be learned from struggle. Sexual harassment is ugly, unprofessional, and unethical. The key to overcoming it lies partially in the law and in institutional commitment. But most of all, it is in the individual's recognizing that the poet May Sarton's perception is accurate: "Pain can make a whole winter bright / Like fever, force us to live deep and hard." And even when they are least expected and wholly undeserved, life's "great shocks" may, in the end, impart courage and strength.

Notes

1. C. Safran, "What Men Do to Women on the Job: A Shocking Look at Sexual Harassment," *Redbook*, November 1996, p. 217.

2. L.F. Fitzgerald, S.L. Schullman, N. Bailey, M. Richards, J. Swecker, Y. Gold, M. Ormerod, and L. Weitzman (1988), "The Incidence and Dimensions of Sexual Harassment in Academia and the Workplace," *Journal of Vocational Behavior*, 32, 152–75.

3. T.C. Fain and D.L. Anderton (1987), "Sexual Harassment: Organizational Context and Diffuse Status," *Sex Roles,* 17, 291–311; B. Lott, M.E. Reilly, and D.R. Howard (1982), "Sexual Assault and Harassment: A Campus Community Case Study," *Signs*, 8, 296–319; P.I. McIntyre and J.C. Renick (1982), "Protecting Public Employees and Employers from Sexual Harassment," *Public Personnel Management Journal*, 282–92.

4. Fain and Anderton, pp. 302–3.

5. See J.W. Adams, J.L. Kottke, and J.S. Padgitt (1983), "Sexual Harassment of University Students," *Journal of College Student Personnel*, 24, 484–90; D.D. Baker, D.E. Terpstra, K. Larntz (1990), "The Influence of Individual Characteristics and Severity of Harassing Behavior on Reactions to Sexual Harassment," *Sex Roles*, 22, pp. 305–25; S. Kenig and J. Ryan (1986), "Sex Differences in Levels of Tolerance and Attribution of Blame for Sexual Harassment on a University Campus," *Sex Roles*, 15, 535–49; S.C. Padgitt and J.S. Padgitt (1986), "Cognitive Structure of Sexual Harassment: Implications for University Policy," *Journal of College Student Personnel*, 34, 34–39.

6. See Lott et al.; A. Metha and J. Nigg (1983), "Sexual Harassment on Campus: An Institutional Response, "*Journal of the National Association for Women Deans, Administrators, and Counselors,* 46, 9–15; M.E. Reilly, B. Lott, and S.M. Gallogly (1986), "Sexual Harassment of University Students," *Sex Roles*, 15, 333–58.

7. See I. W. Jensen and B.A. Gutek (1982), "Attributions and Assignment of Responsibility in Sexual Harassment," *Journal of Social Issues*, 38, 121–36; M. Koss (1990), "Changed Lives: The Psychological Impact of Sexual Harassment," in *Ivory Power: Sexual Harassment on Campus*, ed. M. Paludi (Albany: State University of New York Press); V.C. Rabinowitz (1996), "Coping with Sexual Harassment" in *Sexual Harassment on College Campuses: Abusing the Ivory Power*, ed. M. Paludi (Albany: State University of New York Press); and Reilly (1986).

8. For overviews of coping strategies, see Rabinowitz and L.J. Rubin and S.B. Borgers (1990), "Sexual Harassment in Universities During the 1980's," *Sex Roles*, 23, 297–411.

9. See Adams et al.

10. M. Sullivan and D.I. Bybee (1987), "Female Students and Sexual Harassment: What Factors Predict Reporting Behavior," *Journal of the National Association for Women Deans, Administrators, and Counselors*, 50, 11–16.

11. See S. Riger (1991), "Gender Dilemmas in Sexual Harassment," *American Psychologist*, 46, 497–505.

12. *Id.*, p. 501.

13. B.R. Snyder, *The Hidden Curriculum* (New York: Alfred A. Knopf, 1971), p. 14.

14. G. Farber, "The Student as Nigger," *Daily Bruin Spectra*, Spring 1967, page cite unavailable.

15. M.A. Paludi and R.B. Barickman, "In Their Own Voices: Responses from Individuals Who Have Experienced Sexual Harassment and Supportive Techniques for Dealing with Victims of Sexual Harassment," in *Academic and Workplace Sexual Harassment: A Resource Manual* (Albany: State University of New York Press, 1991), p. 27.

16. D.A. Charney and R.C. Russell (1994), "An Overview of Sexual Harassment," *American Journal of Psychiatry*, 151, p. 14.

17. R. Janoff-Bulman, *Shattered Assumptions: Towards a New Psychology of Trauma* (New York: Free Press, 1992), p. 5.

18. *Id.*, p. 62.

19. *Id.*

20. Koss, p. 76.

21. Charney and Russell, p. 14.

22. C.G. Jung, *The Undiscovered Self* (Boston: Little Brown, 1958), p. 74.

23. Janoff-Bulman, pp. 52, 171–72.

24. Jung, pp. 9–10.

25. Janoff-Bulman, pp. 117, 127.

26. *Id.*, pp. 117–18.

27. *Id.*, p. 123.

28. *Id.*

29. *Id.*, p. 164.

30. Rabinowitz, pp. 210–11.

31. P.A. Frazier and B.B. Cohen (1992), "Research on the Sexual Victimization of Women," *Counseling Psychologist*, 20, 151.

32. *Meritor Savings Bank, FSB. v. Vinson*, 477 U.S. 57 (1986); *Harris v. Forklift Systems, Inc.*, 114 S. Ct. 367 (1993).

33. *Sudtelgte v. Reno*, 1994 U.S. Dist. LEXIS 82, 63 Fair Empl. Prac. Cas. (BNA) 1257 (W.D. Mo. 1/3/94).

34. K. Roiphe, *The Morning After: Sex, Fear and Feminism on Campus* (Boston: Little, Brown & Co., 1993), p. 6.

35. *Id.*, p. 105.

36. *Id.*, p. 101.

37. *Id.*, p. 99.

38. *Id.* p. 90–1.

39. See D. Silverman (1976), "Sexual Harassment: Working Women's Dilemma," *Quest: A Feminist Quarterly*, 3, 15–24.

40.   N.J. Malovich and J.E. Stake (1990), "Sexual Harassment on Campus: Individual Differences in Attitudes and Beliefs," *Psychology of Women Quarterly*, 14, p. 76.

41.   J. Conrad, *The Heart of Darkness*, in *The Norton Anthology of Short Fiction*, ed. R.V. Cassill (New York: W. W. Norton, 1990), p. 158.

42.   J.P. Sartre, *Being and Nothingness* (New York: New York Philosophical Library, 1956), pp. 555–56.

43.   N. Kazantzakis, *Zorba the Greek* (New York: Simon & Schuster, 1952), pp. 120–21.

Chapter Four
Male Students
The Invisible Casualties

Won't you come down here? . . . You haven't got to preach a sermon.
Come down beside me. . . . Have you a little time for me?
　　　　　　　　　　　　　　　　—Franz Kafka, *The Trial*

"Have you a little time for me?" It is a question that resonates among male students on college campuses at the end of the twentieth century, and it is particularly applicable when one considers higher education's response to sexual harassment. If institutions have been negligent about females' predicament, they have also been guilty of neglecting males. The research community has fared little better. After almost two decades of studies, male perceptions of and responses to harassment are discussed almost exclusively by comparing them to those of females, and there has been either indifference to sexual harassment's impact on males or a curious willingness to accept males' self-reports of having been unaffected by it.[1]

Though unwise, this approach was, to some extent, predictable. Designed for males, higher education historically catered to their needs and ways of knowing and behaving. There was and in many cases still is "little time" for females. Thus the emergence of so-called "female" issues like harassment deterred educators and researchers from seeing it in anything but the most simplistic fashion. No one should apologize for the original emphasis on women. They are, after all, overwhelmingly the targets of the behavior, and concern about the "chilly" classroom climates they inhabit has led to greater sensitivity among professors and a better learning environment for all students.

Nevertheless, the time has come for a more inclusive examination of the problem. Few have acknowledged this need. A significant exception did occur in a 1995 article by Harsh K. Luthar, a Bryant College professor who argued that empirical studies of sexual harassment have produced "misleading" information because most have been tainted by "a female perspective and a feminist ideology."[2] Much of the current literature in sexual harassment "borrows heavily but selectively from the rape and sexual aggression literatures without acknowledging this lineage and the limitations associated with it,"[3] Luthar maintained. This has, he concluded, resulted in "intellectual paralysis of the worst kind"[4] and in a paucity of studies of men who have been falsely accused, who are the targets of powerful females in organizations, and who experience legal difficulties following job termination due to sexual harassment allegations. Rather than focusing on the very salient point that we know too little about males' experience with harassment and that we need to ensure gender neutrality in conducting research, Luthar himself used selective research and evidenced the very gender bias he decried.

Most important was that he neglected the small but generally reliable body of information which already exists on males and harassment. He did cite the U.S. Merit System Protection Board's finding that 15 percent of males reported having been targets of harassment in the preceding two years.[5] This statistic supports Barbara Gutek's earlier finding in a study of workplace harassment that "between 9 percent and 37 percent of men [were] sexually harassed by the opposite sex at least once during their working lives."[6] Studies of prevalence rates for males in educational or quasi-educational settings are limited because most of the studies of students have, in fact, concentrated on females, a condition pointed out in L.J. Rubin's and S.B. Borgers's "Sexual Harassment in the Universities During the 1980's."[7] As previously noted, a 1993 article of male medical residents found that 22 percent were subjected to harassment during training,[8] a statistic that is supported by 1991 and 1992 surveys of medical students.[9]

Gutek concluded that attempts to develop demographic profiles of both male and female targets were not "particularly fruitful,"[10] except in the case of marital status. Like women, married men in the workplace are, she observed, less likely to report incidents of harassment, possibly because those "who do not belong to someone else are apparently perceived as fair game and, perhaps, more approachable than other workers."[11] Whether or not a similar condition exists in the case of male students is uncertain, since there has been no research of the phenomenon. It is clear from studies of both the workplace and the campus that the majority of men have narrower definitions of sexual harassment and do not believe its effects to be as serious.[12] Nevertheless, as the Merit Board Survey indicated, they are as unlikely as females to employ formal or informal complaint responses. Very little is known about male responses or reactions, but most studies have found that males are less likely than females to confide in others about the problem.[13]

The area in which the literature on males is most deficient is that which treats consequences. N.J. Malovich and J.E. Stake summarized the prevailing wisdom about the effects of sexual harassment on males.

> *It is well known that the number of men reporting harassment is much smaller than the number of women, and women have been viewed as the primary victims of harassment. In our sample of males, none could be properly labeled as a victim. Some did report harassment as defined by our categories of inappropriate, sexually toned behavior from teachers, yet the responses of our male subjects suggested that rather than feeling harassed, they had enjoyed the experience. The men reported feeling flattered by the attention, and they seemed to view the incident as an interesting learning experience. These reactions are similar to those reported by men in the workplace. . . .*
>
> *That men respond more favorably than women to unsolicited sexual overtures is readily understood in light of the sex-role standards for sexual behavior in our society. A man's status is usually improved by having sexual relations with women, and if women show sexual interest in a man, he and others will usually interpret that interest as a sign of his success as a man. Furthermore, because of the status of men in our society, men are more likely to continue to feel safe and in control, even when they are propositioned by a female teacher or supervisor.[14]*

A limitation in Malovich's and Stake's comments is their leap from finding that male students feel flattered by instructors' "sexually toned" behavior to their assertion that men are less likely than women to feel vulnerable when propositioned. Evaluation of the consequences of sexual harassment should not rest on comparisons of gender abuse but on the individual costs the behavior exacts. Then, too, Malovich and Stake fail to observe that there is a huge difference between being the target of sexually toned behavior and actually being propositioned by a professor, just as there are marked differences between male responses. Whether male students in the aggregate feel safer and more in control than females when confronted with harassment is a moot point when research gives way to reality and a male is forced to endure or witness an incident of harassment. What matters then, as in the case of women targets, is that one incident, however minor, may invoke trauma.

Equally worth noting in light of the seeming consensus among the experts that males are less affected by harassment is that a male's retrospective assessments of experience or his response to an analogue survey may be as fallible as those of females in similar circumstances. If some women tend to deny or diminish harassment, the same is obviously and perhaps more true of males. Yet studies frequently take males' recall and evaluations of their experiences at face value. Researchers would do well to consider Arvey's and Cavanaugh's concern about the extent to which "sexual harassment survey research has to do with the great reliance on self-report methods. . . . Asking respondents to reflect back over 36 months or longer . . . leaves open the question of potential memory distortion and bias. . . . Another problem may occur when the events are accurately recalled, but are perceived differently at later points in time."[15] Though focused on harassment of women in the workplace, Fitzgerald's comments on the ambiguity of analogue studies are also insightful.

With the exception of prevelance surveys, the great majority of sexual harassment research is dominated by analogue studies, most of uncertain generalizability. In particular, the research on gender differences in perceptions rests mainly on a base of relatively weak paper and pencil analogue procedures conducted almost exclusively with college students: the emerging work on coping responses appears to be developing in the same vein. This last is particularly problematic, as it is already clear that actual victims behave very differently than research participants report they would behave.[16]

Not only retrospective but even current accounts and perceptions of sexual harassment must be considered in light of male psychology, which obviously differs considerably from that of females. In *Iron John,* Robert Bly pointed out:

Geneticists have discovered recently that the genetic difference in DNA between men and women amounts to just over three percent. That isn't much. However, the difference exists in every cell of the body. . . .

I think that for this century and this moment it is important to emphasize the three percent difference that makes a person masculine, while not losing sight of the ninety-seven percent that men and women have in common. . . .

Some say, "Well, let's just be human, and not talk about masculine or feminine at all." People who say that imagine they are occupying the moral high ground. I say that we have to be a little gentle here, and allow the word masculine *and the word* feminine *to be spoken, and not be afraid that some moral carpenter will make boxes of those words and imprison us in them.*[17]

Recognizing the hazards of placing males and females in gender "boxes," one can nevertheless allow "the word *masculine* . . . to be spoken" in an effort to stimulate interest in the dynamics of sexual harassment as they pertain to male students. A beginning point is observing that male students, traditional and nontraditional, arrive on campus with the same anxieties, aspirations, and needs as their female counterparts. Traditional students are completing the process of transition to the social, psychological, and economic self-sufficiency of adulthood. Older students experience equally pressing concerns; some return to school out of a desire to better themselves economically; others to discover who they are. The point is that, regardless of age or sex, all are vulnerable in that they submit to the rigors of academe because they believe in the promises it offers. They temporarily relinquish power in order to obtain the financial, social, cultural, and emotional rewards that education promises.

Sacrifice of independence and status is especially trying for males, even when they are young. In "Community and Contest: How Women and Men Construct Their Worlds in Conversational Narrative," B. Johnstone concluded that "men live in a world where they see power as coming from an individual acting in opposition to others and to natural forces. For them, life is a contest in which they are constantly tested and must perform, in order to avoid the risk of failure."[18] This assessment echoes throughout recent studies of males. Popular works like Hazard Adams's *The Hazards of Being Male* and Deborah Tannen's *You Just Don't Understand* chronicle the burdens and misunderstandings that arise when male behaviors and communication styles come into conflict with those of females. Tannen summarized the difference.

Though all humans need both intimacy and independence, women tend to focus on the first and men on the second. . . . If intimacy says, "We're close and the same," and independence says, "We're separate and different," it is easy to see that intimacy and independence dovetail with connection status. The essential element of connection is symmetry: People are the same feeling equally close to each other. The essential element of status is asymmetry. People are not the same; they are differently placed in a hierarchy. . . . The symmetry of connection is what creates community: if two people are struggling for closeness, they are both struggling for the same thing. And the symmetry of status is what creates contest: Two people can't both have the upper hand, so negotiation for status is inherently adversarial.[19]

The asymmetrical, adversarial worldview of males takes perhaps its greatest toll in the realm of feelings. From childhood, boys learn that the route to center stage lies in winning, exhibiting physical prowess, telling jokes well, and eventually in making sexual conquests. There are few rewards, even today, for expressions of vulnerability or emotion; males discover very early that seeking help from others or admitting to self-limitations negates their quest for independence and status.

K. Druck and J.C. Simmons observed in *The Secrets Men Keep*: "Men deny themselves the right to feel uncertain, fearful, and hurt. This is the most central of men's secrets. Men experience a broad range of emotions, no matter how much they may deny it to others and themselves. Contrary to the reality that big boys cry, men are taught from an early age that 'big boys don't cry'—that is, it is not acceptable for men to show their emotions."[20] Similarly, Marc Fasteau noted in *The Male Machine*: "By five or six, boys know they aren't supposed to cry, ever be afraid, or, and this is the essence of the stereotype, be anything like girls. . . . The strain of trying to pretend that we have no 'feminine' feelings of doubt, disappointment, need for love and tenderness creates fear of these emotions in ourselves and hostility toward women, who symbolize these qualities."[21]

Despite contemporary efforts to free males as well as females from stereotypes, it is probably safe to say that even now the stereotypes exercise great control over who and what most men are. Some would prefer that society work toward androgyny; and others, like Bly, believe it is best for the genders to learn to live "between the opposites. To live between means that we not only recognize opposites, but rejoice that they exist."[22] Regardless of the approach one prefers, the reality, at this moment in history, is that the average male on college campuses exhibits predictable behaviors and values that influence his responses to sexual harassment.

Depending upon the circumstances and the participants, there are at least six types of situations involving male students that merit further consideration and research. These include (1) those who are direct targets of harassment, (2) those who refuse to see the behavior when it is directed at themselves or others, (3) those who identify with perpetrators and regard them as role models, (4) those who blame harassees rather than offenders, (5) those who assume assertive responses with harassers, and (6) those who sympathize with the plight of victims but feel impotent to effect change. There are clearly other ways to categorize male reactions, and individuals may shift from one response to another, but in each case distinct male traits are significant in the sexual harassment dynamic.

Male Targets

As women move into positions of greater power and security in the classroom and administration, the likelihood of males becoming subjects of harassment will increase. Female perpetrators are not the only problem, however, since anecdotal evidence and the limited research on males suggests that they most often suffer harassment by members of their own gender. A study of medical residents, for example, found that 55 percent of perpetrators of male targets were men.[23] If males are unlikely to report harassment by females, it is not difficult to comprehend why they would be even less likely to do so when they are the targets of male perpetrators. Given males' socialization and emphasis on masculinity, unwanted attention from gay men may pose catastrophic menace to self-image.

Recognition, response, and consequences may be as difficult for a male student as for a female. While slower to admit their predicaments than females, males may experience the same complex reactions. Psychological and physical stress may take the same toll; threats to self-esteem and academic/career achievement may seem just as real. However, unlike females, who are accustomed to relying on others when troubled, males generally resist seeking help. This may be one reason their plight has gone unnoticed. If some women resent being labeled victims, men are even more likely to spurn such an identification. Female harassees may complicate their situations by turning to close associates who sympathize but lack expertise. Males exacerbate theirs by silence. Thus, in one of the few examinations of males' response to harassment, Bingham and Scherer noted that "the masculine stereotype that defines men as inexpressive, dominant, independent, and always sexually eager . . . may constrain men from talking with friends and relatives about unwanted sexual attention."[24] It may also color their self-reports of sexual harassment, tainting their accounts and responses with masculine bravado and encouraging them to minimize their experiences.

Predictably, males file harassment suits against institutions very rarely, and when they do so the response to their complaints is often dismissive. This was the case when a thirty-three-year-old male student attending a human sexuality class at California State University at Sacramento claimed to be offended by the female professor's use of sex tales, how-to tips, and close-up slides of women's and adolescent girls' genitalia. He alleged that the professor made derogatory remarks about male genitalia and encouraged her female students to masturbate as a way of freeing themselves from the "hardship" of intercourse with males.[25] When the university refused to take action based upon his complaints that he found the professor's lectures offensive, the student filed a civil suit against the school and the professor, maintaining that he felt "raped" and "trapped" by the professor's pedagogical technique. The lawyer for the professor allegedly dismissed the student's action as "fundamentalist Christian

McCarthyism."[26] The attorney for the student responded that "it is unimaginable that a male professor delivering the same lecture while demeaning women wouldn't have been punished."[27] A psychology professor echoed his observation: "[W]e tend to be compassionate to women but there may well be a kind of insensitivity to males."[28]

Powerlessness, perhaps the most destructive of the emotions evoked by sexual harassment, is as damaging to men as it is to women. When it occurs in a male, it may challenge his deepest aspirations toward independence, status, and control. Men have difficulty understanding women's resistance to objectification because they have little or no frame of reference that allows them to comprehend what it is like to be a sex object, so when they are subjected to inappropriate remarks or unwanted sexual attention, some may be even less prepared than their female counterparts to handle the situation. If the student in the California State case was sincerely offended, the institution was obliged to treat his complaint with as much sensitivity and respect as it would that of a female.

Denial

Both male targets of and witnesses to sexual harassment may engage in denial. It is an especially destructive response to sexual harassment. Some males, like females, refuse to admit that they or their associates are the objects of undesired sexual or gender attention. Self-deception is as defeating in these instances as in any other. In closing his eyes to his own and to others' discomfort or pain, the male suppresses feelings of anger and anxiety that, if acknowledged, would make him appear unmanly. One student told of being the butt of jokes for several days in a psychology class while the professor was criticizing Freud's theory of penis envy. When asked whether the so-called humor had caused him discomfort, he replied, "Well, I didn't like it, if that's what you mean. But it was no big deal. He was just trying to be funny, I guess." Having internalized the rules by which males live, the student instinctively adopted the "no big deal" and "I can take a joke" approaches to experience. It never occurred to him that it is a very big deal when an educator's store of teaching methods is so depleted that embarrassing students becomes a means of gaining class attention.

Even more than females, males may be drawn to denial because the prospect of complaining about harassment appears so socially unacceptable. Self-deception and avoidance of problems take energy, and when energy is eroded, students, male and female, react in irresponsible ways. They sleep through classes and appointments they want to avoid. They try to alleviate stress by neglecting their schoolwork and, especially if they are "macho," by drinking too much and too often. They get sick, and their grades suffer. A bizarre cycle, set in motion by a self-indulgent professor, continues because few male students have the internal resources and the external support to say, "Enough!" Unwittingly, they cooperate with the offenders.

Denial of harassment has collective as well as individual consequences. When people refuse to acknowledge a problem, it is unlikely to be solved. Institutions cannot discipline perpetrators without specific complaints from students, so male reluctance to recognize harassment and seek help contributes to the paralysis that exists on many campuses. A Catch-22 thus exists for men as well as women because the average male brings with him to college an established value system and behavioral code that discourage him from engaging in the responses to sexual harassment that would be most successful in deterring it.

Identification with Perpetrators

Equally or perhaps more destructive than denial of the offense is identification with the offender. Little boys, like girls, are taught from their earliest exposure to formal education to "mind" and respect teachers, most of whom are female. Though male children have a harder time accepting discipline, the impact of educators should not be underestimated, especially when male students enter high education and begin to perform at their academic peaks. Poised to enter the "real" world after what may seem an eternity of subjugation in classrooms, the average male student may be presented for the first time with academic role models of his own gender.

Three laboratory studies of sexually harassing behavior by J.B. Pryor and colleagues[29] suggested that social norms and thus role models do indeed influence male tendencies to harass. Having developed the Reliability of the Likelihood to Sexually Harass or LSH scale, which reportedly allows for scientific analysis of the psychological characteristics of potential harassers, Pryor and his associates determined that men high in LSH are likely to harass when social climates make the behavior appear acceptable. In an experiment specifically involving role models, they concluded that "the harassing role model served to define the social norms for behavior in the situation and thus made sexual harassment more socially acceptable for those men who wished to do it."[30]

This is crucial information for institutions if Pryor's experiment is likely to be replicated in the classrooms of perpetrators. Professors dispense information, and "if relations are inherently hierarchical [as men believe], then the one who has more information is framed as higher up on the ladder, by virtue of being more knowledgeable and competent. . . . [Information] is an essential part of the independence that men perceive to be a prerequisite for self-respect."[31] Regardless of male students' personal responses to male professors, they are acutely aware of the independence, power, and status they possess within the confines of academe. The very presence of predominantly male staff is a novelty for most, whose previous educational experiences are likely to have been mostly with women.

It should come as no surprise, then, when male students view male instructors as role models. This is probably an appropriate choice unless the model also happens to be a sexual harasser. If such an individual appears to flourish professionally without intervention from the institution, a male student can easily assume that his behavior is sanctioned and thus acceptable. He carries that lesson with him during his stay on campus and when he leaves it for the world of work. No one should be surprised at this result, and the burden of blame should not be placed on the student. Reminiscent of Samuel Beckett's Clov in *Endgame*, he sends a provocative message to academe: "I use the words you taught me. If they don't mean anything anymore, teach me others."[32] Professors who dismiss the antics of some of their colleagues as harmless or who refuse, in the name of "academic freedom," to criticize them, need to recognize that professional behaviors teach students as much as books, or more, and that if they genuinely care about creating a just society, educators have an obligation to ensure that their words and actions teach males and females the right messages.

Blaming the Victim

Ironically, males who identify with harassers and regard their behaviors as acceptable and those who disapprove of perpetrators' actions often explain harassment in similar ways. They employ a widely recognized defense mechanism of those who are frustrated by their inability to understand a problem or effect change. They blame the victim. This is true even in cases in which they are closely associated with harassees. An architecture student described such a situation: "This prof is bugging my girlfriend like crazy. Every class he makes some little comment about how girls have a hard time when they get out into the world being engineers. Then she goes off on me because she's mad at him, and I try to tell her she doesn't have to take that shit because she's better in math [than I am,] but she won't listen. It pisses me off that she won't do anything to help herself."

In this situation the male refused to understand that the female's way of "handling" the situation may, for the present, simply be to talk it through with him. Sometimes, in recognizing the target's discomfort but focusing on her passivity and refusal to defend herself, the male assuages his own guilt for not acting. By assuming that women who endure crude public jokes and sexist comments without protest "really don't mind" or "like" such behaviors, a male bystander may be relieved of the responsibility of monitoring his own interactions with females. And perhaps academicians, especially those who claim greatest concern about harassment, must accept some degree of culpability for these sorts of uninformed assessments of female behavior. Educational efforts for both students and employees sometimes focus exclusively on the ills of sexual harassment and assume what males may interpret as an accusatory tone. There might be less blaming if there were more effective means of educating college and university communities about the larger issue of gender differences, of encouraging understanding of males' and females' differential responses to sexuality and conflict resolution.

Males may do the most victim-blaming in situations where professors respond sexually to attractive female students, and while only anecdotal evidence supports this theory, it does appear logical. Boys grow to manhood and spend most of their lives in rule-bound endeavors. The games they play as children and enjoy as men are governed by intricate regulations which team players do not violate.

The organizations and work environments males have created are hierarchical and rule-laden. Fair play is an enormous concern for them, and they do not look kindly on those who gain power or status by unfair means. A male struggling to maintain an A average in medical school or a C in Freshman English may view a female peer who attracts professorial attention or, worse still, dates a teacher as a competitor who is violating the rules. His masculine instincts may lead him to ignore or misunderstand the predicament of the person who has been singled out for attention and to assume that she is using her sexuality to manipulate the professor and seize the advantage. The female student may or may not be guilty, but if her male counterpart perceives the former to be the case, higher education will have taught him a lesson about women he will not soon forget. He may generalize from this one negative experience and carry with him for years the impression that femininity is a weapon used to acquire control and unfair advantage over males. Thus both male and female students become casualties when educators misuse their positions for personal self-indulgence.

Intervention

Male students may suffer even when they interpret a sexual harassment situation accurately and attempt to intervene. Female students struggling because of inappropriate professorial behavior are not always open to the advice of their well-meaning male peers. Socialized to be less confrontational, less reliant on formal dispute resolution and more concerned about the effects of their behaviors, women are not comfortable with assertive responses to harassment. Research demonstrates, as noted previously, that while probably 20 percent to 30 percent of females experienced harassment, institutions averaged only 4.3 complaints each year during the 1980s. Hence, the friend of the architectural student defended herself: "I can't make him understand that not everyone is Arnold Schwarzenegger. I'd rather listen to Professor T's craziness than him [her boyfriend] yelling at me to do something when there's no way I can without hurting my grades."

Although there has been no formal research on their experiences, it appears that males who do choose to intervene on behalf of females may encounter censure from friends with locker room mentalities who can't comprehend why a "real guy" would involve himself in a sexual harassment controversy. One freshman clarified this position: "I think Jim is nuts to say he'll talk to the [grievance] committee about Professor N. That guy's the terminator. He'd cut your balls off and not blink an eye. I figure if he thinks he can get it from the girls and nobody's stopping him 'til now, why should any of us act like fags and spill our guts to some committee?"

Males who confront perpetrators appear, at this point in time, relatively rare and report the same anxieties that plague female complainants. "I'm not sorry I went to the hearing with Carol, but I feel like I'll be looking over my shoulder for as long as I'm here," commented one student whose experience taught him that retaliation is a very serious concern for those who agree to take a stand against perpetrators. In some ways the targets of harassment are more protected from the possibility of retaliation than those who support them, and few, if any, institutions have sought to give guidance or encouragement to those willing to support harassees. Institutions are not adverse to monitoring the academic futures of successful complainants, but there are no guarantees for other students—male and female—who may be punished by a resentful harasser or his friends.

This point was illustrated in a letter from a man recalling an experience that occurred twenty years ago.

I was a graduate student working as a research associate for a center at a university. My job was to supervise a team of work-study students in coding data. The faculty of the center began asking me to send them workers to help them. At first they asked for either of two attractive young women, then for just one of them. I suspected their motive, which was confirmed when I overheard the young woman tell that she was being asked to organize books (over and over) high up on shelves. This required her to stand on a step ladder in the days of extremely short skirts. So when one of the faculty asked for the woman, I sent him a young male worker. Shortly thereafter I was called upon the carpet, charged with not properly overseeing the workers, and I was essentially fired.

I never tried to tell my story, and I don't think I even considered filing a grievance. I was so vulnerable, and I had a fine offer from a famous professor back in the department. I was able to avoid the center's faculty because of my many good faculty supporters/friends. If I had not

*been an outstanding graduate student, this incident might have sunk
my chances for the Ph.D. This incident happened twenty years ago but is
clearly burned into my memory.*

Recognition and Powerlessness

Finally, there are the male students who recognize sexual harassment
when it occurs but feel powerless to combat it. This is understandable.
If Professor Q is publicly pursuing or humiliating Jane Jones and she is
unwilling to act on her own behalf, her male classmate, John Smith,
cannot be expected to be eager to come to her aid. Actually, what
usually happens in such cases is that both the female student and her
male peer feel threatened and incapable of exercising control. The only
difference is that the negative reactions of female targets have been
well documented and analyzed, but almost nothing is known about
how observers of sexual harassment fare, especially when they are male.

One possibility is that when a male student witnesses a faculty
member's pursuit of a female peer, he engages in a kind of mental
combat in which he is doomed to failure. Socialization has taught
him to assume that females of his own age and station are, unpalat-
able though the term may seem, his "territory." When a professor
with all the trappings and safeguards of power encroaches on that
"territory," the student finds himself in a no-win situation. If females admire and submit to the professor, the student may feel that
his own status and masculinity are diminished. If, as has been pointed
out, they respond negatively, and he takes the risk of supporting
them, he is liable to suffer peer and academic censure, and thus another form of symbolic emasculation.

If a male student believes a female peer wants and needs his
help and fear of retaliation deters him from giving it, his most basic
nightmares become reality. He flees from confrontation with the
professor, thus psychologically failing the woman and humiliating
himself. He cannot console himself with recollections of a lost but
worthy conflict because he believes he lacked the courage to engage
in struggle. Having deserted what he perceives as his masculine responsibility, he may see himself as impotent by his own choice, and
once again higher education is in the unenviable position of having
helped to promote a distorted and damaging self-image.

Invisibility exacerbates frustration and pain and acts as a deterrent to progress. If the majority of male collegians seem insensitive to the issue of sexual harassment, it is in part because their experience with the problem has been minimized and ignored. If male graduates' understanding of gender issues frequently appears as parochial as that of men denied higher education, it is partially the result of academe's failure to investigate and address their needs.

The predicament of male academicians is equally troubling. Much important leadership and research on sexual harassment has come from males, yet the most pervasive image of the group is that of the lecherous professor. Despite the thousands of pages they have written, presentations they have delivered, and speeches they have made in meetings, the vast majority of male educators have remained silent about sexual harassment. There is little reliable research to indicate how credible they consider it to be as a campus concern, how or whether their perceptions of the problem have changed over time, how the issue has affected their own behavior with students or their attitudes toward and interactions with colleagues who harass. The comment of one English professor may be characteristic: "I'm just trying to survive."

But relations between the genders must be characterized by more than simple survival or "getting by" in a society that demands, as never before, contribution and cooperation from both males and females. It is unfortunate but probable that the numbers of men experiencing sexual harassment will increase as women gain prestige and authority. This is why it is essential that scholars begin now to consider men as crucial a subject of study as women. That is why the campus looms larger than ever as a place for Americans, male and female, to learn to live and work together.

Notes

1.   H.K. Luthar (1995–6), "The Neglect of Critical Issues in the Sexual Harassment Discussion: Implications for Organizational and Public Policies," *Journal of Individual Employment Rights*, 4(4), 261.
2.   *Id.*, p. 261.
3.   *Id.*, p. 262.
4.   *Id.*
5.   "U. S. Merit System Protection Board: Sexual Harassment in the Federal Workplace: An Update," Washington, D.C., U. S. Government Printing Office, 1988.

This study replicates an earlier study, "U. S. Merit System Protection Board: Is it a Problem?" Washington, D.C., U.S. Government Printing Office, 1981.

6. B. Gutek, *Sex and the Workplace: The Impact of Sexual Behavior and Harassment on Women, Men and Organizations*, (San Francisco: Jossey-Bass, 1985), p. 49.

7. See L.J. Rubin and S.B. Borgers (1990), "Sexual Harassment in the Universities During the 1980's," *Sex Roles*, 23, 397–41; J.W. Adams, J.L. Kottke, and J.S. Padgitt (1983), "Sexual Harassment of University Students," *Journal of College and Student Personnel*, 24, 484–90, and A. McCormack (1985), "The Sexual Harassment of Students by Teachers: The Case of Students in Science," *Sex Roles*, 13, 21–32.

8. See M. Komaromy, A.B. Bindman, R.J. Haber, and M.A. Sande (1993), "Sexual Harassment in Medical Training," *New England Journal of Medicine*, 328, 322–26.

9. See D.C. Baldwin, Jr., S.R. Daugherty, and E.J. Eckenfels (1991), "Student Perceptions of Mistreatment and Harassment During Medical School: A Survey of Ten United States Schools." *West Journal of Medicine*, 155, 140–45; D.C. Baldwin, Jr., S.R. Daugherty, and E.J. EcKenfels (1991), "Sexual Harassment in Medical Training," *New England Journal of Medicine*, 325, 1803; J.A. Richman, J.A. Flaherty, K.M. Rospenda, and M.L. Christensen (1992), "Mental Health Consequences and Correlates of Reported Medical Student Abuse," *JAMA*, 267, 692–94.

10. Gutek, p. 57.

11. *Id.*, p. 58.

12. See E.G.C. Collins and T.B. Blodgett (1981), "Sexual Harassment: Some See It . . . Some Won't," *Harvard Business Review*, 59, 76–95; L.F. Fitzgerald and A.J. Ormerod (1991), "Perceptions of Sexual Harassment: The Influence of Gender and Academic Context," *Psychology of Women Quarterly*, 15, 281–94; S. Kenig (1986), "Sex Differences in Levels of Tolerance and Attribution of Blame for Sexual Harassment on a University Campus," *Sex Roles*, 15, 535–49; B. Lott, M.E. Reilly, and D.R. Howard (1982), "Sexual Assault and Harassment: A Campus Community Case Study," *Signs*, 8, 296–319; M.A. Marks (1993), "Sexual Harassment on Campus: Effects of Professor Gender on Perception of Sexualty Harassing Behaviors," *Sex Roles*, 28, 207–17; K. McKinney (1990), "Sexual Harassment of University Faculty by Colleagues and Students," *Sex Roles*, 23, 421–438; P.M. Popovich (1992), "Perceptions of Sexual Harassment as a Function of Sex of Rater and Incident Form and Consequence," *Sex Roles*, 27, 609–625; J.S. Strouse (1994), "Correlates of Attitudes Toward Sexual Harassment among Early Adolescents," *Sex Roles*, 31 (1994), 559–77; C. Struckman-Johnson (1993), "College Men's and Women's Reactions to Hypothetical Sexual Touch Varied by Initiator Gender and Coercion Level," *Sex Roles*, 29, 371–85.

   An exception to these findings is: D.E. Terpstra and D.D. Baker (1987), "A Hierarchy of Sexual Harassment," *Journal of Psychology*, 121, 599–605.

13. See S.G. Bingham (1993), "Factors Associated with Responses to Sexual Harassment and Satisfaction with Outcome," *Sex Roles*, 29, 239–69.

14. N.J. Malovich and J.E. Stake (1990), "Sexual Harassment on Campus: Individual Differences in Attitudes and Beliefs," *Psychology of Women Quarterly*, 14, 79.

15. R.D. Arvey and M.A. Cavanaugh (1995), "Using Surveys to Assess the Prevalence of Sexual Harassment: Some Methodological Problems," *Journal of Social Issues*, 51, 44.

16. L.F. Fitzgerald (1993), "Sexual Harassment: Violence Against Women in the Workplace," *American Psychologist*, 48, 1073.

17. R. Bly, *Iron John: A Book About Men* (Reading, Mass.: Addison-Wesley, 1990), p. 234.

18. B. Johnstone, paraphrased in Deborah Tannen, *You Just Don't Understand* (New York: William Morrow & Co., 1990), p. 178.

19. D. Tannen, *You Just Don't Understand* (New York: William Morrow & Co., 1990), pp. 26, 28–9.

20. K. Druck and J.C. Simmons, *The Secrets Men Keep: Breaking the Silence Barrier* (Garden City, N.Y.: Doubleday, 1985), p. 18.
21. M.F. Fasteau (1975), "The High Price of Macho," *Psychology Today,* 9, 4, p. 60.
22. Bly, p. 174.
23. See Komaromy et al.
24. Bingham, p. 260.
25. A.P. Nomani, "Was Prof's Lecture Academic Freedom or Sexual Harassment?: A Male Student in California Irked by 'Male-Bashing' Asserts It Was the Latter," *Wall Street Journal,* March 7, 1995, Section A1 "W," Column 4.
26. *Id.*
27. *Id.*
28. *Id.*
29. See J.B. Pryor (1987), "Sexual Harassment Proclivities in Men," *Sex Roles,* 17, 269–90; J.B. Pryor, C. LaVite, and L. Stoller, "Sexual Harassment Proclivities in Men" (1993), "A Social Psychological Analysis of Sexual Harassment: The Person/Situation Interaction," *Journal of Vocational Behavior,* 42, 68–83; J.B. Pryor, J.L. Giedd, and K.B. William (1995), "A Social Psychological Model for Predicting Sexual Harassment," *Journal of Social Issues,* 51, 69–84.
30. Pryor (1995), p.79.
31. Tannen, p. 62.
32. S. Beckett, *Endgame,* in *Stages of Drama,* 2nd ed., ed. Carl H. Klaus, Miriam Gilbert, and Bradford S. Field (New York: St. Martin's Press, 1991), p. 942.

Chapter Five
Losing the Way
The Myths of Consent

Midway this way of life we're bound upon,
I woke to find myself in a dark wood
Where the right road was wholly lost and gone.

—Dante, *Inferno*

By its very nature the subject of sexual harassment attracts hyperbole and vacuous rhetoric. Nothing proves this point quite so well as the contrived controversy over what is euphemistically termed "consent" or "consensual" relationships. The Latin for "consent" is *consentire*, which means "to feel or perceive with." The definition suggests why it is impossible to describe intimate relationships between faculty and students as genuinely consensual. To consent, one must be able "to feel or perceive with"; and while equality of feeling between professors and students may arguably be possible, equality of perception clearly is not. Between a student and an individual with academic responsibility for that individual, there is no intervening variable sufficient to outweigh the significance of their unequal status and thus the dissimilarity of their perspectives about one another and their situation. A student may be the same age, race, religion, and nationality as a professor or teaching assistant; he or she may have similar interests, backgrounds, aspirations, and acquaintances. The two may feel enormous physical, emotional, and even spiritual attraction; they may be compatible in every respect. But their perceptions of the relationship will inevitably differ because one hand and only one holds the pen that records the student's grade, and so long as that is the case, the two cannot be regarded as equals.

M.C. Stites, who has done extensive research on consensual relationships in academe, recognized the significance of perception when she observed, "Participants in a faculty-student sexual relationship might have different motivations for engaging in the relationship, different concepts of what type of relationship they have, and different perceptions of how freely the student consented to the relationship with the professor. . . . [An even further complication is] the possibility that the participants' perceptions and motivations might change over the course of a relationship."[1] Despite the explicitness of this point, available studies indicate that only about 17 percent of institutions have policies addressing faculty-student relationships.[2] The reluctance to confront the issue evolves from academicians' hesitancy to deal with controversy, to engage in discussions of ethical responsibilities, and to educate themselves about the costs of intimate relationships between professors and students. Some find it easier to subscribe to the myths that have arisen around consent than to deal with its unsettling truths. Nevertheless, the specter of the law looms large over the academic landscape, making it necessary for educators to differentiate myth from reality, to weigh the inordinate costs of consensual relations, and to accept the responsibilities and complexities involved in developing policies for dealing with the problem.

The Myths

The myths of consent received their most public airing in a 1993 *Harper's* magazine article that aroused considerable controversy. In the article, a moderator and four academicians discussed their opposition to restrictions on faculty-student romances. The editor stated that he could not imagine a debate about such restrictions unfolding ten or twenty years ago.[3] In response, President Leon Botstein of Bard College claimed that contemporary students differ from their predecessors "through the 1960's [who] accepted the idea that higher education was about trying adult clothes on, so they eagerly accepted responsibility for their actions. . . . Rather than say, 'This is my life, I take responsibility,' the reaction today is, 'I have suffered, I wish to be entitled to some reparation.' The ban proponents believe that punishment has a psychic benefit. They want to put the malefactor in stockades and force him to feel the heat of public humiliation."[4]

Professor Joan Blythe of the University of Kentucky added that "most students at eighteen know more about sex than their own parents. . . . The people who voice these concerns [about faculty-student romances] are precisely those who desire the eighteen-year-old. . . . Those pushing for a ban are people who fear real life, especially the protean power of lust. . . . The force that is pushing for these bans is abetted by an administration whose agenda includes castration of the humanities."[5] A professor of English, Blythe contended that today "the only common language among [disparate campus] groups is sexuality. . . . Sexuality is not a simple act but the very air we breathe. People can have orgasms sitting in class listening to a good lecturer."[6]

Professor William Kerrigan of the University of Massachusetts at Amherst offered his experience as an educator who engages in sex with students.

I have been the subject of advances from male and female students for twenty-five years. I've had them come at me right and left. I've had people take their clothes off in my office. And there is a particular kind of student I have responded to. There is a kind of student I've come across in my career who was working through something that only a professor could help her with. I'm talking about a female student who, for one reason or another, has unnaturally prolonged her virginity. Maybe there's a strong father, maybe there's a religious background. And if she loses that virginity with a man who is not a teacher, she's going to marry that man, boom. And I don't think the marriage is going to be very good.

There have been times when this virginity has been presented to me as something that I, not quite another man, half an authority figure, can handle—a thing whose preciousness I realize. These relationships, like all relationships, are hard to describe, and certainly difficult to defend in today's environment. Like all human relationships, they are flawed and sometimes tragic. There usually is this initial idealism—the teacher presents ideas in a beautiful form, and so there is this element of seduction in pedagogy. And then things come down to earth, there often follows disappointment and, on the part of the student, anger. But still, these relationships exist between adults and can be quite beautiful and genuinely transforming. It's very powerful sexually, and psychologically, and because of that power, one can touch a student in a positive way. . . .

Sometimes these affairs last a week, and they're gone. Sometimes a semester or two. Sometimes they grow into things of great constancy, such as my own marriage."[7]

Within this general Myths of Consent articulated in the *Harper's* article lie several fallacious assumptions that arise in debates about bans on faculty-student relationships or that prevent such debates from occurring at all. Some of these are worth examining in detail.

The Historical Myth: Disapproval of amorous relations between faculty and students is a contemporary phenomenon, a response to feminist pressure and a manifestation of invasive campus politics.

Frequency rates of consensual relationships are even more difficult to establish than prevalence statistics for sexual harassment. To date, three studies are usually cited: Glaser and Thorpe's "Unethical Intimacy: A Survey of Sexual Contact and Advances Between Psychology Educators and Female Graduate Students,"[8] Pope, Levenson, and Schover's "Sexual Intimacy in Psychology Training: Results and Implications of a National Survey,"[9] and Fitzgerald, Weitzman, Gold, and Ormerod's "Academic Harassment: Sex and Denial in Scholarly Garb."[10] The first found 17 percent of female psychologists reported sexual contact with former professors. The second reported $16^1/2$ percent of female and 3 percent of male psychology students acknowledged such encounters; it also noted that in a college newspaper survey, 25 percent of faculty responded that they had been amorously involved with students. In the survey by Fitzgerald and colleagues, more than 26 percent of faculty admitted to engaging in sex with students. Yet even if research techniques in all three studies were impeccable, three surveys, two of which sampled individuals in the same discipline, do not seem adequate to justify the conclusion that sex between students and faculty is common.

A far more salient point is that whether or not it is somewhat common in certain disciplines or academic settings, it has never been behavior sanctioned by institutions, educators, or the public. Sex between educators and students has *never* been accepted campus protocol. College professors have access to numerous perquisites not available to other professionals, but bedding their charges is not now and never has been one of these. If it were, offenders of the often unwritten taboos against student-faculty relations would not take such care to hide their activities. The 1960s to which Botstein referred was a singular period in American history, a time in which many contemporary academicians have psychological and philosophical roots, but even then few were likely to flaunt liaisons with students.

Socialization of American females has long served as deterrent to the image of the campus as a benign bordello where students earn not money, but what Kerrigan and Blythe termed "transformation" and "real life" as a result of intercourse with professors. Prior to the 1960s, there was a long history of women being exhorted to protect "reputations" which were judged almost exclusively by sexual behavior. Nor was the typical 1960s female collegian, as opposed to those on whom television cameras focused, likely to bare her breasts in public and offer her body to her history professor.

In his 1967 book, *The College Experience*, M.B. Freedman wrote of the typical college female:

Most educated women are not inclined to surrender the equality of station and outlook they have won. And it is this sense of equality that serves, among women, as a very strong barrier to sex relations in the absence of love. The chances are that a woman who gives of herself in such a relationship has a rather low opinion of herself. She may feel inferior because she is of lower class status than the man; she may feel that she has nothing to give a man of high social station except her body.[11]

Two years later, in his book *Education and Identity*, A.W. Chickering observed of relations between male and female students:

Physical expression of feelings accompanies intimate heterosexual relationships, but a variation in behavior is great. Some couples hold hands and kiss, and manage that limit outside the context of engagement and marriage without great difficulty. For most, kisses and caresses sufficiently complement mutual exploration of self and the other, implemented through continual conversation and closely shared experiences. For a few, close relationships must be accompanied by sexual intercourse. But usually such physical expression is limited to serious relationships where long-term commitment is assumed. . . . Few are promiscuous, be they men or women, and for those that are development of identity and freeing of interpersonal relationships seem stalled.

During the later college years, this pattern shifts. Although the interpersonal ties are stronger—again with persons of both sexes—they are considerably loosened and less binding. Couples don't have to walk with arms around each other or even hold hands. Public necking—that vehicle for personal declaration of attractiveness and likeability, and mutually supportive commitments and assurances—is no longer required. Physical intimacy plays its important part. But again, for most students, the context is one of respect, commitment, and love. Sexual intercourse in the absence of such feelings is infrequent.[12]

Written in the midst of the so-called sexual revolution on campus, such conservative views from academicians may be naive, but they certainly discredit the assertion that intimate relations between students and professors are sanctioned in the American educational tradition. Even now, there is little support for such a myth. Stites's 1993 survey at a large eastern university revealed, for instance, that only 24 percent of male faculty and 22 percent of female graduate students would accept an institution's having no policies to regulate consensual relationships.[13] She further reported that at least 80 percent of this population agreed that such situations create ethical problems for faculty[14] and that 83 percent to 90 percent agreed that women students who engage in sexual activity with professors may suffer detrimental consequences.[15]

Policies discouraging or prohibiting faculty-student romances reflect a longstanding, albeit for many years uncodified, rule in academe. Feminist opposition to sexual harassment undeniably contributed to concern about consensual sex, but it did not create the concern. The invalidity of the Historical Myth has been proven for years in the pages of countless books and articles on college life, works that echo, if they mention sex between students and professors at all, a passage written in 1980, when colleges and universities first demonstrated concern about consensual sex.

Insofar as . . . teaching is taken seriously as a professional activity, there arises a tension between the concepts of professional relationship and the relationship of sexual intimacy. Historically, sexual, or for that matter, familial intimacy has been seen as distorting clear professional judgment. The Hippocratic Oath, for example, prohibits sex between physicians and their patients. Beyond the issue of professional judgment, the professional may be viewed not so much as one who has achieved some high level of useful, specialized skill (an apt description of an accomplished athlete or good plumber), but rather as someone who is accorded special status, income, or security in exchange for which he or she agrees to an ethic of placing the client's interest above all else. A teacher who gains satisfaction for sexual wants and needs through students may have considerable difficulty maintaining the student's interests as primary.[16]

The Marriage Myth: A significant number of student-faculty romances end amicably or in marriage; therefore, sex between faculty and students is acceptable.

Those who oppose bans against consensual relationships are fond of citing instances in which educators marry student lovers. The irony is that such statements assume the tone of defense or justification, as if the speaker acknowledges an existent taboo. The implication seems to be, "If I married her, my having intercourse with her when she was a student can't be wrong, even though people thought it was." Opponents of bans are also eager to provide illustrations of famous educators who wed students, as if renown somehow sanitizes a behavior with which they are uncomfortable. It is amusing to note the *Harper's* article, for instance, which cites John Kenneth Galbraith's half-century marriage to a former student and then includes an excerpt from the letters of Abélard, the twelfth-century philosopher who fell in love with and married his student, Héloïse. The introductory passage to the Abélard quotation makes scant reference to the fate of the two: "When news of their union spread, Abélard was castrated by an angry mob. [He] became a monk; Héloïse, a nun."[17]

John Kenneth Galbraith's matrimonial success and Abélard's fate aside, there are telling observations that should be made about the Marriage Myth. One of the most memorable is that of Fitzgerald and associates: "that [a] relationship [between professor and student] was a success, or that the couple married, in essence represents a *post hoc* rationale that cannot be used as a guide to ethical behavior since one has no way of knowing beforehand which relationships will be 'successful' and which will not."[18] Secondly, although there is scant research on the topic, anecdotal evidence suggests that the number of students who marry educators is minuscule. The pages of alumni bulletins are replete with reports from former collegians who wed peers, not professors, and administrators receive more headaches from infrequent incidents of faculty-student romances than they do wedding invitations from colleagues marrying students.

Most important is that no occasional marriage, even a remarkably happy one, can atone for the far more widespread and greater pain of those whose lives are irrevocably altered by unwise decisions to engage in sex with educators. For every testament to wedded bliss from a John Kenneth Galbraith or a William Kerrigan, there is a wealth of reports on the damage incurred by so-called consensual sex acts or relationships. Glaser and Thorpe's study of former female graduate students who were sexually involved with professors or clinical supervisors during a graduate program in psychology reported that, while in school, only 49 percent of the women felt the liaisons to be problematic but that the figure rose to 68 percent once they graduated.[19] During the relationship, 72 percent reported no feelings of having been coerced by the faculty member. That figure changed to 49 percent once they left school.[20] In the Stites survey, only 26 percent of male faculty and 33 percent of female graduate students agreed that a professor can be viewed as acting ethically if his consensual relationship with a student for whom he has had responsibility leads to marriage.[21]

Professor Kerrigan acknowledged that after the "initial idealism . . . things come down to earth, and there often follows disappointment and, on the part of the student, anger."[22] What he did not consider was the toll exacted on the student who must discover ways to channel disappointment and anger toward a superior whose power may alter the course of his or her life. Nor does the Marriage Myth address the discrepancy between romantic fantasies of students and the more jaded realizations of academicians who share Kerrigan's view that "sometimes these affairs last a week, and they're gone."[23] "Gone" for the professor does not necessarily mean "gone" for the student, who may feel humiliation, anger, or intimidation in classrooms controlled by an ex-lover and his colleagues.

The Student Support Myth: Consensual relationships are acceptable because they have widespread student support.

This myth rests upon inadequate knowledge of the total student population. While it is possible to arouse a vocal segment of a student body by claiming bans threaten students' rights or denigrate their judgment and maturity, students also express pronounced concern about sexual harassment and professorial abuse of power. Stites's survey did find that 85 percent of female graduate students believed bans on all consensual relationships would violate individuals' rights to privacy in cases in which the professor had no professional responsibility for students.[24] But she also reported that 87 percent supported a discouragement-type policy on consensual relations;[25] that 57 percent would accept a policy that prohibited such relationships when a professor taught, advised, or supervised a student;[26] and that 97 percent believed other graduate students might assume favoritism on the part of a faculty member who had professional responsibility for a student with whom he was intimate.[27]

Professors Kerrigan and John Boswell of Yale, who also participated in the *Harper's* forum, contended that students "absolutely throw themselves"[28] at them, but the majority of college students seem unlikely to do so, since they are far more conservative about sexuality than the *Harper's* academicians assumed. This fact has been repeatedly reinforced in the prestigious thirty-one-year-old survey of American college freshmen conducted by the Higher Education Research Institute at the University of California at Los Angeles. Contrary to the assumption that college students support indiscriminate sexual activity, only 42.2 percent agreed with the statement that "if two people really like each other, it's all right for them to have sex even if they've known each other for only a short time."[29] The reality is that the typical American collegian is more interested in passing examinations than in winning the right to have intercourse with educators; and if the campus is, in fact, in a state of perpetual tumescence, as Blythe, Boswell, and Kerrigan assert, such an environment probably derives more from the mutual attractions of healthy male and female students than it does from the fantasies of those lusting after professors whose words move them to public orgasm.

The Composed Student Myth: Consensual situations are acceptable because students can effectively differentiate between the classroom and the bedroom.

This myth derives from lack of knowledge of or insensitivity to gender relations. Human beings cannot easily separate work and school from the successes, frustrations, and failures of personal relationships; from the expectations, needs, and demands of spouses or lovers. It is ludicrous to assume that a student will be able to maintain perfect calm while her professor-lover lectures on a John Updike novel if she suspects him of infidelity or fears he is about to reject her. Nor is it likely that one would be receptive to hearing about differential equations from a math professor with whom she's had a quarrel about living arrangements. Former students' retrospective assessments of affairs with educators are revealing. Glaser and Thorpe noted of the respondents in their survey: "Although only 28% said they experienced some degree of coercion at the time of contact, 51% now see some degree of coercion, and although 36% saw an ethical problem then, 55% see one now. Finally, 40% saw some hindrance to the working relationship then, but 51% see some hindrance now."[30]

Females, who tend to emphasize relationships and to derive self-esteem primarily from winning the approval of others, are especially at risk as a result of the Composed Student Myth. Inarguably, students depend for academic survival on the approval of their teachers. If a student becomes romantically and/or sexually involved with a professor, her need for his acceptance is greatly multiplied; in a sense, her world is diminished because she has so much invested in one person's opinions. If she falls short intellectually, she relinquishes the approbation of her lover as well as her teacher; if she fails to meet his expectations in bed, she will feel that not even brilliant academic performance can restore her tarnished image.

Conversely, differentiating genuine academic achievement from favoritism becomes difficult. How can she know if an A means exceptional work, reward for compliance, or acknowledgment of exceptional sexual accomplishment? And what about a D or an F?

Does it imply her lover has no respect for her ability or that he cares so little about her feelings and her future that he treats her as any other student or, worse still, as a stranger? Does it suggest that he plans to abandon her for someone brighter or that he will devote special attention to her that is unavailable to others?

Lecherous professors' expectations of student sex partners are curious. They tend to argue that students are capable of responding objectively to the omnipresent judgments inherent in teacher-student relations. What they don't mention is the frequency with which educators charged with sexual harassment rationalize affairs with students by citing their own emotional frailties or vulnerabilities. Excuses range from "She was so young, beautiful, and irresistible" to "She pursued me and rendered me helpless" to "My wife emasculated me and drove me into the student's arms." When experienced professionals use lack of control to defend their behaviors, they cannot expect students to behave unemotionally and objectively in confusing or traumatic situations.

The Mechanical Professor Myth: Consensual relationships are not unprofessional or unethical because educators are capable of distinguishing personal from professional behavior.

Although most educators are equipped to evaluate accurately the performance of those to whom they are physically attracted or with whom they are romantically entangled, the impetus to do so is limited. Once an educator becomes intimate with a student, grades and recommendations may serve as tools to cajole, encourage, reward, threaten, or punish. In the Stites study, 87 percent of male faculty agreed that a professor is behaving unethically if he maintains a professional relationship with a graduate student with whom he is having an affair.[31]

Academicians, like physicians, are discouraged from working with members of their families because personal interest poses dangers to professional objectivity. And yet, unlike psychologists, physicians, attorneys, and social workers, who have adopted ethical codes to protect clients or patients from potential abuses of power, trust, and authority, the American Association of University Professors has refused to establish prohibitions against consensual relationships. The justification for this abandonment is far from clear in light of the threat of economic liability and the potential for damage to institutions' reputations. What is clear, however, is that adherence to this head-in-the-sand position frees faculty who choose to engage in activity which puts them, institutions, and, most importantly, students at risk. In June 1995, Committee W on the Status of Women in the Academic Profession of the AAUP did publish a policy statement regarding consensual relationships between faculty and students.

Sexual relations between students and faculty members with whom they also have an academic or evaluative relationship are fraught with the potential for exploitation. The respect and trust accorded a professor by a student, as well as the power exercised by the professor in an academic or evaluative role, make voluntary consent by the student suspect. Even when both parties initially have consented, the development of a sexual relationship renders both the faculty member and the institution vulnerable to possible later allegations of sexual harassment in light of the significant power differential that exists between faculty members and students.

In their relationship with students, members of the faculty are expected to be aware of their professional responsibilities and avoid apparent or actual conflicts of interest, favoritism, or bias. When a sexual relationship exists, effective steps should be taken to ensure unbiased evaluation or supervision of the student.[32]

Unfortunately, this statement overestimates the realities of faculty-student relationships and underestimates the power of human passion to overcome logic, reason, and objectivity. Despite the desire to place educators in a class separate from other professions, they too are human and when in the throes of passion or great romantic attachment can be expected to adhere to physical or emotional rather than rational dictates. When this occurs as a result of a faculty-student romance, the faculty member compromises his or her professional role, and the institution must ensure that not only the student but also other students are protected from the professor's lack of objectivity.

There are, of course, cases in which instructors do maintain professional distance while carrying on affairs with students, but these usually involve an insidious dynamic. Students who submit to the advances of the "objective" professor seldom foresee the time when the passion will subside and the attraction be revealed as ephemeral. An interesting example of this type of behavior was contained in a letter that a self-proclaimed reformed sexual harasser wrote in response to reading *The Lecherous Professor.*

Since I am a lecherous ex-professor, I must remain anonymous, even though I'm now in industry rather than the academic world. . . . I taught for fourteen years at five different colleges and universities in the West, South, and Northeast. I was asked to resign from two of the schools. At a school in the South, I went to the Academic Dean at the beginning of my second year there, and asked him what to do about the situation. His reply was that since I was not married, I was free to date any girl over 18. His only stipulations were to avoid freshmen and to keep all dating off-campus, and to avoid girls in my classes. Of course, avoiding girls in my classes was impossible, because even if they weren't in my classes to start with, they'd be in them the following semester. . . .

There was only one semester in the 28 semesters I taught when I was not involved with one or more coeds. There was one semester when I was involved with nine different girls, leaving me virtually no time to prepare for my classes. I was asked to resign from that school, and I was almost glad it happened. I have to admit that in 75% of the cases, I was the instigator.

The Vindictive Student Myth: The only difficulty that consensual relationships may pose is that they place faculty at the mercy of vindictive ex-lovers who refuse to take responsibility for their part in affairs.

Since both anecdotal evidence and research indicate that the typical college student is not overly enthusiastic about engaging in sexual activity with faculty, the possibility exists that a significant proportion of those who become intimate with professors may exhibit greater vulnerability and emotional need or greater rebelliousness and willingness to experiment than is the norm. If this is the case, faculty who are imprudent enough to take advantage of such students should recognize that they may not always behave according to professorial scripts and can thus pose considerable personal and professional threat. The contention that the danger and damage of consensual affairs is mitigated by an occasional student's initiating a grievance or lawsuit against a former faculty lover is illogical, and the image of the naive, duped professor is deceptive.

People capable of earning three college degrees are sophisticated enough to comprehend the personal and professional risks of excessive involvement with students, and in the final analysis nothing a student says or does should compromise their ethical and legal obligations. The vulnerabilities and enthusiasms of students are not typical determinants of professorial behavior, so they are not valid explanations for educators' sexual exploits. A student may slink into an instructor's office, remove his/her clothing, lie prone on the floor, and cry, "I need a good grade in your class. Take me!" The student may be overwhelmingly appealing, the offer may be completely earnest, and the odds against discovery minuscule. Nevertheless, the obligation of the professional must be to respond, "Young woman/man, get off my floor, replace your clothing, take yourself to the school therapist's office, and when you are emotionally prepared to do so, I will show you what to study so that you can do well in my course." His second responsibility is to report the incident to the proper authorities so that he and the institution will be protected and the student made aware of the inappropriateness of such behavior.

One participant in the *Harper's* discussion contended that when consensual relationships sour, students "today [demand] reparation . . . the desire for punishment . . . fame . . . displace[ment] of guilt [and] disavowal of responsibility."[33] As has been previously demonstrated, the reality is that nearly two decades of research, campus experience, and litigation prove that reports of sexual harassment are extraordinarily low in comparison to actual incidence of the behavior, and a wealth of anecdotal evidence suggests that participants in consensual relationships are the least likely to come forward. Spurned lovers occasionally bring complaints and create headaches for college administrators and fascinating stories for the media, but the vast majority are known to neither. The reasons are obvious. They emanate not from the students' disavowal of responsibility but rather from fear of retaliation, excessive assumption of obligation, and self-blame. Students feel guilty, embarrassed, frightened, violated, and often simply stupid. Their initial reactions are almost always, "I know I brought this on myself." Superhuman intelligence is not required to realize that the average eighteen-year-old will not blithely request that her parents finance a lawsuit against a former faculty lover so that she can become famous. Nor do middle-aged married collegians or divorcees routinely expiate guilt by initiating arduous grievances over failed affairs.

Even if every student who ever committed the foolish error of having sex with a teacher did file a grievance or a lawsuit, the educators involved would still have violated the ethics of a profession which expects its members to exercise appropriate care for those placed in their charge. An academician cannot be absolved of unethical, irresponsible, or unprofessional behavior simply by labeling students vindictive, and labels do not relieve institutions of the responsibility of making judgments about situations in which students may be entitled to vindication and retribution.

The Costs of Consent

Beyond the myths and romantic accounts of teachers and students who fell in love at first sight and remain blissfully joined after decades lie the harsh realities of "consent." It is always dangerous, always intimidating—if not to the student and the professor, then to the institution and to the other students for whom it bears responsibility. But more often than not, both the student and the professor are likely to suffer. Two recent cases prove this point.

Susan H, a student in a graduate counselor education program, began receiving advice from one of her instructors about problems she was having. In the spring or early summer of 1979, the instructor, Professor K, approached her while she was in the central department office. He took her to his office and threatened to have her discharged from the program unless she had intercourse with him. Over the next several months he forced her to perform various sexual acts with him on seven additional occasions. Some would object to use of the term "forced" and prefer the terminology "she agreed to perform various sexual acts." They might also be disconcerted to learn that she did not bring charges against the professor until almost fifteen years later.

The difficulty with such objections, as with Professor K's assumption that he could walk away unscathed after bedding this woman and several other students, is that they rest on inadequate knowledge of the predicament of Susan H. Some years after her "affair" with Professor K, Susan became an instructor at the institution where she had done her graduate work. Although an excellent teacher, she experienced severe personal problems that led her to seek therapy. Ultimately, she was diagnosed by one of the most prestigious experts in the country as a victim of multiple personality disorder. The experience with Professor K surfaced in the course of the therapy when one of her personalities, who serves the role of "protector" in her personality system, revealed it to the treating therapist. Susan, the core personality, was unaware of the situation because a protective personality had emerged each time Professor K made a demand. The continuing theme in her complaint was that she felt responsible not only for what happened to her but for other women who succumbed to Professor K.

While most would consider this a bizarre case and argue the impossibility of finding the instructor guilty based on Susan's accusations, an examination of her experience would not be complete without observing that in providing a deposition to the court, the professor sealed his own fate when he complacently admitted to having sex not only with her but at least four other students. Susan's lawyer indicated there was reason to believe there were probably others, but the most interesting point is that in every incident Professor K described in his deposition, the student was the "aggressor." "Consent" always occurred because the student was attracted to him.

[Student A] said, "What would you say if I told you that I wanted to have an affair with you?". . . I said that I would consider that a compliment. And I think with—with the rejection that I had felt, and was still feeling . . . by my own wife . . . that I felt positive affirmations like that, it felt real good. . . . So we had an affair.

[Student B] was a person who was—she would dress, you know, short shorts. . . . I guess she was attracted to me. When I found that out I was attracted to her . . . [I knew that by her] actions . . . how she was dressed. She was dressed in short-shorts and as—she was a well-endowed person and she had on a tight sweater or a tight top.

[With Student C] I think there was a mutual attraction. She came in to see me and I think I recognized that and felt attracted. She felt attracted to me.

[With Student D] we felt a mutual attraction toward one another. . . . I don't know how that reaction got understood, communicated. But it was one time. We had sexual intercourse one time.

Susan's lawyer was able to identify only one of the women about whom Professor K spoke. She denied his contention that she initiated a relationship. In addition to Susan and these four women, another student not in his class reported to the lawyer that Professor K attempted intercourse with her during the course of her affair with one of his married colleagues. Still another of Professor K's students indicated that when she sought counseling from him about marital difficulties, he hugged her and began stroking her in a manner she thought inappropriate. She discontinued the counseling sessions but indicated she was still "frightened" of him.

The lurid details of these "consensual" encounters do not paint an attractive picture of the academic profession, and this is unfortunate because educators like Professor K are hardly the majority. In this situation everyone suffered. When the case was settled out of court, the costs of the additional therapy Susan required greatly exceeded the financial settlement she received. The institution lost money and an even greater amount of prestige. Professor K was forced to retire early. The law firm that handled Susan's case did not profit but determined early on that it would persist. Her lawyer explained the reasoning.

When the student first came into our office, it was clear that she had been ill served by her professor. After commencing the suit, the attorneys for the University tried all manner of legal maneuvers to avoid addressing the underlying problem. Their conduct merely reinforced the idea that the student had not been treated properly. The professor took the position that his conduct was not inappropriate. The University did not see that it had any responsibility for the conduct of its professors, which had not been authorized by their administration. Those positions were so contrary to the law, that they made the decision to pursue the case to resolution an easy one.

Unlike Susan, most complainants do not find altruistic counsel to guide them through institutional legal maneuvering, yet anyone seeking reparations from institutions rapidly discovers that legal representation is essential. Chris Ruh, a student at the University of Wisconsin-Milwaukee came to this realization after claiming she had a brief affair with Stephen Samaerjan, a professor at her institution's School of Fine Arts. She maintained that while she accepted responsibility for her part in the relationship, the professor's subsequent retaliation (failure to observe appointments, lowering her grades, verbal attacks, and refusing to critique her work in class) led to her filing charges of harassment. It was a classic he said/she said situation that became unique only in light of the institution's questionable behavior, which Ruh described as "far more outrageous" than the original problem.

Ruh claimed that she endured retaliation from Samaerjan for approximately two years, at which time she dropped out of school, filed a complaint, and began a nine-year ordeal that left her without a degree and $20,000 in debt from school loans and psychological counseling. Her frustration and anger were directed primarily at the institution, which she argued left her "living on the edge, unable to get [her] life together" when it supported other student complaints with details of her own case "but never even acknowledged that anything happened to [her]."[34]

After a decade of confusion and contradictions, the university's most definitive decision appears at present to be that voiced by its chancellor: "Since the UWM policy in effect at the time of [Ruh's] relationship with Professor Stephen Samaerjan did not prohibit consensual relationships between instructors and students, there was no violation in [her] case."[35] University correspondence to Ruh consistently addressed the consensual issue but avoided that of retaliation, which was the substance of the complaint. It was the kind of behavior that led one Milwaukee newspaper to conclude: "Ruh was bedeviled by a bureaucracy bent on preserving its own. She was ignored, stalled, lied to, called crazy and given the run-around for years."[36] Ruh herself maintained:

Up to this point the University has seen me as an adversary. I am not. I think education is our last hope in this culture for resolving any of our

difficulties. . . . If the University cannot discipline itself, if the one insti-
tution in our society whose sole purpose is the pursuit of knowledge and
truth would rather embrace ignorance and deceit in an effort to protect
some small part of itself, then a greater value is lost. Not only to me, but
to our vision of ourselves as society.[37]

It is uncertain whether Ruh will ever pursue her case with a
lawyer who can clear the legal hurdles and give her the day in court
she believes she deserves, but while she, like many complainants,
sees herself as ineffectual and defeated, she may realize precisely the
opposite over time. Her case reveals the crippling effects that lecherous faculty and consensual affairs can have on an institution, its
personnel, students, and support constituencies. Nevertheless, pub-
licity about Ruh's situation encouraged both professors and students
to agitate about discrimination and harassment on her campus, and
the results were significant. Samaerjan resigned as department head
and was eventually given a one-year suspension without pay because
of an intimate relationship with another student. One of his department colleagues was dismissed after having been allegedly served
with twenty-two complaints.

Six years after Chris Ruh's first complaint, the Wisconsin State
Legislative Audit Bureau concluded in a thirty-two-page report,
"UWM does not effectively investigate complaints of harassment or
discrimination."[38] In reaching this conclusion, it noted that in a
three-year period the university had had "336 reports, or one report
every third day, of discrimination or sexual harassment filed."[39]
Asked whether she views herself as "vindictive," Ruh replied:

This process has taught me that there are times when it's okay to be angry
and to demand vindication. The process of fighting back and seeing this
thing through to the end has kept me going. Every step I've taken has made
me realize what this is all about. At first I thought it was about me, about
being some fragile victim. Then I thought it was about him and professors
seducing students. Then it seemed to be about UWM and its attempt to
humiliate me and then use information I'd given them to solve other com-
plaints. Lately though, as the issue gets bigger and bigger, I can see light at
the end of the tunnel. I know this is about courts that won't try hostile
environment sexual harassment cases and politicians who avoid seeing the

problem. In trying to have an impact on the legal system, the university, the legislators and the public, I recognize that their refusal or failure to do anything has absolutely nothing to do with me, and I think that recognition will soon give me the power I need to go on.

While Chris Ruh's and Susan's cases represent extreme examples of the problems inherent in consenting relations, they demonstrate emphatically and, hopefully, unforgettably the paramount issue to be made about the Myths of Consent: amorous relationships between faculty and students are, above all, dangerous. They are dangerous to the parties immediately involved, to their families and acquaintances, to other students, to the institution, and to the academic profession. Members of the latter are too often negatively portrayed in the media because of the antics of a few who are unrepresentative of the whole. Institutions lose money, credibility, and respect when they are judged incapable of controlling the erotic impulses of their employees, and the educational environment is contaminated for students forced to be spectators of campus romances.

The Case for Bans

Prior to the Supreme Court's 1992 ruling in *Franklin v. Gwinnet County Public Schools,* institutions could afford to be somewhat casual about policing faculty-student affairs because, as E.N. Wagner argued in "Colleges Need Outright Bans on Sexual Fraternization," "Lawyers once took Title IX cases in something of a spirit of altruism, but the Court's ruling in *Franklin* gave federal courts freedom to award monetary damages to students of both public and private educational institutions and thus made sexual harassment cases under Title IX far more attractive for attorneys and far more risky for colleges and universities."[40] Even before *Franklin,* however, people were arguing the importance of institutional policies on consent. In 1988, P. DeChiara asserted in an article in the *Columbia Journal of Law and Social Problems*:

Sexual relationships between teachers and students present problems which universities should confront. By intervening in such relationships, universities can help prevent favoritism, sexual harassment and situations in which students make pressured decisions about whether to enter a sexual relationship. . . . Universities should approach the problem of faculty-student relationships by promulgating written rules. . . . Rules both give warning to potential violators and discourage officials from discriminating in their intervention against certain groups of teachers.

The rules universities fashion should ban all relationships in which the teacher is in a position to evaluate the student officially; such relationships are presumptively problematic. Other relationships require officials to decide whether the interests of the student are threatened. In making such a decision, universities should strive to protect the student's freedom—both her freedom from pressure to enter a relationship, and her freedom to enter a relationship when no such pressure exists.

Two years later in "Consensual Relationships and Institutional Policy," E.N. Keller[41] discussed the most characteristic approaches to the issue of faculty-student romance. Keller noted that some institutions ignore the matter altogether, but she contended that this exposes both faculty and students to capricious treatment by university officials. Another approach was to write policy statements expressing concern about but no specific prohibitions or sanctions on such relations; these, however, plunge institutions and their faculties into ambiguity and possibly unenforceable disciplinary circumstances. Keller described a third method as defining exploitative relationships and establishing sanctions to be used against those initiating them. The difficulties she identified in this alternative were the complexities involved in investigations of such relationships and the unjustified intrusions they would pose in settings where faculty and students might naturally meet beyond the classroom. The other two approaches she discussed were prohibitions on all romantic relationships with specific penalties for violations and bans only on intimate associations when the educator supervises the student's work. Of the five alternatives, Keller maintained, the latter is preferable, predominantly because it safeguards the privacy interests of the involved parties.

Stites identified somewhat similar approaches to consensual relationships that institutions employ: prohibition policies, discouragement-type policies, potential conflict-of-interest policies, and total-ban policies. Prohibition policies, like those of the University of Iowa, Temple, and Harvard, ban intimate relationships between students and professors only when they have advisory, supervisory, teaching, or grading responsibilities.[42] Discouragement-type policies, like those of the Universities of Minnesota and Connecticut and the New York University School of Law, provide "a statement of a university's preference regarding faculty members' sexual relationships with students. Such . . . policies express concern, discourage, or warn professors about engaging in sexual relationships with students over whom they have some authority."[43] In the Stites survey, discouragement policies were the most acceptable to both male faculty (88 percent) and female graduate students (87 percent).[44] However, like Keller, Stites noted that such approaches are vaguer than prohibition policies and are difficult, perhaps impossible, to enforce. In addition, she concluded that "collegial solutions and discouragement-type policies often serve as a means for academic departments to avoid addressing the conflicts of interest in faculty-student sexual relationships."[45]

According to Stites, both Harvard and the University of Iowa include in their prohibition policies the potential for faculty to have future conflicts of interest with students with whom they have consensual sexual relationships but no current professional relations. She expressed discomfort with these as well as a fourth kind of policy which bans all sexual relations between faculty and students, even when the professor has no professional responsibility for the student. Stites observed, "Warnings about potential conflicts of interest could inhibit sexual relationships between professors and students where no conflict of interest ever arises and appears to some faculty members to be an unfair intrusion by the university on their personal lives."[46] Her position was similar to those of Keller and DeChiara, who shared the view held by many that in the absence of direct responsibility for a student, a professor may ethically and safely engage in a sexual relationship with him or her. DeChiara wrote: "No flat ban should apply to faculty-student relationships in which the teacher has no evaluative role. Not all faculty-student relationships present problems, and to ban them all would be unreasonably to deny to teachers and students one channel through which a mutually fulfilling relationship might arise."[47] Keller opposed total bans from a slightly different perspective: "Outside the instructional context, the presumption that an intimate faculty-student relationship results from coercion cannot be justified. Since the faculty member does not academically supervise the student, the university has no reason to question the consensual nature of the association. The faculty person cannot use the threat of reprisal or the promise of reward to manipulate the student. Also, little reason would exist for others to suspect academic favoritism."[48]

There are numerous fallacies in these assumptions. The first is the view that colleges and universities are appropriate and desirable "channels" through which "mutually fulfilling relationships" should arise. To state the point bluntly, the campus is not a dating service. It is not the only and certainly not the best location for students and professors to seek potential mates. Students are on campus primarily to be educated, and faculty to teach and engage in scholarly activity. Faculty contracts do not specify and students do not pay tuition for opportunities to engage in amorous adventures. When faculty-student romances are prohibited, educators are obliged to pursue sexual release with more appropriate partners, and students are less likely to engage in behavior that places them at risk.

Another fallacy is the assumption that faculty-student affairs can be divorced from the main activities of the institution. It is impossible to ensure that the paths of a professor and his student-partner will never cross or never cast a shadow on the paths of others. Even when the faculty member does not bear direct responsibility for the student, there are always means by which he or she could exercise influence on the student's fate. If, for instance, a romance ends in serious acrimony and the student attends a class conducted by the ex-lover's best friend or office mate, the student may have very legitimate reasons to feel vulnerable. In very small departments or programs there is also a genuine likelihood that eventually the student would have no choice but to take a course from the partner in the failed relationship.

Nor is there a way to prevent other students from being affected by a consensual relationship. If Professor G is involved in a very public romance with a law student, Katie S, and their relationship leads to close and frequent interactions with his best friend, who is one of Katie's professors, other students would have justifiable reason for assuming that her interactions with Professor G's friend have influenced her standing in the tightly packed competitive structure. This situation could easily work in reverse if the student's roommate were enrolled in Professor G's class. As long as there are fraternities and sororities, groups of students majoring in a discipline, dormitories and student life activities, there will be a "grapevine" to trace the course of a consensual relationship and a constituency that can claim to be damaged by it. Then too there is the negative influence that a highly publicized romantic disaster can have on an entire campus. Few students, faculty members, or administrators enjoy being associated with an institution that is subjected to inquiry and dissension as a result of public scandal over an ugly ending to a faculty-student liaison. When the media focuses its attention on a titillating story, it seldom bothers to record whether the ex-lovers met in the classroom or off campus; its primary interest is to record the details of an affair between unlikely partners whose relationship may damage an entire institution.

Another criticism of restrictions on all intimate student-faculty relations is that they are not only intrusive but also unpopular. Stites reported that only 23 percent of female students and male faculty in her survey would find total bans acceptable,[49] and the potential for controversy over such policies is probably a major influence on administrations' and oversight boards' reluctance to propose them. This is curious because popularity and acceptability are not typical criteria for determining most campus policy and procedures, nor is it possible for students' and faculty's opinions to be the primary arbiters of activity on the modern campus. Grades and tuition are not popular with most students, and a significant number, in some environments the vast majority, of faculty object to athletic programs; but grades, tuition, and sports are nevertheless integral parts of campus life. Students and faculty may desire input into decisions about the financial investments of the modern university, but they cannot assume authority for determining how it will invest its money. If consensus is not required in these situations, it is difficult to understand why it is necessary in determining policy on consensual relationships. Probably more often than not, "consent" ends in acrimony and pain, and when that happens, the result is damage to students. Failed romances place institutions as well as students at risk, so the ultimate determinant in discussions of total bans must not be whether they are popular but whether they serve as deterrents and help to protect the financial and legal interests of institutions.

Yet another criticism of total bans and indeed any prohibitions on faculty-student relationships is that they violate individuals' rights to privacy under the Constitution. Although the courts have yet to rule specifically on the issue, it appears at this writing that such measures could survive judicial review if it could be demonstrated that the institution had a compelling interest which outweighed the student's and professor's rights to privacy in a consensual relationship. It should be noted that the privacy concern is relevant only to state-supported institutions since the privacy right derives primarily from the Fourteenth Amendment, which applies only to acts by states. Three frequently cited higher education cases, *Naragon v. Wharton*,[50] *Korf v. Ball State University*,[51] and *Board of Trustees v. Stubblefield*[52] are often used as proof that state institutions may intervene in faculty-student romances.

In *Korf*, the Seventh Circuit Court of Appeals ruled that a university could fire a gay professor who admitted having sex with one student but denied having made advances at others and having offered to trade grades for sexual favors. Despite the fact that Ball State had no consent policy, the court ruled that the professor could be dismissed because he violated his ethical obligations under AAUP Guidelines.[53] In *Naragon*, the Fifth Circuit Court of Appeals upheld Louisiana State's right not to renew the contract of an instructor who had a lesbian relationship with a student for whom she had professional responsibility.[54] A faculty committee recommended continuing the instructor's teaching assignment despite complaints from the student's parents, but the administration chose not to renew her contract on general standards of professional and ethical conduct.[55] Naragon alleged that her rights to free association and to privacy had been violated and that she had been treated differently from heterosexuals.[56] The court, however, concluded that the university had legitimate interests which took precedence over Naragon's right to engage in an intimate relationship.

A romantic relationship between a teacher and a student may give the impression of an abuse of authority; it may appear to create a conflict of interest even if in fact no such conflict directly results; it tends to create in the minds of other students a perception of unfairness; it tends to and most probably does affect other students' opinions of the teacher.[57]

In *Board of Trustees v. Stubblefield*, a California court upheld a junior college's decision to terminate a professor who injured a sheriff when he sped away after being caught engaging in sexual relations with a student while parked on a public street.[58] Although the court was more concerned with the unusual behavior of the professor, who had to be forced by the student to stop his car, it did acknowledge that the consensual sexual encounter threatened the "integrity of the educational system under which teachers wield considerable power in the grading of students and the granting and withholding of certificates and diplomas."[59]

Having examined the constitutionality issue in depth, DeChiara concluded:

Since faculty-student relationships are probably not shielded by the right to privacy, intervention by universities is probably constitutional. For intervention to pass a test of constitutionality, a university would need only show that the intervention is a rational means of achieving legitimate ends. Since protecting students from coercion and favoritism are legitimate ends, and intervening in a faculty-student relationship is an arguably rational means of achieving these ends, the university's actions would probably pass this low level of constitutional scrutiny with ease.[60]

Some case law from the workplace fortifies the contention that sexual relationships between consenting adults are not necessarily protected by the right to privacy. A significant example occurred in *Hollenbaugh v. Carnegie Free Library*. When two employees of a public library were discharged for nonmarital cohabitation, the Third Circuit affirmed the lower court's decision that their dismissal did not violate the Equal Protection Clause or their constitutional right to privacy.[61] In *Shawgo v. Spradlin*,[62] the Fifth Circuit upheld a lower court's finding that two police officers could be disciplined for an intimate relationship because their "romantic involvement" was not protected by the Constitution and violated their employer's regulation that "[n]o member shall engage in any personal conduct or act which, if brought to the attention of the public, could result in justified unfavorable criticism of that member or the department."[63]

While most colleges and universities have avoided the issue and the courts have been inconsistent in rulings regarding consensual relationships,[64] many employers have attempted to deal with the problem of amorous affairs between employees. Apple Computer, Inc. and Arthur Anderson & Company prohibit romances between supervisors and subordinates. IBM requires that employees inform management when they become involved in dating relationships and then transfers one of the two to a different department. Wal-Mart originally instituted a total nonfraternization ban but modified it when confronted with lawsuits; now employees who are equal in status may date, but supervisors may not become involved with subordinates. The theme from the workplace regarding consensual relationships remains ambiguous, but while businesses appear undecided about romances between co-workers, most are of necessity definitive in their prohibition of intimate relationships between supervisors and subordinates. The irony—or perhaps the tragedy—is that on most American campuses educators have chosen to ignore the far more troubling situation of teachers dating and having sex with students.

Yale University, the first institution of higher education to feel the legal force of the sexual harassment issue, is one of the most recent to discover that problems do not disappear simply by establishing policies that discourage sexual relationships between faculty and students and by assuming that professionals will have the wisdom to comply. Since Connecticut's privacy laws prohibit release of personnel information without employee's consent, little is known about the charges brought by a female freshman who had a two-month affair with Assistant Mathematics Professor Jay Jorgensen. Nevertheless, in 1996, one year after a sexual harassment grievance board found Jorgensen guilty, Yale announced that it has proposed altering its former policy of merely discouraging consensual relations to a policy that bans all sexual involvements between faculty and students.

If implemented in 1998, the ban would add a conflict-of-interest provision to the institution's sexual relations policy. It would be published in the Faculty Handbook with the sexual harassment policy enforced by Title IX. The new rule defines any sexual relationship between undergraduate and graduate students and their teaching assistants and professors as an inherent conflict of interest likely to jeopardize the learning environment. It allows for romantic involvements between faculty and students not engaged in teaching or mentoring situations only if they do not later initiate professional relationships in addition to their personal entanglements.

Yale's proposed approach, the first substantive change in its policy's eighteen-year history, reflects recognition of the increasing complexities of sexual harassment policy and law. It acknowledges the ambiguity underlying the notion of consent between individuals of unequal status and, by adding the conflict of interest rule, clarifies faculty responsibility. Under the rule, a professor can no longer argue that he or she bears no responsibility when a student initiates a sexual relationship and later classifies it as coercive. In some respects even more significant is that the new addition provides stronger justification for third parties to complain when they perceive themselves affected by faculty-student romances. A teacher's behaviors, especially those involving conflict of interest, influence all participants in the educational environment, and the Yale ban would send other colleges and universities a reminder of a burgeoning area of grievance and litigation.

When the University of Virginia committed itself to addressing the problem of consent, it did so with less foresight and more controversy. The Advisory Committee on Women's Concerns, appointed by John Casteen, the institution's president, wrote the first of three documents regarding consensual relationships. Soundly rejected by the faculty senate, it included the following provisions:

The complexity of the University requires that any policy take into account the different kinds of faculty members and students who constitute the community. Policy number one, outlined below, covers teaching assistants: policies two and three cover faculty. For purposes of this policy, "faculty" shall include all full-time or part-time university personnel who hold positions on the academic or general faculty or who teach, coach, or evaluate students, allocate benefits among students, or carry out research.

1. A teaching assistant or grader shall not make romantic or sexual overtures to, or engage in sexual relations with, any student currently in his or her class.

2. A faculty member may not make romantic or sexual overtures to, or engage in sexual relations with, any undergraduate student.

3. A faculty member may not make romantic or sexual overtures to, or engage in sexual relations with, any graduate/professional student in the same department who has not completed all of his or her coursework or any graduate/professional student currently enrolled in a course offered by the faculty member, or any graduate/professional student currently working for or being supervised by the faculty member.

4. A faculty member who allocates funds or other benefits among student applicants, may not make romantic or sexual overtures to, or engage in sexual relations with, any student who is receiving, or is in a position to receive, those benefits.

After the policy was defeated, the committee submitted a compromise resolution written by the dean of faculty. It was passed by the Faculty Senate.

It is the policy of the University of Virginia that a member of the faculty shall not engage in amorous or sexual relations with, or make amorous or sexual overtures to, any student over whom he or she holds a position of authority with regard to academic or administrative judgments and decisions.

For purposes of this policy "faculty" shall include all teaching assistants and graders, as well as all full or part-time university personnel who hold positions on the academic or general faculty, or who teach, coach or evaluate students, allocate benefits or conduct research.

Violators of this policy will be subject to sanctions ranging from letters of reprimand to dismissal, according to the severity of the offense.

Before this second draft could be submitted to the university's Board of Visitors, the administration wrote a third discouragement policy, which is the one now in effect.

As a matter of sound judgment and professional ethics . . . faculty members have a responsibility to avoid any apparent or actual conflict between their professional responsibilities and personal interests in terms of their dealings or relationships with students. . . . It is . . . the responsibility of faculty members to avoid sexual relationships with or making sexual overtures to students over whom they are in a position of authority by virtue of their specific teaching, research, or administrative assign-

*ments. These professional constraints derive from AAUP ethical stan-
dards and the University's policy prohibiting conflict of interests, in order to ensure that the evaluation of students is conducted fairly and
without any perception of favoritism or bias. Perhaps less obvious, but
equally compelling, is the interest in avoiding potential harm to students
as well as the liability that could occur, for example, if facts regarding a
sexual relationship or sexual overture are demonstrated that support a
legal claim of sexual harassment by either party.*

*In this context, the term "faculty members" broadly includes all
full-time and part-time University personnel who hold positions on the
academic or general faculty, as well as all graduate teaching assistants,
graders, and coaches.*

The evolution from a policy which banned consensual relationships to one which simply discourages them has not altered the view
of Ann Lane, professor of history, who served on the Advisory Committee on Women's Concerns.

*I continue to believe that the only serious policy is one that prohibits all
relationships of a sexual or amorous nature between all undergraduates
and faculty/staff/administrators. The inevitable power embedded in a
relationship between a professor and a student and the resulting asymmetrical nature of that relationship makes suspect the idea of a student
as a consenting adult. The mission of a university or college is to provide
the most expansive educational opportunities possible to students, and
such a goal is undermined by intimate relationships between faculty
and students. A teacher's role is to provide intellectual guidance and
nurturance, academic and professional support and advice. Such a role
is inherently antithetical to that of lover, and constitutes an abuse of
power and betrayal of trust.*

*Sexual relations between a professor and a student also address con-
cerns beyond the privacy of two people. Their conduct is not only private
conduct; it affects others, the community they share with other students
and other teachers, all of whom are inevitably affected by their presence
and their behavior.*

Lane's position is sound, and even if professional ethics were
not a problem, the legal and monetary risks for individuals and in-

stitutions are simply too great to justify any course but banning consensual relationships. Wagner summarized this point.

*Given the current case law on sexual harassment, the conclusion is ines-
capable: colleges and universities whose federal funding brings them under
Title IX cannot tolerate a faculty-student sexual relationship, regardless
of the student's age, regardless of the student's willingness to enter such a
relationship, regardless of the student's undergraduate or graduate status, and regardless of whether the student comes under the direct supervision of the teacher or not.*

*Colleges should issue unequivocal statements that sexual fraterni-
zation is cause for termination. Although faculty members may rail that
such a prohibition violates their rights to privacy, given institutions' legal and financial liability under Title IX, administrators' reluctance to
issue clear prohibitions represents a great injustice to faculty members.
Fair or not, the fact is that teachers facing charges of sexual misconduct
with students now bear a "strict liability" burden of proof. In other words,
the blame automatically falls on the teacher, with little or no concern
about the student's capability. . . .*

*Once a teacher-student sexual relationship turns sour, once the
teacher is tempted to use pedagogical authority to influence the
relationship's direction, once the student balks at the teacher's sexual
demands, or indeed once the favored student flaunts the special status
to less favored students, there's trouble ahead. The Supreme Court has
said that when such trouble develops, damages may be collected and
no limits on the amount have been set. And colleges and universities
have what lawyers love to call "deep pockets." You can bet that many
students who simply faded into the sexual reveries of their philander-
ing teachers will return summons in hand, to haunt the whole
institution's nightmares.*[65]

Even with formal prohibitions against all faculty-student romances, the problems will not cease. Proponents of bans must be
prepared to convince courts that they, as outsiders, are in positions
to judge the potential harm of faculty-student relationships and to
prove that such harm will almost always occur but for the intervention of the court. This means that courts will have to agree to assume very paternalistic views in order to uphold prohibitions against

consensual relationships. Such paternalism, in the eyes of many, denigrates students and implies that they are incapable of mature judgment. To an extent, this is true; bans are based on recognition that wisdom and objectivity do not typically motivate those who are infatuated, moved by erotic impulses, and/or in love. This is especially true when power, status and age disparities intervene. Yet such bans are not novel and should be no more denigrating for students than they are for adults who have benefited from them for centuries when dealing with other professionals such as lawyers, physicians, psychologists, and nurses. For every atypical student complaining of feeling "put down," there are hundreds who view the restrictions as protections. To the extent that the population she surveyed is representative, Stites's statistics bear repeating: only 22 percent of female graduate students would accept an institution's having no policy on consensual romances; at least 80 percent believe ethical problems are inherent in such relationships.

Students would benefit from considering that educators who support bans may have their best interests at heart. Every professor wants as much freedom of choice as possible, but most of those who have seen the results of disastrous faculty-student affairs recognize that the cost of gaining the "right" to date students is too high. An English instructor at a large midwestern university pointed out:

It's easy to work these people up about their rights and how they're not respected if we impose restrictions, but let's face it, we're not talking about a Rodney Dangerfield situation here. This is not about not respecting my students; it's about respecting and caring about them so much that you try to protect them from people and situations they're too inexperienced to visualize. I work with a guy who would sleep with every female he's ever had in class if he weren't stopped. Am I supposed to give him carte blanche to do that just because some of these academics have a theoretical, pie-in-the-sky commitment to freedom? My freedom as a person ends where my students' freedom and need for protection begins. When I agreed to work here, I agreed to put the interests of my students first, and that's what bans do.

The most authentic argument against total-ban policies is that they are, to a large extent, unenforceable. But this is also true of the partial prohibition approaches that discourage intimacy only between students and professors who have professional responsibility for them. A college cannot realistically employ ban-enforcement personnel to supervise the private lives of all those suspected of violating school policy, but this is not what proponents of restrictions typically intend anyway. Although bans cannot prevent amorous relationships, they do discourage them. They establish legal and ethical positions for faculty, administrators, and institutions. They communicate to the campus a required standard of behavior. They send a message that faculty and students disregard at their own risk and, in so doing, alleviate the potential for problems at the institution's expense when consensual affairs sour.

Prohibition is not prevention, but it does offer a safeguard, and that is the best that beleaguered institutions can hope for as they struggle with more complexities and challenges than ever before. In 1998, the vast majority of college students are over eighteen years of age, old enough chronologically to choose their own sex partners but academically inexperienced and powerless to protect themselves when such partners are also their professors. The society that made millionaires of Madonna and the 2 Live Crew also produced William Bennett and Pat Robertson, and how is higher education to determine what that society expects of it? Within the context of American history, sexual harassment law and theory are in their infancy at a time when in loco parentis ideals have fallen prey to deep-pocket realities and when people obsessed with individual rights are also preoccupied with concerns about abuses of power.

Tomorrow it may be possible to distinguish the lecherous from the "in love" professor, tomorrow institutions may be able to determine what students and society really want of them, tomorrow legal and constitutional parameters may be clearer. But institutions cannot afford to operate in the future. Today, amid all the myths and controversy, one fact remains: amorous relationships between academicians and students are dangerous—to students, to faculty, to institutions. Until there is a way to prevent personal, professional, and legal risks, "consent" remains a chimera that places both individuals and institutions in unnecessary peril.

Notes

1.   M.C. Stites (1996), "University Consensual Relationship Policies," *Sexual Harassment on College Campuses: Abusing the Ivory Power*, ed. M.A. Paludi (Albany: State University of New York Press), p. 154. ("1")

2.   *Id.*, p. 153.

3.   "New Rules about Sex on Campus" (1993), *Harper's* (September 1993), p. 34.

4.   *Id.*, p. 42.

5.   *Id.*, pp. 37–38.

6.   *Id.*, p. 41.

7.   *Id.*, pp. 35–36.

8.   See R. Glaser and J. Thorpe (1986), "Unethical Intimacy: A Survey of Contact and Advances Between Psychology Educators and Female Graduate Students," *American Psychologist*, 41, 43–51.

9.   K. Pope, L. Schover, and H. Levenson (1980), "Sexual Behavior Between Clinical Supervisors and Trainees: Implications for Professional Standards," *Professional Psychology*, 11, 158.

10. See L.F. Fitzgerald, L.M. Weitzman, Yael Gold, and M. Ormerod (1988), "Academic Harassment: Sex and Denial in Scholarly Garb," *Psychology of Women Quarterly*, 12, 329–40.

11. M.B. Freedman, *The College Experience* (San Francisco: Jossey-Bass, 1967), p. 120.

12. A.W. Chickering, *Education and Identity* (San Francisco: Jossey-Bass, 1969), p. 105.

13. Stites (1), p. 153.

14. M.C. Stites (1996), "What's Wrong with Faculty-Student Consensual Relationships?" *Sexual Harassment on College Campuses: Abusing the Ivory Power*, ed. M.A. Paludi (Albany: State University of New York Press), p. 120. ("2")

15. *Id.*, (2), p. 131.

16. See Pope et al., p. 158.

17. *Harper's*, p. 40.

18. Fitzgerald, p. 339.

19. Glaser and Thorpe, p. 46.

20. *Id.*

21. Stites (2), p. 122.

22. *Harper's*, p. 36.

23. *Id.*, p. 38.

24. Stites (1), p. 160.

25. *Id.*, (1), p. 158.

26. *Id.*, (1), p. 157.

27. Stites (2), p. 125.

28. *Harper's*, p. 37.

29. *American Freshman: National Norms for Fall 1997* (1997) (Los Angeles: Cooperative Institutional Research Program of the Higher Education Research Institute of the University of California, Los Angeles), p. 27.

30. Glaser and Thorpe, p. 49.

31. Stites (2), p. 121.

32. "Sexual Harassment: Suggested Policy and Procedures for Handling Complaints" (1995), *Academe*, 81, 64.

33. *Harper's*, p. 42.

34. S. Kerr, "UWM Sex Harassment Coverups Charged," *Shepherd Express*, November 8–15, 1990, p. 17.

35. *Id.*

36. A. Henzel, "Audit Slams UWM's Affirmative Action Office," *The UWM Post*, March 5, 1992, p. 1.

37. *Id.*

38. E.N. Wagner (1993), "Fantasies of True Love in Academe," *Chronicle of Higher Education*, 26, B2.

39. P. DeChiara (1988), "The Need for Universities to Have Rules on Consensual Sexual Relationships Between Faculty Members and Students," *Columbia Journal of Law and Social Problems*, 21, 162.

40. See E.A. Keller (1990), "Consensual Relationships and Institutional Policy," *Academe*, 76, 29–32.

41. Stites (1), p. 155.

42. *Id.* (1), p. 158.

43. *Id.*

44. *Id.* (1), p. 160.

45. *Id.* (1), p. 162.

46. DeChiara, pp. 155–56.

47. E.A. Keller (1988), "Consensual Amorous Relationships Between Faculty and Students: The Constitutional Right to Privacy," *Journal of College and University Law*, 15(1), 40–41.

48. Stites (1), p. 160.

49. *Naragon v. Wharton*, 737 F.2d 1403 (5th Cir. 1984).

50. *Korf v. Ball State University*, 726 F. 2d 1222 (7th Cir. 1984).

51. *Board of Trustees v. Stubblefield*, 16 Cal. App. 3d 820, 94 Cal. Rptr. 318 (1971).

52. *Korf v. Ball State University*, 726 F. 2d 1222 (7th Cir. 1984).

53. *Naragon v. Wharton*, 737 F. 2d 1403 (5th Cir. 1984).

54. *Id.*

55. *Id.*

56. *Naragon v. Wharton*, 572 F. Supp. 1117, 1121 (M.D. La. 1983).

57. *Board of Trustees v. Stubblefield*, 16 Cal. App. 3d 820, 94 Cal. Rptr. 318 (1971).

58. *Id.* at 827, 94 Cal. Rptr. at 323.

59. DeChiara, p. 152.

60. *Hollenbaugh v. Carnegie*, 436 F. Supp. 1328 (W. D. Pa. 1977), aff'd mem., 578 F. 2d 1374 (3rd Cir. 1978), cert. denied, 439 U. S. 1052 (1978).

61. *Id.*

62. *Shawgo v. Spradlin*, 701 F. 2d 470 (5th Cir. 1983), cert. denied, sub nom. *Whisenhut v. Spradlin*, 464 U. S. 965 (1983).

63. *Id.* at 473.

64. *Briggs v. North Muskegon Police Department*, 563 F. Supp. 585 (W.D. Mich. 1983), aff'd, 746 F. 2d 1475 (6th Cir. 1984), *cert. denied*, 473 U. S. 909 (1985), differs significantly from the cases described above. The court in *Briggs* held that public employees do, in fact, enjoy a constitutional right to privacy regarding their living arrangements and that that right cannot be infringed upon "simply because of a general community disapproval of the protected conduct." *Id.* at 590.

65. Wagner, p. B3.

Chapter Six
Facing the Future
Common Sense and Professionalism

Thus they in mutual accusation spent
The fruitless hours, but neither self-condemning:
And of their vain contest appeared no end.

—John Milton

Let us return to imperfection's school.
No longer wander after Plato's ghost.
Seeking the garden where all fruit is flawless,
We must at last renounce the ultimate blue
And take a walk in other kinds of weather.

—Adrienne Rich

I learn by going where I have to go.

—Theodore Roethke

Two decades ago who would have predicted that as the twentieth century drew to a close, sexual harassment would be a more controversial issue than ever? Back then most people thought it meant males in power propositioning females or, as it was crudely labeled in descriptions of the campus, "an 'A' for a lay." Those who opposed creation of institutional policies claimed that educators were above such behavior (the "nonissue" approach), or that they were responding naturally to sexual cues (the "boys will be boys" and "male as victim of female wiles" approaches), or that academe would collapse under the weight of capricious sexual harassment complaints. Most rapidly forgot these arguments in the face of grim statistics and rare, but high-visibility and thus high-cost, grievances and lawsuits. Today's discussion focuses not only on male-female harassment but on same-

sex and peer abuses, indirectly affected third parties, political correctness, victimization culture, and gender disparities. Not only has
the problem not been resolved, in twenty years it has grown more
complicated and potentially divisive.

Despite Supreme Court cases and thousands of complaints, the
complexities remain. Is the intention or the effect the final determinant in disputes? Who should ultimately interpret the meaning of
"hostile," "offensive," "intimidating," and "unwelcome"? Should
hostile environment offenses be considered as serious as quid pro
quo harassment? How do institutions differentiate insensitive from
intentionally inappropriate behavior, and should they sanction the
two differently? How do organizations discourage harassment without creating stressful, contentious environments? In many instances
there are no easy answers to these questions because even now not
enough is known about the offense. This was J. Wood's point in
"Naming and Interpreting Sexual Harassment: A Conceptual Framework for Scholarship."

*We need to know a great deal more about why individuals initiate,
tolerate, and/or resist sexual harassment, what professional, psychological, and cognitive consequences (both payoffs and problems) it entails,
and what conditions in individuals, relationships, organizations, and
culture legitimate, perpetuate, and sometimes promote it. Insight into
these issues is prerequisite to any informed effort to empower victims and
eliminate—or at least reduce—the incidence and occurrence.[1]*

The controversy surrounding sexual harassment has become, if
nothing else, a reminder of the Talmudic assertion "We do not see
things as they are. We see them as we are."[2] People view the issue
through the prisms of gender, generational, and personal experience;
race, religion, politics, and even regional culture influence perceptions and responses. Some ways of seeing harassment are so intrinsic
to the individual that people cannot process information that supports divergent conceptions of reality. But this is precisely what they
must learn to do because society has altered radically since the days
when sexual harassment had no name. Case law has begun to mount,
and the issue is not going to disappear. From namelessness to
superstardom in the Hill-Thomas hearings, from toleration to po-

litical correctness to reassessment, the issue of harassment has run a tumultuous course, and its omnipresent ambiguities cannot be eliminated by oversimplification or scapegoating.

In many respects academe has been the most curious of all cultures or professions to define in its approach to harassment, since it has led inquiry into the issue and provided direction for the workplace at the same time that its own house has been far from ordered. When Wal-Mart managers are prohibited from dating cashiers but physics professors insist they have the right to engage in sex with students, something is amiss. One academic administrator put the point most succinctly when he said, "Our people write policies for people in the real world that we wouldn't consider abiding by ourselves." Sensitive to historic power inequities, campus women, by both choice and default, early on assumed ownership of the sexual harassment issue. For those who had long felt disenfranchised, harassment represented the most egregious example of male domination and irresponsibility. Male academicians, even those aware of the need for policies, educational programs, and sanctions for offenders, at times felt the tone of discourse to be so heightened that it was perceived as "male-bashing." Thus, more often than not, the gender component of harassment obscured the equally compelling professional concerns it involves; but while gender must always be at the core of the issue, the time has come for educators to acknowledge that sexual harassment raises serious questions about the profession and the priorities of some of its members and to realize that it is in many respects a wake-up call for a profession that has been arrogant and insular too often.

The 1994 case of *Silva v. University of New Hampshire* provides an example of the need to recognize that professional responsibility, as well as gender, informs the sexual harassment dynamic on campus. Silva's dispute with his university evolved from sexual harassment complaints brought against him by a number of students. They involved a series of comments or statements he made both inside and outside the classroom. During the period between February 7 and March 2, 1992, nine females filed formal complaints, alleging Silva had sexually harassed them. While some complainants took issue with comments directed at them outside of class, the focus of the court's analysis centered on the professor's in-class comments.

The most notable was an explanation of the process of "focusing" that he shared with his technical writing class.

I will put focus in terms of sex, so you can better understand it. Focus is like sex. You seek a target. You zero in on your subject. You move from side to side. You close in on the subject. You bracket the subject and center on it. Focus connects the experience and the language. You and the subject become one.[3]

Two days later, in an alleged attempt to illustrate how a good definition combines a general classification with concrete specifics in a metaphor, Silva said to his class, "Belly dancing is like jello on a plate with a vibrator under the plate."[4]

Immediately following the "vibrator" discussion, six students began what would become one of academe's most publicized recent cases. Several of Silva's students reported that in addition to his classroom statements, he had also made derogatory comments to them outside class. One said he had implied she was having a lesbian relationship with another student when, in response to his offer of assistance, she informed him, "[N]o, I'm with her."[5] Another alleged that after observing her on her knees looking into the bottom drawer of a card catalog, he commented, "It looks like you've had a lot of experience down there."[6] Yet another maintained she was intimidated by Silva's asking, "How would you like to get an 'A' for the class?"[7] When a student told a classmate that she was going to "jump on the computer,"[8] Silva responded to listeners nearby, "I'd like to see that."[9]

Several students maintained they felt trapped because the instructor's writing class was a required part of the curriculum. They eventually sought the aid of another professor, who encouraged them to file a formal complaint with the university's administration. The matter was reviewed by the appeals board of the university, which concluded that Silva's repeated and sustained comments and behavior of a sexual and otherwise intrusive nature had the effect of creating a hostile and intimidating academic environment. It also found that given his years of experience teaching communication and language, the professor should have known that his conduct would be offensive to the students. Silva's reaction to the board's findings was less than conciliatory. He defended his actions by asserting, "The students were immature and in need of better training in the use and interpretation of language."[10] In light of the fact that this was the second time in a two-year period that Silva had been disciplined about his use of sexually explicit remarks, the following sanctions were imposed: (1) suspension without pay for one year, (2) psychological counseling at his own expense by a counselor selected by the university, and (3) no contact with or retaliation against the students who filed the complaints against him.

In response, Silva filed an action seeking injunctive relief to prevent the imposition of the sanctions. He maintained that the university's action violated his right to free speech under the First and Fourth Amendments, his civil rights, right to due process, and various contract and tort laws of the state of New Hampshire. Silva claimed that he "[did] not understand the relationship between the [university's] Sexual Harassment Policy and the remarks he made in class"[11] and maintained that his statements were related, at least in part, to the instruction he was providing in the classroom.

The university's sexual harassment policy was similar to that of other institutions. The court in *Silva* described sexual harassment as the following.

Unwelcome sexual advances, requests for sexual favors and other verbal or physical conduct of a sexual nature constitute sexual harassment when:

- *such conduct has the purpose or effect of unreasonably interfering with an individual's work performance or creating a hostile or offensive working or academic environment.*
- *submission to or rejection of such conduct by an individual is used as the basis for employment or academic decisions affecting that individual.*
- *submission to such conduct is made either explicitly or implicitly a term or condition of an individual's employment or academic work. [citations omitted]*

Examples of conduct which may, if continued or repeated, constitute sexual harassment are

- *unwelcome sexual propositions*
- *graphic comments about a person's body*
- *sexually suggestive objects or pictures in the workplace*
- *sexually degrading words to describe a person*
- *derogatory or sexually explicit statements about an actual or supposed sexual relationship*
- *unwelcome touching, patting, pinching or leering*
- *derogatory gender-based humor*

Such conduct whether intended or not constitutes sexual harassment and is illegal under both State and Federal law. Violations of this policy will not be permitted. Any faculty, staff or student who violates this policy will be subject to discipline up to and including dismissal.[12]

In a lengthy opinion, the federal district court reviewed each of Silva's claims, beginning with his argument that the university violated his right to free speech. Reviewing the claim, the court focused on only the classroom comments and did not consider those made individually to students. In applying constitutional law principles, it concluded that it was likely that Silva's freedom of speech had been infringed upon by the university in its attempt to censor his classroom comments. It stated, "Silva's classroom statements advanced his valid educational objective of conveying certain principles related to the subject matter of his course."[13] In addition, it found that because "Silva's classroom statements were made in a professionally appropriate manner as part of a college lecture,"[14] the university did not have sufficient basis for restricting such speech and was not within its right to discipline him based upon those statements.

Silva's action also alleged a violation of his right to due process. He maintained, and the court agreed, that an allegation of sexual harassment "implicates [Silva's] liberty interests in his good name and reputation because the charge . . . and the subsequent sanctions . . . 'might seriously damage his standing and associations in his community.' [citations omitted]"[15] While the court determined that there was insufficient evidence for a finding that Silva was likely to succeed on the merits of his due process claim, as required when seeking injunctive relief, it refused to grant the university's request that this charge be dismissed in its summary judgment motion. The questions the court felt needed to be resolved through trial were whether Silva received adequate notice that the incidents not mentioned in the students' complaints and incidents upon which no evidence was presented at the hearing would be considered by the hearing panel and whether the bias of a member of the appeals board compromised its impartiality and independence.

James E. Perley, president of the American Association of University Professors, referred to the Silva case in a 1995 address.

Sexual harassment is an issue involving aspects of academic freedom whose time seems to have come. We read about a professor in New Hampshire who uses sex metaphors in a technical writing class and the use of these illustrations is seen as sexual harassment. This, at a time when real examples of sexual harassment are being exposed and remedied. . . . The EEOC regulations talk about verbal conduct. It is hard to understand how verbal conduct is not speech. If there are prohibitions on what is not speech, if there are prohibitions on what can and cannot be said in the classroom, particularly if the guidelines for interpreting what is acceptable is the comfort level of students, then we have had the nature of what happens in the classroom radically altered for us.[16]

Perley failed to note that several faculty members, administrators, and students at the University of New Hampshire had for years found Silva's behaviors to be "real" sexual harassment and that, regardless of the court's decision, they will continue to believe that he acted inappropriately. But if emphasis were placed only on private definitions of "real" sexual harassment or exaggerated concern about academic freedom, the debate about this case would rage on forever. The one indisputable point that deserves attention is that something went wrong in Silva's interactions with students. It happened more often than simply in the 1992 incident, and it was serious enough to cause several students to take the highly unusual step of complaining both formally and informally. Excerpts from the students' responses to the jello-vibrator-belly-dancing and the intercourse analogies are revealing.

There are a hundred different ways to give an example of something without being sexual about it.[17]

I feel that as a professor of English he could have illustrated the definition of "analysis" in a much more appropriate manner. He insinuated that every student present had first-hand knowledge of his illustration, and furthermore, that it was the only one we would understand.[18]

He could have used other explanations, and if he couldn't then he was better off saying nothing at all.[19]

I am not a prude, but his is not an appropriate way for a writing teacher to communicate with his students.[20]

The comments demonstrate that Silva's students' concerns about harassment existed within a larger context that cannot be divorced from discussions of academic freedom and constitutional rights. At the same time that some cheer Silva's victory, they should ask themselves serious questions about the intersection of academic freedom and professional responsibility. The University of New Hampshire may or may not have been inept in handling the case; Silva's academic freedom and First Amendment rights may or may not have been an issue; his behavior may or may not have constituted "real" sexual harassment.

Nevertheless, amid all the ambiguity one point *is* certain: good teachers pay attention to the comfort level of students. This does not mean they avoid controversial subjects or texts, but rather that they are articulate and considerate enough of students to place controversy within contexts that help minimize discomfort and wrong impressions. Good teachers are attentive to the social, political, and legal debates occurring in the world around them; they do not operate in a time warp and court trouble when they and their students would be "better off saying nothing at all." They do not, as did Silva in his response to the charges made against him, dismiss multiple complaints from students as "hypersensitiv[e],"[21] "exceedingly emotional,"[22] and "immature,"[23] and they do not refuse to consider modifying behavior that has created trouble for them, their students, and their institutions.

This is the point made in an *ABA Journal* article by L. Hirshman, who received an award as best teacher of the year while a visiting professor at Northwestern University School of Law.

Professors like Silva and their defenders say that the students should lighten up. Such sex talk is important, they say. Yet the more I know about the offending teachers, the more I realize that what really matters to them is the privilege of sexual abuse. The academics' attachment to acting out has made me realize the importance of this issue. . . .

College tuition these days is a pretty high price to pay for something you can get from a 900 number for a lot less money. . . .

The professor's defenders invoke the serious and worthy value of "academic freedom," implying that nothing less than the future of Western Civilization rests on the freedom to engage in such exhibitions. This suggestion defames the very concept of "teachers."

Since women entered higher education in numbers, a whole generation of American women have been lucky enough to know teachers who managed to achieve excellence without insulting female students.[24]

R.N. O'Neil echoed her argument in a *Chronicle of Higher Education* article.

If classroom language creates a hostile climate but does not fall within the bounds of what the courts allow to be proscribed, the language still cannot be ignored by institutions. Indeed, the cases that have ended up in court would never have got that far if the academic system had been working properly. College teachers who create a hostile classroom climate, however acceptable their teaching styles may be to some students, must be warned of the corrosive effects of their behavior. They need to be guided by deans, department heads, and other colleagues in the quest for teaching methods and materials that enliven classes without offending or demeaning their students.[25]

Professional educators at the end of the twentieth century should be sophisticated enough to recognize that gender differences have an enormous impact on teaching and learning, and that they cannot assume, as Silva reportedly did, that their conversation is "natural"[26] and will be understood and accepted by everyone. Most of the research demonstrates that, throughout their lives, men tend to be more interested in erotic materials than women; they tell more jokes and use more off-color language and sexual innuendo. This is neither abnormal nor immoral; to many males, it is as natural as donning a bathrobe to watch television late at night. But the workplace and the classroom are governed both by laws and unwritten codes of behavior that discourage people from doing what happens to seem normal or comes most easily to them. While bedroom attire is perfectly appropriate in one's home, it is clearly not acceptable in the office, and off-color language is no different.

Unless teaching can be perceived as a wholly private experience, one's own concept of "natural" cannot serve as the determinant of appropriate pedagogical behavior. It is tempting to speculate about Silva's response if a female professor taught the concept of focus in writing with one of the most familiar analogies from her experience: "I will put focus in terms of [inserting a tampon], so you can better understand it. Focus is like inserting [a tampon]. You seek [the] target. You zero in on your subject. You move [the tampon] from side to side. You close in on the subject. You bracket the subject and center on it. . . . You and the subject become one."

There are good reasons for not taking this approach in the classroom: (1) The professor suspects that a significant number of students will be unfamiliar with the experience used to make the analogy. (2) She can safely assume that, however "natural" it seems to her, it is certain eventually to offend or embarrass someone, male or female. (3) She recognizes that there are other more neutral and easily generalizable ways of making a point. Nor does she teach essay organization by using the stages of the menstrual cycle as an example. She knows that while her husband may be accustomed to hearing about her bodily functions, she cannot measure all males by one, so she keeps illustrations of ovulation to herself, just as well-intentioned male professors choose the appropriate audience and the right time to discuss intercourse.

The message that institutions need to convey to employees is that people can work together and teach students without engaging in behavior that, while intrinsic to them, creates embarrassment for others. The issue is that simple. Much of the pontificating about First Amendment rights and academic freedom is really a way of arguing that one's own tastes and habits take precedence over professional responsibility. No one defends professors who use physical handicaps, race, or religion to make pedagogical points or inject humor into lectures, and gender is no less significant an issue. The classroom is not a laboratory for testing the limits of civil rights. It is a place where a small number of people wield immense power over the lives of others and where those in authority need to be reminded that self-indulgence can cause unnecessary conflict and irreparable damage.

It is true that sometimes the issue of appropriate behavior seems less clear than in the Silva case. College professors, like many contemporary males, are predictably sensitive about the confusion and ambiguity in hostile environment law. For example, given the amount of time they spend with attractive young women, some fear that simply looking at a female could be interpreted as "ogling" and provide impetus for an harassment claim. Most are not comforted by arguments that such behavior would have to be very extreme to be judged an acceptable basis for a complaint; to them, the concern is genuine. This is so in part because they have been subjected to half truths and horror stories, but also because their normal responsiveness to physical appearance can create a sense of unease. But even in this ambiguous area of the law, the solution is not to decry regulations that protect students from truly lecherous professors, but rather to accept basic realities of gender interaction.

Many men, college professors among them, regard staring at an attractive female or complimenting her on her appearance not as a lecherous act, but as an expression of appreciation for which she should be grateful. The problem is that if the receiver of the action is rendered uncomfortable by it, she will not "get" the message of appreciation, so responsible educators recognize that contrary to the myth that women universally enjoy male attention, there is no "female perspective" determining reactions to males. Women differ radically in their attitudes toward male attention. Some tolerate it. Some welcome it and even appear to seek it; some use dress as a means of attracting it. Yet clothing is a very inexact measure, since women choose their attire for as many different reasons as men find various kinds of dress "sexy." Young collegians may experiment with clothing styles much as they try on identities in their progress to maturity, and some are discomfited or offended when males, even peers, observe them too long or too closely. Since women's clothing, faces, and body language convey indeterminate messages that only familiarity or carefully considered communication can decipher, the ambiguity surrounding female students', colleagues', and staff's physical appearance make prolonged observation by male educators an ill-advised behavior, an activity that has probably always been imprudent, but has been criticized only now that females feel free to express their discomfort.

Discussion of hostile environment concerns needs to be more realistic and less hyperbolic. In the ideal academic environment, male (and female) professors would never be physically attracted to colleagues, staff, or students, and they would never harbor fantasies about them. In the real world, many do, but the test of professional responsibility is not an emotion or a fantasy, but rather how one acts in response to emotions and fantasies. Arguments about whether college professors have a "right" to stare, and students or other institutional employees a "right" to be offended in reaction, accomplish little except to exacerbate tensions. Contrary to the hyperbole of females who see a rapist lurking behind every male face or the exaggerations of perpetrators who demean their gender by proclaiming it captive to testosterone, men, especially college professors, should not be controlled by their sexual appetites. Just as they restrain themselves from attempting intercourse with every woman to whom they are attracted, so too are they capable of managing their facial expressions and eye responses. Similarly, women, especially adult professionals, should be able to accept responsibility for using clear verbal and nonverbal cues to indicate when a male's attention is welcome; and by both role modeling and direct instruction, educators can teach collegians that sexual attention from professors is inappropriate.

One of the most effective and least used techniques for preventing hostile environment complaints from students is student evaluation of faculty, which could easily be adapted to raise educators' consciousness about students' perceptions of their treatment of the genders. Assessment forms, including brief questions about students' comfort level, would allow professors to review their interactions with collegians and address problems before they escalate. A single global question could be revealing: "Does this instructor engage in behaviors or make statements that cause you to feel discomfort or intimidation as a result of your race, nationality, religion, or gender? If so, explain." *No one other than the professor should be given access to*

such information; it should be employed solely as a professional develop-
ment tool to inform and guide the instructor in interacting with stu-
dents. If faculty fear that students' responses could be misused by
administrators or colleagues, then they should gather such information on their own, recognizing that negative responses may occasionally occur and that they must make informed decisions about
the point at which criticism should be taken seriously.

Today it is apparent, as never before, that professional judgment must be a focus in discussions about sexual harassment in academe. The Silva debacle happened when some students were, in
effect, a "captive" audience in a required course, but trouble can
occur even, or perhaps especially, when students seek out professors
promising unorthodox teaching experiences. No case proves this point
or the labyrinthine nature of the harassment issue more clearly than
that of University of Wisconsin-Milwaukee feminist Jane Gallop,
who was accused by two students of sexual harassment. Gallop described herself as a "power" or "pro-sex feminist,"[27] terminology which
was apparently meant to distinguish her from feminist colleagues
whom she criticized for taking "the standard, protectionist path"[28]
of supporting bans on consensual relations. She argued that "denying women the right to consent . . . infantilizes [them], denies
[them] full humanity."[29] Gallop authenticated her position by citing her own experience "as a woman who, when [she was] a student . . . aggressively pursued sexual relations with teachers."[30] She
maintained that her "friends . . . feminist academics of [her] generation"[31] followed a similar course; it was, she explained, a "part of our
embrace of the intellectual life."[32]

In a book discussing the sexual harassment charges brought
against her, Gallop included an overview of previous exploits. Describing her attraction to two professors on her dissertation committee, she stated that although they initially rejected her, she continued to attempt to seduce them. After finally having sex once with
each, she concluded, "To be honest, I think I wanted to get them
into bed in order to make them more human, more vulnerable. Screw-
ing these guys definitely did not keep me from taking myself seriously as a student . . . . I learned and excelled; I desired and I fucked
my teachers."[33] (It should be noted that in recounting her own
motivation as a student engaging in sex with an instructor, Gallop

reinforced one of the most urgent reasons faculty should avoid so-called consensual sex: it makes them vulnerable.)

Gallop then recounted an affair with a graduate student that she claimed did not affect her evaluation of his work or her attitude toward other students in class. She added, "But I will admit both of us found our secret titillating: it was a perverse thrill to treat him in class just like the other students though all the while we also had this sexual relation outside of class."[34] (Her statement indicates no aware-ness that when one shares a "titillating secret" with a student and finds "perverse thrill" in his presence in the classroom, she cannot logically be responding to him "just like . . . other students.") When the graduate student left her for another woman, she acknowledged feelings of rejection and loneliness and observed that she was con-soled by having a casual sexual relationship with an undergraduate who intended "to cheer [her] up by sleeping with [her]."[35] When this student visited her on her birthday "to make sure [she] got laid,"[36] Gallop felt "the thought was sweet"[37] but assured readers, "His real devotion to me was intellectual."[38]

These anecdotes were followed by the professor's account of sexual relations with two lesbian students whose standing joke when they passed her apartment was to suggest to each other "SBFJ (Stop by, Fuck Jane)."[39] After the two students parted, Gallop noted that she was "thrilled" to be seduced by one and equally delighted to accept a similar invitation from the other a year later. Gallop, like William Kerrigan, John Boswell, and Professor K., saw herself as exceedingly desirable and completely free of blame in all of these situations since it was, she maintained, the students who initiated the sex.

Described by a former colleague as a "troubled but well-connected exhibitionist," Gallop asserted in a newspaper interview that she found "fair [and] . . . accurate [and] . . . enjoyed"[40] "the flamboyant bad-girl persona she cultivates [as] . . . a sort of post-structural Mae West. In critiquing the notion of a disembodied mind, she loves to flaunt her own body."[41] Her troubles began when she was accused of sexual harassment by two graduate students drawn to her theories of personalized pedagogy. Eventually she would describe the asso-ciation with one of the women as "neither a sexual relation nor even a romantic dating one; it was a teaching relation where both parties were interested in writing and talking about the erotic dynamics underpinning the student-teacher relation. Add to that adventure-some topic a teacher and student whose styles tend toward the peda-gogy of shocking performance—and what was never anything but a teaching relation found itself proscribed by university policy."[42] The "adventuresome" student-teacher relationship cited by Gallop in-cluded, in the university's investigation of the charges against her, meeting "regularly (both in private and in the company of others) for drinks after class and for lunch or dinner. . . . Communicating in [a] sexual banter mode . . . 'confessional honesty, exploration of sexual ambiguity, and provocative performativity' [Gallop's termi-nology], as well as a 'standard goodbye'—a hug and a kiss."[43] Gallop denied being attracted to the complainant but stated "that on . . . one occasion . . . [when] she had noticed how [the student's] breasts looked in a tank top . . . [she] felt attraction in the form of . . . re-marking to [herself] that [she] remembered how nice [the student] looked in that tank top."[44]

The student charged that "by repeatedly introducing a sexual element into [their] working relationship, [Professor Gallop] cre-ated an environment in which [her] intellectual performance was not the only performance for which [she] was being judged."[45] She stated that during a session of a conference on gay and lesbian stud-ies, "Gallop expressed her sexual preference for graduate students"[46] and that later at a bar they had a conversation that led to the professor's French-kissing her.

At the bar, I [asked] her what she meant by her announcement and said something to the effect of, "So you're not interested in me as a person as much as someone over which you have power?" At this point she pulls me between her legs (she is sitting on a bar stool) and sa[id], "Yes, but I told [my companion] I thought you wanted to f—— the teacher out of me." She strokes my shoulders and breasts. I do not reciprocate and sit there awkwardly trying to figure out what to do. I remember being struck that no one seemed shocked. Maybe because I wasn't registering a reaction. I just felt numb. . . . Afterwards, I rounded up the people who came with me and was leaving when Jane said, "Aren't you going to kiss me goodnight?" She mashed her lips against mine and shoved her tongue in my mouth and just sat there. So I kissed her until she responded, more as a vindictive act than a reciprocally sexual one.[47]

Gallop's account of the incident differed considerably.

[The student] and I embraced as had become customary upon our partings. This time we kissed on the lips and, to my surprise, [the student's] kiss felt not like a peck but like a kiss. When [she] started putting her tongue in my mouth, I understood this as some sort of performance for the sake of the assembled conference participants. . . . I wished to support her attempt at provocative performance and so I went along with this performance kiss.[48]

It is not necessary to delineate all the charges made by the student in order to comment on the disquiet one experiences in reading simply this excerpt from Gallop's reportedly ninety-four-page response. If not disingenuous, it describes professional behavior which is, at best, reckless; and while the institution issued a slap on the wrist to Gallop by finding her not guilty of sexual harassment but in violation of its policy on consensual relationships, it avoided confrontation with the thorny concerns inherent in the case. The charges of sexual harassment were obviously difficult to resolve. Gallop argued in various public forums that she did not engage in harassment. The student maintained that she did do so and that the institutional process protected Gallop even though it did not exonerate her.

Despite the ambiguous or unknowable elements of the case, it is indisputable that the university was long cognizant of Gallop's personal and professional behavior and philosophy. No one could argue that she was deceptive in describing her style or her intentions. The introduction to her publication *Around 1981* read, "To my students, the bright, hot, hip women who fire my thoughts, my loins, my prose."[49] She consistently maintained her belief that "erotic dynamics" underlie the pedagogical relationship. In her response to the charges against her, she admitted that she "explored" the erotic nature of her relationship with the student because it was, according to the university's finding, "an important aspect of her research."[50] Such rhetoric recalled her observation in *Thinking Through the Body*: "[This essay] is my attempt to understand the sexuality that underlies my chosen profession. . . . Pedantry is undoubtedly a useful paradigm for Classic European pedagogy. A greater man penetrates a lesser man with his knowledge. The student is empty, a receptacle for the phallus; the teacher is the phallic fullness of knowledge."[51]

Students Against Sexual Harassment (SASH) apparently did not share this approach to pedagogy. According to Gallop, the group was organized by the students who accused her of sexual harassment. She reported that they and their supporters had a table outside a conference she had arranged and sold bumper stickers reading "Distinguished Professors Do It Pedagogically."[52] They also distributed handouts that exhorted readers, "Do not allow yourselves to be co-opted into Jane's deluded world."[53] In reviewing Gallop's accounts of her experience, even the most sympathetic witness of Gallop's behavior must wonder why she would put herself and her institution at such risk, why she could not see that there are demarcations between students' "personal" and private revelations, between "shocking" and invasive pedagogy. Gallop admitted that for approximately a decade students who seek out her presumably elective feminist seminars have not been universally pleased with her teaching and describe her as authoritarian. Nevertheless, she dismissed the students' perceptions:

In the context of feminism, these complaints of sexual harassment are saying the same thing: that I abuse my power, get off on my power at students' expense, that I am just as bad as men. . . . Feminists often condemn the woman who is like a man as a traitor to feminism, a traitor to her sex.[54]

Such criticism of feminist students is indicative of a larger irony that pervaded Gallop's self-defense: in order to portray herself as not guilty of sexual harassment, she was forced to abandon the "power feminist" position she claimed to occupy and to assume instead the role of the victim. According to her account, she was at the mercy of a variety of forces—the two complainants, SASH, other women faculty, "victim feminists," male power, administrators, attorneys, and sexual harassment policymakers. Ultimately, she argued that the two grievants, with the approbation of her university's affirmative action officer, who assisted in composition of the complaints, were requesting that the university restrict her writing and speech and "police [her] thinking"[55] when they asked that she not be permitted to use their case as "the subject of intellectual inquiry."[56]

Many scholars might wonder whether self-defense can legitimately be termed "intellectual inquiry," but more significant is that upon declaring herself the victim of an attempt to "police her thinking," Gallop did not mention that her version of the events was and will remain the sole public record. The journal *Academe* and Duke University Press, which published her accounts, do not frequently accept manuscripts from students; thus, in hospitable forums, Gallop exercised a formidable gesture of power and effectively silenced and chastised those less powerful who had questioned her behavior. It is not known whether her university recognizes that many campuses have "research on human subjects" regulations requiring professors to submit documentation explaining "research" that deals with human subjects, to acquire subjects' consent to be used in such "research," and to guarantee that subjects will not be harmed by faculty members' work.

In this, as in the Silva case, controversy over sexual harassment became symptomatic of greater contention and inertia in academe. Sooner or later higher education must face the troubling issue of whether, in the name of academic freedom and intellectual inquiry, it can justify, economically, politically, and ethically, perilous professional behavior. In examining three recent hostile environment cases, Silva's among them, K. Jost stated in the *ABA Journal* that "on close examination [they turned] out to have at least as much to do with poor judgment as with academic freedom."[57] He then observed of a conversation with Jordan Kurland, associate general secretary of the AAUP, "Kurland says the association, a watchdog for the classroom and financial interests of faculty, has never made an official finding of a violation of academic freedom in any sexual harassment case."[58]

It is interesting that nowhere in the fourteen-page determination of the Gallop case was consideration paid to the reception that the professor's "provocative" theories would receive not only from students but also from taxpayers, businesses, prospective enrollees, and alumni who support her institution. Yet the unadorned truth is that when institutions are scrambling for funds to survive and to support services for students with limited academic skills, they will ultimately have to prioritize and defend their goals. Although it goes without saying that the public would not label "research" into the "erotic dynamics" of the teacher-student relationship and "the pedagogy of shocking performance" as genuinely academic, it remains to be seen whether educators will place them high on the priority list. Nevertheless, it is tempting to regard these, like other exotic academic pursuits, as analogous to the situation of the Castalians in Herman Hesse's *Magister Ludi.*

In this novel, Hesse described life in Castalia, an isolated community in which a group of scholars devote their lives to playing the Glass Bead Game, an esoteric exercise carried out by an intellectual elite supported by the general populace. Ultimately, Joseph Knecht, a player who rises to the highest station in the community, defects. His comments in doing so should be provocative to a profession facing inevitable change as government, one of its primary supports, undergoes redefinition and retrenchment. Hesse's Knecht, troubled by his peers' hubris, poses troubling questions:

Does [the present-day Castalian] not often suffer from a severe lack of insight into his place in the structure of the nation? . . . Does he have any notion of the sacrifices the nation makes for his sake, by feeding and clothing him, by underwriting his schooling and his manifold studies? And does he care very much about the meaning of our special position?

The average Castalian may regard the man of the outside world, the man who is not a scholar, without contempt, envy, or malice, but he does not regard him as a brother, does not see him as his employer, does not in the least feel that he shares responsibility for what is going on outside in the world. The purpose of his life seems to him to be cultivation of the scholarly disciplines for their own sake, or perhaps even to be taking pleasurable strolls in the garden of a culture that pretends to be universal culture without ever being quite that. . . .

But as it happens, we Castalians are dependent not only on our own morality and rationality. We depend vitally on the condition of the country and the will of the people. We eat our bread, use our libraries, expand our schools and archives—but if the nation no longer wants to authorize this, or if it should be struck by impoverishment, war, and so on, then our life and studying would be over in a minute. Some day our country might decide that its Castalia and our culture are a luxury it can no longer afford. Instead of being genially proud of us, it may come round to regarding us as noxious parasites, tricksters, and enemies. Those are the external dangers that threaten us.[59]

At the end of the twentieth century, institutional "impoverish-ment" and the likelihood of being regarded by the public as "trick-sters," or even "parasites [and] enemies," are omnipresent realities for academicians. Regardless of one's response to the general thesis of controversial works like W.A. Henry III's *In Defense of Elitism*, it is clear that a significant number of Americans share his view.

The best reasons for skepticism about mass higher education . . . reach far beyond the decline in meaning of a degree. The opening of the academy's doors has imposed great economic costs on the American people while delivering dubious benefits to many of the individuals supposedly being helped. The total bill for higher education is about one hundred fifty billion dollars per year. . . . Some expenditures are offset through tuition, endowment income, and so on, [but] even the gross total is mean-ingful as an index of the scale of national commitment. President Clinton refers to this sort of spending as an investment in human capital. If that is so, it seems reasonable to ask whether the investment pays a worth-while rate of return. At its present size, the American style of mass edu-cation probably ought to be judged a mistake.[60]

Financial exigency and diminishing confidence in the profes-sion have posed serious problems since the 1970s, and in the con-temporary climate, which shows no signs of change, creative inter-pretations of academic freedom, especially with regard to gender and sex, invite significant risk. This is not to suggest that such inter-pretations be disallowed but simply that they be approached with recognition of the repercussions they might stimulate. The concept of academic freedom was intended to protect scholars engaged in controversial or unorthodox research and teaching from the shifting moods and prejudices of the public; but unlike constitutional privi-leges, which are limited only by recognition of the rights of others, academic freedom implies responsibility. Clearly, it is not a license to engage in sexual harassment, and institutions are becoming in-creasingly impatient with faculty who place them at risk. The Col-lege of William and Mary filed a federal court complaint against a professor, contending he alone was responsible for damages stem-ming from a student's sexual harassment suit. When the student's complaint was settled out of court, charges against the professor were dropped, but the case suggested that changes are coming. The *Chronicle of Higher Education* noted:

The college says that it had prohibited sexual harassment and that Mr. Abdalla [the alleged perpetrator], if guilty, failed to follow the rules. The professor, it says, "had a duty to act in ways that did not expose the college, his employer, to liability."

Guy W. Horsley, a senior assistant attorney general in Virginia, is working on the case for William and Mary, a public college. He says, "The college wants to pass any liability on to the professor because he was the actor." The institution "doesn't have control over professors on a day-to-day basis, and if one professor goes out and does something wrong the college shouldn't be held liable." He believes that William and Mary's action may start a trend. . . .

[Lee B. Liggett, President of the National Association of College and University Attorneys, agrees.] "Institutions are asking what they can do to protect themselves. . . . Why are we responsible for the acts of an employee when we didn't hire them to do what they did?" he asks.[61]

In the not too distant past the profession enjoyed considerable approbation from a public beguiled by its mystique. When only the privileged had access to the college campus and few academics sought or received media attention, blemishes on the ivory tower were easier to obscure. But familiarity breeds, if not contempt, awareness of imperfections; and today, with approximately 62 percent of high school graduates seeking further education, academe is an easy target for critics acquainted with its foibles. Even a brief stay on campus acquaints present and future taxpayers with the lifestyle differences of the professoriate and other workers. The average citizen labors a minimum of forty discernible hours a week, for fifty weeks per year, at readily measurable tasks; failure to achieve hypothesized results is seldom an option, and job termination is an ever present possibility. Given these conditions, outsiders cannot easily comprehend the lifestyle and employment concerns of academicians, whose work they subsidize though taxes and tuition.

Academicians have paid too little attention to the skepticism that these discrepancies arouse, and the sexual harassment issue has only accentuated them. Some, like Thomas Wagner, former vice president for Student Affairs and Services at the University of Cincinnati, are aware that the sexual harassment issue has raised increasingly serious concerns for educators.

Our natural response is to rally around the flag of academic freedom in even the most questionable instances because the next case might be legitimate, but the academy needs to gather the courage to say to those who harass or experiment with students, "No matter what words you impose on what you do, your behavior is inappropriate." If we allow questionable behavior to be protected for the sake of a few, we lose the freedom to pursue legitimate research and pedagogy.

As society and academe struggle to clarify higher education's place in contemporary culture, the spectacles of a few atypical educators have emerged to complicate the situation further. The first and most persuasive message from the campus was that sexual harassment is an educational and societal malignancy that demands definition, analysis, and control. In an unfortunate twist, the imperative from some quarters of academe now appears to be: Do as we say, not as we do. We have the right to indulge our own prurient interests, to invade students' privacy in the name of pedagogy, and to use the security of consent to bed subordinates. And even those of us who would never engage in such behaviors will defend to the utmost colleagues who choose to do so because academic freedom and faculty rights are sacrosanct, paramount among all other professional commitments.

The issue of sexual harassment lays bare all of higher education's contradictions and weaknesses. It demonstrates that many of the people who claim to know so much about the past, present, and even the future have limited objective grasp of the multifaceted cultures in which they work. It reveals that not all academicians are as rational and high-minded as they claim to be. Their intellectual pursuits and allegiances may derive from fierce emotions, and their commitments may be driven as much by self-interest as magnanimity. Sexual harassment reminds the profession that it cannot survive in isolation and that dependence on the larger community necessitates keeping its affairs in order unless it wishes to avoid external control. The harassment issue has gradually but inexorably forced higher education toward what it likes least—defining moments, moments of choice and decision.

But the most difficult decisions have already been made. After years of ignorance and denial, most academicians have committed themselves to recognizing and preventing sexual harassment. Although the path to eradicating the behavior has been treacherous and marked by impediments along the way, progress cannot be undone by extremists or those who use students and institutions to further personal agendas. In the end, discussion has come full circle to the place it most belongs—the campus itself. The law has made an essential contribution by establishing a framework to define unacceptable behavior and by creating a last resort to maintain control, but only educators can ensure that freedom, opportunity, and respect are extended to everyone on the American campus.

Notes

1. J.T. Wood, "Naming and Interpreting Sexual Harassment: A Conceptual Framework for Scholarship," in *Sexual Harassment: Communication Implications*, ed. Gary L. Kreps (Cresskill, N.J.: Hampton Press, 1993), p. 9.
2. Talmud, attribution information unavailable.
3. *Silva v. University of New Hampshire*, 888 F. Supp. 293, 299 (D.N.H. 1994).
4. *Id.*
5. *Id.* at 302.
6. *Id.* at 310.
7. *Id.*
8. *Id.*
9. *Id.*
10. *Id.* at 311.
11. *Id.* at 299.
12. *Id.* at 298.
13. *Id.* at 313.
14. *Id.*
15. *Id.* at 317.
16. J.E. Perley, Reprint of speech presented at the University of Cincinnati, in *AAUP Works for You* 2, 3 (February 1995): p. 3.
17. *Silva v. University of New Hampshire*, 888 F. Supp. 293, 301 (D.N.H. 1994).
18. *Id.*
19. *Id.*
20. *Id.*
21. *Id.* at 309.
22. *Id.*
23. *Id.* at 311.
24. L. Kirschman (1994), "First Amendment: Do 'Hostile Environment' Charges Chill Academic Freedom?" *ABA Journal*, 80, 41.
25. R.M. O'Neil (1996), "Protecting Free Speech When the Issue Is Sexual Harassment," *Chronicle of Higher Education*, 43, 3, B4.
26. *Id.*, p. 300.

27.   J. Gallop, *Feminist Accused of Sexual harassment* (Durham, N.C.: Duke University Press, 1997), p. 71. ("1")
28.   J. Gallop (1994), "Sex and Sexism: Feminism and Harassment Policy," *Academe*, 80, 22. ("2")
29.   *Id.*
30.   *Id.*
31.   *Id.*
32.   *Id.*
33.   Gallop (1), pp. 40–42.
34.   Gallop (1), p. 44.
35.   *Id.*, (1), p. 45
36.   *Id.*
37.   *Id.*
38.   *Id.*
39.   *Id.*
40.   M. Kissinger, "She's No Plain Jane," *The Milwaukee Journal*, November 8, 1994, p. A2.
41.   *Id.*
42.   Gallop, p. 18 (2).
43.   D. Beckelman, charging party, and J. Gallop, respondent, EOP Case No. 044 (University of Wisconsin-Milwaukee Office of Equal Opportunity Programs, 1993), pp. 4–5.
44.   *Id.*, p. 5.
45.   *Id.*, p. 1.
46.   *Id.*, p. 2.
47.   *Id.*, pp. 2–3.
48.   *Id.*, p. 5.
49.   J. Gallop, "Dedication" in *Around 1981: Academic Feminist Literary Theory* (New York: Routledge, 1992).
50.   D. Beckelman, charging party, and Jane Gallop, respondent, EOP Case No. 044 (University of Wisconsin-Milwaukee Office of Equal Opportunity Programs, 1993), p. 13.
51.   J. Gallop, *Thinking Through the Body* (New York: Columbia University Press, 1988), pp. 3, 43.
52.   Gallop (1), p. 68.
53.   *Id.*
54.   *Id.* (1), pp. 21, 23.
55.   *Id.* (1), p. 79.
56.   *Id.* (1), p. 78.
57.   K. Jost (1994), "Questionable Conduct," *ABA Journal*, 80, 71.
58.   *Id.* p. 72.
59.   H. Hesse, *Magister Ludi* (New York: Bantam, 1972), pp. 321–22.
60.   W.H. Henry III, *In Defense of Elitism* (New York: Doubleday, 1994), pp. 153–54.
61.   R. Wilson (1995), "William and Mary Seeks to Shift Liability for Damages to Professor in Federal Sexual Harassment Case," *Chronicle of Higher Education*, 41, A20.

Appendix
Selected Cases Related to Sexual Harassment/Discrimination in College and University Settings
Citations

The following, while not an exhaustive list, is an overview of cases related to sexual harassment and/or discrimination in college and university settings.

Abrams v. Baylor College of Medicine, 805 F.2d 528 (5th Cir. 1986).

Abramson v. University of Hawaii, 594 F.2d 202 (9th Cir. 1979).

Adams v. University of Washington, 106 Wash.2d 312, 722 P.2d 74 (Wash. 1986).

Al-Hamdani v. State University of New York, 438 F.Supp. 299 (W.D.N.Y. 1977).

Aldridge v. Tougaloo College, 847 F.Supp. 480 (S.D.Miss. 1994).

Alexander v. Yale University, 459 F.Supp. 1 (D.C.Conn. 1977).

Amoss v. University of Washington, 40 Wash.App. 666, 700 P.2d 350 (Wash.App. 1985).

Anderson v. University Health Center of Pittsburgh, 623 F.Supp. 795 (W.D. Pa. 1985).

Anderson v. University of Northern Iowa, 779 F.2d 441 (8th Cir. 1985).

Andriakos v. University of Southern Indiana, 867 F.Supp. (S.D. Ind 1992).

Arcuragi v. Miami Univ., 103 Ohio App.3d 455, 659 N.E.2d 869 (Ohio App. 12 Dist. 1995).

Arriaga v. Loma Linda University, 10 Cal.App.4th 1556, 13 Cal.Rptr.2d 619 (Cal.App. 4 Dist. 1992).

Atherton v. Chicago State Univ., 1997 U.S. Dist. Lexis 7427 (N.D. Ill. 1997).

Ballou v. University of Kansas Medical Center, 871 F.Supp. 1384 (D.Kan. 1994).

Barrett v. University of Colorado Health Sciences Center, 851 P.2d 258 (Colo.App. 1993).

Bartges v. University of North Carolina at Charlotte, 908 F.Supp. 1312 (W.D.N.C. 1995).

Bawa v. Brookhaven Nat'l Lab., 968 F. Supp. 865 (E.D. N.Y. 1997).

Beasley v. Alabama State Univ., 1998 U.S. Dist. Lexis 3695 (M.D. Al. 1998).

Belanoff v. Grayson, 98 A.D.2d 353, 471 N.Y.S.2d 91 (N.Y.A.D. 1 Dept. 1984).

Benzo v. New York State Div. of Human Rights, 1997 U.S. Dist. Lexis 901 (S.D. N.Y. 1997).

Berry v. Board of Sup'rs of Louisiana State University, 783 F.2d 1270 (5th Cir. 1986).

Bickley v. University of Maryland, 527 F.Supp. 174 (D.C.Md. 1981).

Bilut v. Northwestern University, 269 Ill.App.3d 125, 645 N.E.2d 536 (Ill.App. 1 Dist. 1994).

Board of Community College Trustees for Baltimore County v. Adams, 701 A.2d 1113 (Md. Ct. Spec. App. 1997).

Board of Governors of Wayne State University v. Perry, 1976 WL 10, 17 Fair Empl. Prac. Cases (BNA) 457 (E.D.Mich.1976).

Board of Higher Ed. in City of New York v. Professional Staff Congress/CUNY, 105 Misc.2d 497, 432 N.Y.S.2d 451 (N.Y.Sup. 1980).

Board of Regents for Regency Universities v. Human Rights Com'n, 196 Ill.App.3d 187, 552 N.E.2d 1373 (Ill.App. 4 Dist. 1990).

Board of Trustees v. Stubblefield, 16 Cal. App. 3d 820, 94 Cal. Rptr. 318 (1971).

Bougher v. University of Pittsburgh, 713 F. Supp. 139 (W.D.Pa. 1989), aff'd, 882 F.2d 74 (3rd Cir. 1989).

Dacus v. Southern College of Optometry, 657 F.2d (6th Cir. 1981).

Dasgupta v. University of Wisconsin Bd. of Regents, 121 F.3d 1138 (7th Cir. 1997).

Davis v. Weidner, 421 F. Supp. 594 (E.D.Wis. 1976).

Delgrande v. Temple Univ., 1997 U.S. Dist. Lexis 12122 (E.D. Penn. 1997).

Deli v. University of Minnesota, 863 F. Supp. 958 (D.Minn. 1994).

Dinsmore v. University of Maine System, 1994 WL 774519, 66 Fair Empl. Prac. Cases (BNA) 852 (D.Me. 1994).

Dixon v. Rutgers, The State University of New Jersey, 215 N.J.Super. 333, 521 A.2d 1315 (N.J. 1987).

Dixon v. Rutgers, The State University of New Jersey, 110 N.J. 432, 541 A.2d 1046 (N.J. 1988).

Dixon v. Rutgers, The State University of New Jersey, 215 N.J.Super. 333, 521 A.2d 1315 (N.J. 1987).

Doe v. University of Illinois, 1998 U.S. App. Lexis 3881 (7th Cir. 1998).

Donnelly v. Rhode Island Bd. of Governors for Higher Educ., 929 F. Supp. 583 (D.R.I. 1996).

Duello v. Board of Regents of University of Wisconsin System, 170 Wis.2d 27, 487 N.W.2d 56 (Wis.App. 1992).

Dugan v. Ball State University, 815 F.2d 1132 (7th Cir. 1987).

Duke v. University of Texas at El Paso, 729 F.2d 994 (5th Cir. 1984).

Duke University, 27 Fair Empl. Prac. Cases (BNA) 1389 (5th Cir. 1981).

E.E.O.C. v. Board of Governors of State Colleges and Universities, 665 F. Supp. 630 (N.D.Ill. 1987).

E.E.O.C. v. Cleveland State University, 1982 WL 439, 30 Empl. Prac. Dec. P 33,193 (N.D.Ohio 1982).

E.E.O.C. v. Cleveland State University, 1982 WL 320, 28 Fair Empl. Prac. Cases (BNA) 1782 (N.D.Ohio 1982).

E.E.O.C. v. Cleveland State University, 1982 WL 226, 28 Fair Empl. Prac. Cases (BNA) 441 (N.D.Ohio 1982).

E.E.O.C. v. Maricopa County Community College Dist., 736 F.2d 510 (9th Cir. 1984).

E.E.O.C. v. Strasburger, Price, Kelton, Martin and Unis, 626 F.2d 1272, 24 Fair Empl. Prac. Cases (BNA) 1279 (5th Cir. 1980).

E.E.O.C. v. University of Pittsburgh, 643 F.2d 983 (3rd Cir. 1981).

E.E.O.C. v. University of Pittsburgh, 487 F. Supp. 1071 (W.D.Pa. 1980).

Eaton v. University of Illinois, 1995 WL 506060 (N.D.Ill. 1995).

Einhorn v. Presbyterian University Hosp., 1981 WL 27096, 26 Fair Empl. Prac. Cases (BNA) 911 (W.D.Pa. 1981).

Elliott v. Board of Trustees of Montgomery County Community College, 104 Md.App. 93, 655 A.2d 46 (Md.App. 1995).

El-Marazki v. University of Wisconsin Sys. Bd. of Regents, 1998 U.S. App. Lexis 307 (7th Cir. 1998).

Ende v. Board of Regents of Regency Universities, 757 F.2d 176 (7th Cir. 1985).

Estate of Scott by Scott v. deLeon, 603 F. Supp. 1328 (E.D.Mich. 1985).

Ettinger v. State Univ. of New York Sate College of Optometry, U.S. Dist. Lexis 2289 (S.D. N.Y. 1998).

Farlow v. University of North Carolina Through Its Bd. of Governors, 624 F. Supp. 434 (M.D.N.C. 1985).

Faulkner-King v. Board of Trustees of University of Illinois, 757 F. Supp. 951 (C.D.Ill. 1991).

Feng v. Sandrik, 636 F. Supp. 77 (N.D.Ill. 1986).

Fields v. Clark University, 817 F.2d 931 (1st Cir. 1987).

Flanders v. William Paterson College of New Jersey, 163 N.J.Super. 225, 394 A.2d 855 (N.J.Super. 1976).

Fonseca v. Michigan State University, 214 Mich.App. 28, 542 N.W.2d 273 (Mich.App. 1995).

Ford v. Nicks, 741 F.2d 858 (6th Cir. 1984).

Fortunato v. Keene State College, 1994 WL 269340 (D.N.H.1994).

Franklin v. Herbert Lehman College, 508 F. Supp. (S.D.N.Y. 1981).

Fuchilla v. Layman, 109 N.J. 319, 537 A.2d 652 (N.J. 1988).

Fuchilla v. Layman, 210 N.J.Super. 574, 510 A.2d 281 (N.J.Super. 1986).

Fuchilla v. Prockop, 682 F. Supp. 247 (D.N.J. 1987).

Gallo v. Board of Regents of University of California, 916 F. Supp. 1005 (S.D.Cal. 1995).

Garvey v. Dickinson College, 775 F. Supp. 788 (M.D.Pa. 1991).

Garvey v. Dickinson College, 763 F. Supp. 796 (M.D.Pa. 1991).

Garvey v. Dickinson College, 761 F. Supp. 1175 (M.D.Pa. 1991).

Gay and Lesbian Law Students Ass'n at University of Connecticut School of Law v. Board of Trustees, University of Connecticut, 236 Conn. 453, 673 A.2d 484, (Conn. 1996).

Gehrt v. University of Illinois at Urbana-Champaign Coop. Extension Serv., 974 F. Supp. 1178 (C.D. Ill. 1997).

Gentner v. Cheyney University of Pennsylvania, 1996 WL 525323 (E.D.Pa. 1996).

Gerardi v. Hofstra University, 897 F. Supp. 50 (E.D.N.Y. 1995).

Gilinsky v. Columbia University, 1974 WL 255, 8 Fair Empl. Prac. Cases (BNA) 846 (D.C.N.Y. 1974).

Giordano v. William Paterson College of New Jersey, 804 F. Supp. 637 (D.N.J. 1992).

Gold v. Gallaudet College, 630 F. Supp. 1176 (D.D.C. 1986).

Gomez v. Medical College of Pennsylvania, 1994 WL 423847 (E.D.Pa. 1994).

Goodman v. Board of Trustees of Community College Dist., 498 F. Supp. 1329 (N.D.Ill. 1980).

Gottlieb v. Tulane University of Louisiana, 809 F.2d 278 (5th Cir. 1987).

Goulianos v. Ramapo College of New Jersey, 1986 WL 7649, 41 Fair Empl. Prac. Cases (BNA) 329 (D.N.J. 1986).

Gradine v. College of St. Scholastica, 426 N.W.2d 459 (Minn.App. 1988).

Grassinger v. Welty, 818 F. Supp. 862 (W.D.Pa. 1992).

Gray v. Wilberforce University, 1971 WL 122, 3 Fair Empl. Prac. Cases (BNA) 516 (S.D.Ohio 1971).

Green v. Howard University, 1992 WL 724733, 63 Fair Empl. Prac. Cases (BNA) 1607 (D.C. Super.1992).

Griffin v. Board of Regents of Regency Universities, 795 F.2d 1281 (7th Cir. 1986).

Grove City College v. Bell, 687 F.2d 684 (3rd Cir. 1982).

Guckenberger v. Boston Univ., 974 F. Supp. 106 (D. Mass. 1997).

Hansbury v. Regents of University of Cal., 596 F.2d 944 (10th Cir. 1979).

Harmond v. Board of Regents, University System of Georgia, 1983 WL 30385, 31 Fair Empl. Prac. Cases (BNA) 940 (S.D.Ga. 1983).

Hart v. University System of New Hampshire, 938 F. Supp. 104 (D.N.H. 1996).

Hart v. University of Texas at Houston, 474 F. Supp. 465 (S.D.Tex. 1979).

Harvey v. Board of Trustees of University of Illinois, 1989 WL 152536 (N.D.Ill. 1989).

Hatton v. Hunt, 780 F. Supp. 1157 (W.D.Tenn. 1991).

Hayne v. Rutgers, 1990 WL 484133, 55 Fair Empl. Prac. Cases (BNA) 1838 (D.N.J. 1990).

Heagney v. University of Washington, 642 F.2d 1157 (9th Cir. 1981).

Hedman v. Coppin State College, 1982 WL 31054, 35 Fair Empl. Prac. Cases (BNA) 7 (D.C.Md. 1982).

Henschke v. New York Hospital-Cornell Medical Center, 821 F. Supp. 166 (S.D.N.Y. 1993).

Hermann v. Fairleigh Dickinson University, 183 N.J.Super. 500, 444 A.2d 614 (N.J.Super. 1982).

Heyliger v. State Univ. & Community College Sys. of Tennessee, 126 F.3d 849 (6th Cir. 1997), *cert. denied*, 118 S. Ct. 1054, 140 L. Ed. 2d 117 (1998).

Hollenbaugh v. Carnegie, 436 F. Supp. 1328 (W. D. Pa. 1977), *aff'd mem.*, 578 F. 2d 1374 (3rd Cir. 1978), *cert. denied*, 439 U. S. 1052 (1978).

Holm v. Ithaca College, 1998 N.Y. Misc. Lexis 41 (N.Y. S. Ct. 1998).

Hooker v. Tufts University, 581 F. Supp. 104 (D.C.Mass. 1983).

Hooker v. Tufts University, 581 F. Supp. 98 (D.C.Mass. 1983).
Hooten v. Pennsylvania College of Optometry, 601 F. Supp. 1151 (E.D.Pa. 1984).
Hoth v. Grinnell College, 1980 WL 302, 23 Fair Empl. Prac. Cases (BNA) 528 (S.D. Iowa 1980).
Howard University v. Best, 484 A.2d 958 (D.C.App. 1984).
Howard University v. Green, 652 A.2d 41 (D.C.App. 1994).
Hudak v. Curators of University of Missouri, 586 F.2d 105 (8th Cir. 1978).
Huffman v. Youngstown State University, 885 F.2d 871 (Table, Text in WESTLAW), Unpublished Disposition, 1989 WL 109752 (6th Cir. 1989).
Ivan v. Kent State University, 863 F. Supp. 581 (N.D.Ohio 1994).
Jacobs v. College of William and Mary, 495 F. Supp. 183 (E.D.Va. 1980).
Jew v. University of Iowa, 749 F. Supp. 946 (S.D.Iowa 1990).
Jew v. University of Iowa, 398 N.W.2d 861 (Iowa 1987).
Jochnowitz v. Junior College of Albany, A Div. of Russell Sage College, 96 A.D.2d 1131, 467 N.Y.S.2d 732 (N.Y.A.D. 3 Dept. 1983).
Johnson v. University of Bridgeport and Local 1199, Drug and Hosp. Union 1979 WL 15349, 20 Fair Empl. Prac. Cases (BNA) 1766 (D.Conn. 1979).
Johnson v. University of Pittsburgh, 435 F. Supp. 1328 (W.D.Pa. 1977).
Johnson v. University of Pittsburgh, 359 F. Supp. 1002 (W.D.Pa. 1973).
Johnson v. University Surgical Group Associates of Cincinnati, 871 F. Supp. 979 (S.D. Ohio 1994).
Jolley v. Phillips Educ. Group of Central Florida, Inc., 1996 WL 529202, 71 Fair Empl. Prac. Cases (BNA) 916 (M.D.Fla.1996).
Jones v. Los Angeles Community College Dist., 702 F.2d 203 (9th Cir. 1983).
Jungels v. State University College of New York, 922 F. Supp. 779 (W.D.N.Y. 1996).
Junior College Dist. of St. Louis v. Califano, 455 F. Supp. 1212 (W.D.Mo. 1978).
Junior College Dist. of St. Louis v. Califano, 597 F.2d 119 (8th Cir. 1979).
Kadiki v. Virginia Commonwealth University, 892 F. Supp. 746 (E.D.Va. 1995).
Karibian v. Columbia University, 812 F. Supp. 413 (S.D.N.Y. 1993).
Karibian v. Columbia University, 930 F. Supp. 134 (S.D.N.Y. 1996).
Kelecic v. Board of Regents of Regency Universities, 1994 WL 702814 (N.D. Ill. 1994).
Kelecic v. Board of Regents of Regency Univs., U.S. Dist. Lexis 7991 (N.D. Ill. 1997).
Keller v. University of Michigan, 411 F. Supp. 1055 (E.D.Mich. 1974).
Keller v. University of Michigan, 1976 WL 13272, 16 Fair Empl. Prac. Cases (BNA) 1601 (E.D. Mich. 1976).
Kelley v. Troy State University, 923 F. Supp. 1494 (M.D. Ala. 1996).
Kemp v. State Bd. of Agriculture, 790 P.2d 870 (Colo.App. 1989).
Kennamore v. Alabama A & M University, 1991 WL 350047, 58 Fair Empl. Prac. Cases (BNA) 1539 (N.D.Ala. 1991).
Kern v. University of Notre Dame Du Lac, 1997 U.S. Dist. Lexis 21158 (N.D. Ind. 1997).
Keyes v. Lenoir Rhyne College, 1976 WL 13229, 15 Fair Empl. Prac. Cases (BNA) 914 (W.D.N.C. 1976).
Klemencic v. Ohio State Univ., 111 F.3d 131 (Table, Text in Lexis), Unpublished Disposition, 1997 U.S. App. Lexis 12962 (6th Cir. 1997).
Korf v. Ball State University, 726 F. 2d 1222 (7th Cir. 1984).
Kracunas v. Iona College, 119 F.3d 80 (2nd Cir. 1997).
Kumar v. Temple Univ. Cancer Ctr., 1997 U.S. Dist. Lexis 13576 (E.D. Penn. 1997).
Kunda v. Muhlenberg College, 463 F. Supp. 294 (E.D. Pa.1978).
Kunda v. Muhlenberg College, 621 F.2d 532 (3rd Cir. 1980).
Laborde v. Regents of University of California, 1980 WL 285, 24 Empl. Prac. Dec. P 31,448 (C.D. Cal. 1980).
Laborde v. Regents of University of California, 686 F.2d 715 (9th Cir. 1982).
Lam v. Curators of the Univ. of Missouri, 122 F.3d 654 (8th Cir. 1997).
Lamphere v. Brown University, 798 F.2d 532 (1st Cir. 1986).
Lamphere v. Brown University, 685 F.2d 743 (1st Cir. 1982).
Lamphere v. Brown University, 875 F.2d 916 (1st Cir. 1989).

Lamphere v. Brown University, 71 F.R.D. 641 (D.C.R.I. 1976).

Lamphere v. Brown University, 690 F. Supp. 125 (D.R.I. 1988).

Langland v. Vanderbilt University, 589 F. Supp. 995 (M.D.Tenn. 1984).

Langland v. Vanderbilt University, 772 F.2d 907 (Table, Text in WESTLAW) Unpublished
    Disposition, 1985 WL 13611 (6th Cir. 1985).

Lanyon v. University of Delaware, 544 F. Supp. 1262 (D.C.Del. 1982).

Leake v. University of Cincinnati, 93 F.R.D. 460 (S.D.Ohio 1982).

Leake v. University of Cincinnati, 605 F.2d 255 (6th Cir. 1979).

Lee v. Junior College Dist., 1995 WL 363723 (E.D.Mo. 1995).

LeGare v. University of Pennsylvania Medical School, 488 F. Supp. 1250 (E.D.Pa. 1980).

Lever v. Northwestern University, 1987 WL 11365, 50 Fair Empl. Prac. Cases (BNA)
    1183 (N.D. Ill. 1987).

Levitt v. University of Texas at El Paso, 847 F.2d 221 (5th Cir. 1988).

Lewis and Clark College v. Bureau of Labor, 43 Or.App. 245, 602 P.2d 1161 (Or.App. 979).

Lieberman v. Gant, 474 F. Supp. 848 (D.C.Conn. 1979).

Lindsay v. Valley Forge Military Academy and Junior College, 1993 WL 409855 (E.D.
    Pa. 1993).

Linson v. Trustees of University of Pennsylvania, 1996 WL 637810 (E.D.Pa. 1996).

Linson v. Trustees of University of Pennsylvania, 1996 WL 479532 (E.D.Pa. 1996).

Lipsett v. University of Puerto Rico, 864 F.2d 881 (1st Cir. 1988).

Lipsett v. University of Puerto Rico, 576 F. Supp. 1217 (D.C. Puerto Rico 1983).

Lockhart v. Commonwealth Educ. Systems Corp., 247 Va. 98, 439 S.E.2d 328 (Va. 1994).

Long v. Laramie County Community College Dist., 840 F.2d 743 (10th Cir. 1988).

Longmire v. Alabama State University, 151 F.R.D. 414 (M.D.Ala. 1992).

Loren v. Feerick, 1997 U.S. Dist. Lexis 11381 (S.D. N.Y. 1997).

Lorick v. York Technical College, 1994 WL 780205 (S.C.Com.Pl. 1994).

Loyola University of Chicago v. Illinois Human Rights Com'n, 149 Ill.App.3d 8, 500
    N.E.2d 639 (Ill.App. 1 Dist. 1986).

Lyford v. Schilling, 750 F.2d 1341 (5th Cir. 1985).

Lynn v. Regents of University of California, 656 F.2d 1337 (9th Cir. 1981).

Maas v. Cornell Univ., 666 N.Y.S.2d 743 (N.Y. App. Div. 1997).

*Mabry v. State Bd. of Community Colleges and Occupational Educ.,*813 F.2d 311 (10th
    Cir. 1987).

Mabry v. State Bd. for Community Colleges and Occupational Educ., 597 F. Supp. 1235
    (D.C. Colo. 1984).

Maguire v. Marquette University, 627 F. Supp. 1499 (E.D.Wis. 1986).

Maguire v. Marquette University, 814 F.2d 1213 (7th Cir. 1987).

Mansfield State College v. Kovich, 46 Pa.Cmwlth. 399, 407 A.2d 1387 (Pa.Cmwlth. 1979).

Marino v. Louisiana State Univ. Bd. of Supervisors, 1997 U.S. Dist. Lexis 8966 (E.D. La.
    1997).

Marshall v. University of Hawaii, 9 Haw.App. 21, 821 P.2d 937 (Hawai'i App. 1991).

Matthews v. Superior Court (Regents of University of California), 34 Cal.App.4th 598,
    40 Cal.Rptr.2d 350 (Cal.App. 2 Dist. 1995).

McClellan v. Board of Regents of State University, 921 S.W.2d 684 (Tenn. 1996).

Merrill v. Southern Methodist University, 806 F.2d 600 (5th Cir. 1986).

Middleton-Keirn v. Stone, 655 F.2d 609 (5th Cir. 1981).

Miles v. New York Univ., 979 F. Supp. 248 (S.D. N.Y. 1997).

Miller v. Long Island University, 85 Misc.2d 393, 380 N.Y.S.2d 917 (N.Y.Sup. 1976).

Milligan-Jensen v. Michigan Technological University, 767 F. Supp. 1403 (W.D. Mich.
    1991).

Mitchell v. Los Angeles Community College Dist., 861 F.2d 198 (9th Cir. 1988).

Mitchell v. Peralta Community College Dist., 766 F. Supp. 834 (N.D.Cal. 1991).

Moire v. Temple University School of Medicine, 613 F. Supp. 1360 (E.D. Pa. 1985).

Moisi v. College of Sequoias Community College Dist., 25 Cal.Rptr.2d 165, Ordered
    Not Published, Previously published at 19 Cal.App.4th 564, 63 Fair Empl. Prac.
    Cases (BNA) 69 (Cal.App. 5 Dist. 1993).

Molthan v. Temple University of Commonwealth System of Higher Ed., 442 F. Supp. 448 (E.D. Pa. 1977).

Molthan v. Temple University of Commonwealth System of Higher Ed., 778 F.2d 955 (3rd Cir. 1985).

Moore v. Alabama State University, 945 F. Supp. 235 (M.D. Ala. 1996).

Morpurgo v. Board of Higher Ed. in City of New York, 423 F. Supp. 704 (S.D.N.Y. 1976).

Morrison v. Brandeis University, 125 F.R.D. 14 (D. Mass. 1989).

Morrow v. Auburn Univ. at Montgomery, 973 F. Supp. 1392 (M.D. Al. 1997).

Mortenson v. Syracuse University, 1974 WL 10604, 10 Fair Empl. Prac. Cases (BNA) 1312 (N.D.N.Y. 1974).

Munsey v. Walla Walla College, 80 Wash.App. 92, 906 P.2d 988 (Wash.App. Div. 3 1995).

Myers v. Chestnut Hill College, 1996 WL 67612 (E.D. Pa. 1996).

Namenwirth v. Board of Regents of University of Wisconsin System, 769 F.2d 1235 (7th Cir. 1985).

Naragon v. Wharton, 737 F.2d 1403 (5th Cir. 1984).

Naragon v. Wharton, 572 F. Supp. 1117 (M.D. La. 1983).

Nayar v. Howard University, 881 F. Supp. 15 (D.D.C. 1995).

Neibauer v. Philadelphia College of Pharmacy and Science, 1992 WL 151321, 61 Empl. Prac. Dec. P 42,319 (E.D.Pa. 1992).

Nelson v. Temple University, 920 F. Supp. 633 (E.D. Pa. 1996).

Nelson v. University of Maine System, 923 F. Supp. 275 (D. Me. 1996).

Neptune v. Burlington County College, 1993 WL 273995, 66 Fair Empl. Prac. Cases (BNA) 897 (E.D. Pa. 1993).

Newton v. Southern Methodist Univ., 1998 U.S. Dist. Lexis 3481 (N.D. Tex. 1998).

Nogueras v. University of Puerto Rico, 890 F. Supp. 60 (D. Puerto Rico 1995).

Northern Illinois University v. Fair Employment Practices Commission, 58 Ill.App.3d 992, 374 N.E.2d 748 (Ill.App. 2 Dist. 1978).

O'Connell v. Teachers College, 63 F.R.D. 638 (S.D.N.Y. 1974).

O'Connor v. Peru State College, 781 F.2d 632 (8th Cir. 1986).

Ohio Dominican College v. Krone, 54 Ohio App.3d 29, 560 N.E.2d 1340 (Ohio App. 1990).

Orbovich v. Macalester College, 119 F.R.D. 411 (D. Minn. 1988).

Ostrach v. Regents of the Univ. of California, 957 F. Supp. 196 (E.D. Cal. 1997).

Ottaviani v. State University of New York at New Paltz, 679 F. Supp. 288 (S.D.N.Y. 1988).

Ottaviani v. State University of New York at New Paltz, 1979 WL 206, 26 Fair Empl. Prac. Cases (BNA) 181 (D.C.N.Y. 1979).

Pace College v. Commission on Human Rights of City of New York, 38 N.Y.2d 28, 339 N.E.2d 880 (N.Y. 1975).

Paddio v. Board of Trustees for State Colleges and Universities, 1993 WL 30302, 61 Fair Empl. Prac. Cases (BNA) 86 (E.D. La. 1993).

Pallett v. Palma, 914 F. Supp. 1018 (S.D.N.Y. 1996).

Park v. Howard University, 1994 WL 780903, 71 Fair Empl. Prac. Cases (BNA) 977 (D.D.C. 1994).

Passonno v. State University of New York, University at Albany, 889 F. Supp. 602 (N.D.N.Y. 1995).

Patel v. Board of Governors of State Colleges & Univs., 1997 U.S. Dist. Lexis 10221 (N.D. Ill. 1997).

Paton v. Dallas County Community College Dist., 1996 WL 722071 (N.D. Tex. 1996).

Pearlstein v. Staten Island University Hosp., 886 F. Supp. 260 (E.D.N.Y. 1995).

Pell v. Trustees of Columbia Univ. in New York, 1998 U.S. Dist. Lexis 407 (S.D. N.Y. 1998).

Penn v. Iowa State Bd. of Regents, 1998 Iowa Sup. Lexis 48 (Iowa 1998).

Peper v. Princeton University Bd. of Trustees, 151 N.J.Super. 15, 376 A.2d 535 (N.J.Super. 1977).

Peper v. Princeton University Bd. of Trustees, 77 N.J. 55, 389 A.2d 465 (N.J. 1978).

Peralta Community College Dist. v. Fair Employment and Housing Com'n (Brown), 52 Cal.3d 40, 801 P.2d 357 (Cal. 1990).

Peralta Community College Dist. v. Fair Employment and Housing Com'n (Brown), 226 Cal.Rptr. 794, Previously published at 214 Cal.App.3d 1222 (Cal.App. 1 Dist. 1986).

Perham v. Ladd, 436 F. Supp. 1101 (N.D. Ill. 1977).

Peric v. Board of Trustees of University of Illinois, 1996 WL 515175, 71 Fair Empl. Prac. Cases (BNA) 1760 (N.D. Ill. 1996).

Peric v. Board of Trustees of the Univ. of Illinois, 1997 U.S. Dist. Lexis 2693 (N.D. Ill. 1997).

Peters v. Wayne State University, 691 F.2d 235 (6th Cir. 1982).

Peterson v. City College of City University of New York, 160 F.R.D. 22 (S.D.N.Y. 1994).

Petrone v. Cleveland State Univ., 1998 U.S. Dist. Lexis 1309 (N.D. Ohio 1998).

Presseisen v. Swarthmore College, 442 F. Supp. 593 (E.D. Pa. 1977).

Presseisen v. Swarthmore College, 386 F. Supp. 1337 (E.D. Pa. 1974).

Professional Staff Congress/City University of New York v. Board of Higher Ed. of City of New York, 39 N.Y.2d 319, 347 N.E.2d 918 (N.Y. 1976).

Pyo v. Stockton State College, 603 F. Supp. 1278 (D.C.N.J. 1985).

Rackin v. University of Pennsylvania, 386 F. Supp. 992 (E.D. Pa. 1974).

Rajender v. University of Minnesota, 1978 WL 212, 24 Fair Empl. Prac. Cases (BNA) 1045 (D. Minn. 1978).

Rajender v. University of Minnesota, 1979 WL 287, 24 Fair Empl. Prac. Cases (BNA) 1051 (D. Minn. 1979).

Reitmeier v. Converse College, 1991 WL 433732, 125 Lab.Cas. P 57,438 (S.C.Com.Pl. 1991).

Rice v. New England College, 676 F.2d 9 (1st Cir. 1982).

Roberson v. University of Tennessee, 829 S.W.2d 149 (Tenn.App. 1992).

Roberts v. College of the Desert, 861 F.2d 1163 (9th Cir. 1988).

Rodriguez v. Hunter College of the City Univ. of New York, 1997 U.S. Dist. Lexis 3543 (S.D. N.Y. 1997).

Rosenberg v. University of Cincinnati, 118 F.R.D. 591 (S.D.Ohio 1987).

Rosetti v. Hudson Valley Community College, 1997 U.S. Dist. Lexis 13949 (N.D. N.Y. 1997).

Rothman v. Emory University, 123 F.3d 446 (7th Cir. 1997).

Samper v. University of Rochester, 144 A.D.2d 940, 535 N.Y.S.2d 281 (N.Y.A.D. 4 Dept. 1988).

Sanbonmatsu v. Boyer, 45 A.D.2d 249, 357 N.Y.S.2d 245 (N.Y.A.D. 4 Dept. 1974).

Schanzer v. Rutgers University, 934 F. Supp. 669 (D.N.J. 1996).

Schier v. Temple University, 576 F. Supp. 1569 (E.D. Pa. 1984).

Schneider v. Northwestern University, 1995 WL 38994 (N.D. Ill. 1995).

Schneider v. Northwestern University, 925 F. Supp. 1347 (N.D. Ill. 1996).

Schneider v. Northwestern University, 1995 WL 33140 (N.D. Ill. 1995).

Schofield v. Trustees of University of Pennsylvania, 894 F. Supp. 194 (E.D. Pa. 1995).

Schofield v. Trustees of University of Pennsylvania, 919 F. Supp. 821 (E.D. Pa. 1996).

Schweitzer v. University of Texas Health Center at Tyler, 688 F. Supp. 278 (E.D. Tex. 1988).

Seattle University v. U.S. Dept. of Health, Ed. and Welfare, 1978 WL 31, 16 Fair Empl. Prac. Cases (BNA) 719 (W.D. Wash. 1978).

Seattle University v. U.S. Dept. of Health, Ed. and Welfare, 621 F.2d 992 (9th Cir. 1980).

Sellers v. Delgado College, 781 F.2d 503 (5th Cir. 1986).

Shawer v. Indiana University of Pennsylvania, 602 F.2d 1161 (3rd Cir. 1979).

Shawgo v. Spradlin, 701 F. 2d 470 (5th Cir. 1983), *cert. denied*, sub nom. *Whisenhut v. Spradlin*, 464 U.S. 965 (1983).

Silver v. City University of New York, 767 F. Supp. 494 (S.D.N.Y. 1991).

Silverman v. Lehigh University, 1976 WL 13357, 19 Fair Empl. Prac. Cases (BNA) 983 (D.C. Pa. 1976).

Sime v. Trustees of California State University and Colleges, 526 F.2d 1112 (9th Cir. 1975).
Sinha v. State University of New York at Farmingdale, 764 F. Supp. 765 (E.D.N.Y. 1991).
Slater v. Marshall, 906 F. Supp. 256 (E.D.Pa. 1995).
Slippery Rock State College v. Pennsylvania Human Relations Commission
    11 Pa.Cmwlth. 501, 314 A.2d 344 (Pa.Cmwlth. 1974).
Smith v. St. Louis Univ., 109 F.3d 1261 (8th Cir. 1997).
Smith v. University of North Carolina, 632 F.2d 316 (4th Cir. 1980).
Smith v. Virginia Commonwealth University, 856 F. Supp. 1088 (E.D. Va. 1994).
Smith College v. Massachusetts Commission Against Discrimination, 376 Mass. 221,
    380 N.E.2d 121 (Mass. 1978).
Smithgall v. Trustees of University of Pennsylvania, 855 F. Supp. 750 (E.D. Pa. 1994).
Sobel v. Yeshiva University, 1976 WL 13341, 13 Fair Empl. Prac. Cases (BNA) 1339
    (D.C.N.Y. 1976).
Sobel v. Yeshiva University, 566 F. Supp. 1166 (S.D.N.Y. 1983).
Sobel v. Yeshiva University, 477 F. Supp. 1161 (S.D.N.Y. 1979).
Sobel v. Yeshiva University, 619 F. Supp. 839 (S.D.N.Y. 1985).
Sobel v. Yeshiva University, 1976 WL 611, 12 Empl. Prac. Dec. P 11,157 (D.C.N.Y.
    1976).
Sormani v. Orange County Community College, 659 N.Y.S.2d 507 (N.Y. App. Div.
    1997).
Southern Methodist University Ass'n of Women Law Students v. Wynne & Jaffe, 599
    F.2d 707 (5th Cir. 1979).
Spaulding v. University of Washington, 740 F.2d 686 (9th Cir. 1984).
Spirt v. Teachers Ins. and Annuity Ass'n, 93 F.R.D. 627 (S.D.N.Y. 1982).
Spirt v. Teachers Ins. and Annuity Ass'n, 475 F. Supp. 1298 (S.D.N.Y.1979).
Spirt v. Teachers Ins. and Annuity Ass'n, 691 F.2d 1054 (2nd Cir. 1982).
Starishevsky v. Hofstra University, 161 Misc.2d 137, 612 N.Y.S.2d 794 (N.Y.Sup. 1994).
State University of New York at Albany v. State Human Rights Appeal Bd., 81 A.D.2d
    688, 438 N.Y.S.2d 643 (N.Y.A.D. 3 Dept. 1981).
State by Cooper v. Moorhead State University, 455 N.W.2d 79 (Minn.App. 1990).
State Division of Human Rights v. Columbia University in City of New York, 39 N.Y.2d
    612, 350 N.E.2d 396 (N.Y. 1976).
State Division of Human Rights on Complaint of Morris v. Hamilton College,113 A.D.2d
    1006, 494 N.Y.S.2d 570 (N.Y.A.D. 4 Dept. 1985).
State Division of Human Rights on Complaint of Noble v. University of Rochester, 53
    A.D.2d 1020, 386 N.Y.S.2d 147 (N.Y.A.D. 4 Dept. 1976).
Stevens v. St. Louis University Medical Center, 831 F. Supp. 737 (E.D. Mo. 1993).
Stoll v. New York State College of Veterinary Medicine at Cornell University, 652
    N.Y.S.2d 478 (N.Y. 1996).
Suhr v. North Carolina State University Agr. Research Service, 1987 WL 5853 (E.D.N.C.
    1987).
SUNY College of Environmental Science and Forestry v. State Div. of Human Rights,
    144 A.D.2d 962, 534 N.Y.S.2d 270 (N.Y.A.D. 4 Dept. 1988).
Sweeney v. Board of Trustees of Keene State College, 569 F.2d 169 (1st Cir. 1978).
Sweeney v. Board of Trustees of Keene State College, 1977 WL 15495, 14 Fair Empl.
    Prac. Cases (BNA) 1220 (D.N.H. 1977).
Sweeney v. Research Foundation of State University of New York, 711 F.2d 1179 (2nd
    Cir. 1983).
Sweeney v. Research Foundation of State University of New York,1982 WL 31082, 30
    Fair Empl. Prac. Cases (BNA) 986 (N.D.N.Y. 1982).
Taylor v. Faculty-Student Ass'n of State University College at Fredonia, Inc., 1986 WL
    4048, 40 Fair Empl. Prac. Cases (BNA) 1292 (W.D.N.Y. 1986).
Thomas v. Trustees of Livingstone College Inc., 1987 WL 13316, 43 Fair Empl. Prac.
    Cases (BNA) 885 (M.D.N.C. 1987).
Thomasko v. University of South Carolina, Coastal Carolina College, 1985 WL 6455, 41
    Fair Empl. Prac. Cases (BNA) 1032 (D.S.C. 1985).

Thompkins v. Morris Brown College, 752 F.2d 558 (11th Cir. 1985).

Thomson v. Olson, 866 F.Supp. 1267, 72 Fair Empl. Prac. Cases (BNA) 24 (D.N.D. 1994).

Torres v. New York University, 1996 WL 393565, 71 Fair Empl. Prac. Cases (BNA) 837 (S.D.N.Y. 1996).

Torres v. Pisano, 116 F.3d 625 (2nd Cir.), *cert. denied*, 118 S. Ct. 563, 139 L. Ed. 2d 404 (1997).

Tracy v. Mount Ida College, 1995 WL 464909 (D. Mass. 1995).

U.S. v. Baylor University Medical Center, 736 F.2d 1039 (5th Cir. 1984).

University of Southern California v. Superior Court (Miller), 222 Cal.App.3d 1028, 272 Cal.Rptr. 264 (Cal.App. 2 Dist. 1990).

University of Texas at Austin v. Ables, 914 S.W.2d 712 (Tex.App.-Austin 1996).

University of Toledo v. U. S. Dept. of HEW., 464 F. Supp. 693 (N.D. Ohio 1979).

University of Utah v. Industrial Com'n of Utah, 736 P.2d 630 (Utah 1987).

Vincent v. West Texas State University, 895 S.W.2d 469 (Tex.App.-Amarillo 1995).

Vinson v. Superior Court (Peralta Community College Dist.), 43 Cal.3d 833, 740 P.2d 404 (Cal. 1987).

Wagner v. Texas A & M University, 939 F. Supp. 1297 (S.D. Tex. 1996).

Walker v. Columbia University, 407 F. Supp. 1370 (S.D.N.Y. 1976).

Walters v. President and Fellows of Harvard College, 616 F. Supp. 471 (D.C. Mass. 1985).

Ward v. Johns Hopkins University, 861 F. Supp. 367 (D. Md. 1994).

Washington v. Oklahoma State Univ. Bd. of Regents, 113 F.3d 1247 (Table, Text in Lexis), Unpublished Disposition, 1997 U.S. App. Lexis 12614 (10th Cir. 1997).

Wedding v. University of Toledo, 862 F. Supp. 201 (N.D. Ohio 1994).

Weisbord v. Michigan State University, 495 F. Supp. 1347 (W.D. Mich. 1980).

Wheelock College v. Massachusetts Commission Against Discrimination, 371 Mass. 130, 355 N.E.2d 309 (Mass. 1976).

Whittingham v. Amherst College, 164 F.R.D. 124 (D. Mass. 1995).

Wilkins v. University of Houston, 471 F. Supp. 1054 (S.D. Tex. 1979).

Willett v. Emory and Henry College, 569 F.2d 212 (4th Cir. 1978).

Wilson v. Glenwood Intermountain Properties, Inc., 876 F. Supp. 1231 (D. Utah 1995).

Wilson v. University of Texas Health Center at Tyler, 773 F. Supp. 958 (E.D. Tex. 1991).

Winkes v. Brown University in Providence in State of R.I., 1983 WL 2105, 32 Fair Empl. Prac. Cases (BNA) 1041 (D.R.I. 1983).

Winston v. Maine Technical College System, 631 A.2d 70 (Me. 1993).

Wu v. Thomas, 863 F.2d 1543 (11th Cir. 1989).

Young v. Columbia University College of Physicians and Surgeons, 1980 WL 177, 23 Empl. Prac. Dec. P 31,058 (D.C.N.Y. 1980).

Yourse v. Miller, 1982 WL 31062, 38 Fair Empl. Prac. Cases (BNA) 287 (M.D.N.C. 1982).

Zahorik v. Cornell University, 1981 WL 27033, 34 Fair Empl. Prac. Cases (BNA) 147 (N.D.N.Y. 1981).

Selected Bibliography

Abbey, A. (1982). " Sex Differences in Attributions for Friendly Behavior: Do Males
    Misperceive Females' Friendliness?" *Journal of Personality and Social Psychol-
    ogy* 42: 830–38.
Adams, J. W., Kotke, J. L., and Padgitt, J. S. (1983). "Sexual Harassment of University
    Students," *Journal of College Student Personnel* 24: 484–90.
Allen, D., and Okawa, J. B. (1987). "A Counseling Center Looks at Harassment," *Jour-
    nal of the National Association for Women Deans, Administrators, and Counse-
    lors* 51: 9–16.
Alliance Against Sexual Coercion (1980). *University Grievance Procedures, Title IX, and
    Sexual Harassment on Campus.* Boston: Alliance Against Sexual Coercion.
American Association of State Colleges and Universities (1981). *Policy Statement on
    Sexual Harassment.* Washington, D.C.: American Association of State Colleges
    and Universities.
American Association of University Professors (1990). "Sexual Harassment: Sug-
    gested Policy and Procedures for Handling Complaints." In *Policy Documents
    and Reports,* 113–15. Washington, D.C.: American Association of University
    Professors.
American Association of University Women (1993). *Hostile Hallways: The AAUW Sur-
    vey on Sexual Harassment in America's Schools.* Washington, D.C.: American
    Association of University Women.
American Council on Education (1986). *Sexual Harassment on Campus: Suggestions
    for Reviewing Campus Policy and Educational Programs.* Washington, D.C.:
    American Council on Education.
American Council on Education (1989). *Sexual Harassment.* Newsletter. Washington,
    D.C.: American Council on Education.
American Council on Eduction (1992). *Sexual Harassment on Campus: A Policy and
    Program of Deterrence.* Washington, D.C.: American Council on Education.
American Council on Education (1992). *Women Chief Executive Officers in U.S. Col-
    leges and Universities, Table XIII, April 15, 1992.* Washington, D.C.: American
    Council on Education, Office of Women in Higher Education.
American Freshman: National Norms for Los Angeles (1997). *Cooperative Institutional
    Research Program of the Higher Education Research Institute of the University
    of California, Los Angeles.*
Antioch College (1996). *Sexual Offense Policy.* Yellow Springs, Ohio: Antioch College.
Arliss, L. P. (1991). *Gender Communication.* Englewood Cliffs, N.J.: Prentice-Hall.
Arvey, R. D., and Cavanaugh, M. A. (1995). "Using Surveys to Assess the Prevalence
    of Sexual Harassment: Some Methodological Problems," *Journal of Social Issues.*
    51: 44.
Association of American Colleges (1978). *Sexual Harassment: A Hidden Issue.* Wash-
    ington, D.C.: Project on the Status and Education of Women, Association of
    American Colleges. ED 157 481.8 pp. MF–01; PC–01.

Association of American Colleges (1980). *Title VII Sexual Harassment Guidelines and Educational Employment.* Washington, D.C.: Project on the Status and Education of Women, Association of American Colleges. ED 2000 097.7 pp. MF–01; PC–01.

Association of American Colleges (1988). *Peer Harassment: Hassles for Women on Campus.* Washington, D.C.: Project on the Status and Education of Women, Association of American Colleges.

Astin, A. (1981). Proposals for Change in College Administration. In *Maximizing Leadership Effectiveness*, ed. A. Astin and R. Scherrei. San Francisco: Jossey-Bass.

Backhouse, C., and Cohen, L. (1981). *Sexual Harassment on the Job.* Englewood Cliffs, N.J. Prentice-Hall.

Baker, D. D., and Terpstra, D. E. (1986). "Locus of Control and Self-Esteem versus Demographics Factors as Predictors of Attitudes Toward Women," *Basic and Applied Social Psychology* 7: 163–72.

Baker, D. D., Terpstra, D. E., and Cutler, B. D. (1990). "Perceptions of Sexual Harassment: A Re-examination of Gender Differences," *The Journal of Psychology* 124: 409–16.

Baker, D. D., Terpstra, D. E., and Larntz, K. (1990). "The Influence of Individual Characteristics and Severity of Harassing Behavior on Reactions to Sexual Harassment," *Sex Roles* 22: 305–25.

Baldwin, D. C., Jr., Daugherty, S. R., and Eckenfels, E. J. (1991). "Sexual Harassment in Medical Training," *New England Journal of Medicine* 325: 1803.

Baldwin, D. C., Jr., Daugherty, S. R., and Eckenfels, E. J. (1991). "Student Perceptions of Mistreatment and Harrassment During Medical School: A Survey of Ten United States Schools," *West Journal of Medicine* 155: 140–45.

Bate, B. (1988). *Communication and the Sexes.* New York: Harper and Row.

Bayly, S. (1990). "Meritor and Related Cases," *Synthesis: Law and Policy in Higher Education*: 114–19.

Beauvais, K. (1986). "Workshops to Combat Sexual Harassment: A Case Study of Changing Attitudes," *Signs* 12, 130–45.

Beckett, S. (1991). *Endgame.* In *Stages of Drama*, 2nd ed., ed. C. H. Klaus, M. Gilbert, and B. S. Bradford. New York: St. Martin's Press.

Belenky, M. F., Clincy, B. M., Goldberger, N. R., and Tarule, J. M. (1986). *Women's Ways of Knowing: The Development of Self, Voice, and Mind.* New York: Basic Books.

Bellah, N. R., Madsen, R., Sullivan, W. M., Swidler, A., and Tipton, S. M. (1991). *The Good Society.* New York: Alfred A. Knopf.

Bennis, W., and Nanus, B. (1985). *Leaders: The Strategies for Taking Charge.* New York: Harper & Row.

Benson, D. J., and Thompson, G. E. (1982). "Sexual Harassment on a University Campus: The Confluence of Authority Relations, Sexual Interest, and Gender Stratification," *Social Problems* 29(3): 236–51.

Berryman-Fink, C. (1993). "Preventing Sexual Harassment Through Male-Female Communication Training." In *Sexual Harassment: Communication Implications*, ed. G. L. Kreps. Cresskill, N.J.: Hampton Press.

Betts, N., and Newman, G. (1982). " Defining the Issues: Sexual Harassment in College and University Life," *Contemporary Education* 54: 48–52.

Betz, N., and Fitzgerald, L. (1987). *The Career Psychology of Women.* New York: Academic Press.

Biaggio, M., Watts, D., and Brownell, A. (1990). "Addressing Sexual Harassment: Strategies for Prevention and Change." In *Ivory Power: Sexual Harassment on Campus*, ed. M. Paludi, 213–30. Albany: State University of New York Press.

Bingham, S. G. (1991). "Communications Strategies for Managing Sexual Harassment in Organizations: Understanding Message Options and Their Effects," *Journal of Applied Communication Research* 19(2): 88–115.

Bingham, S. G. (1993). "Factors Assocated with Responses to Sexual Harassment and Satisfaction with Outcome," *Sex Roles* 29: 239–69.

Bingham, S. G., and Burleson, B. R. (1989). "Multiple Effects of Messages with Multiple Goals: Some Perceived Outcomes of Responses to Sexual Harassment," *Human Communication Research* 16(2): 184–216.

Bly, R. (1990). *Iron John: A Book about Men.* Reading, Mass.: Addison-Wesley.

Bond, M. (1988). "Division 27 Sexual Harassment Survey: Definition, Impact and Environmental Context," *The Community Psychologist* 21: 7–10.

Booth-Butterfield, M. (1989). "Perceptions of Harassing Communication as a Function of Locus of Control, Work Force Participation, and Gender," *Communication Quarterly* 37: 262–75.

Bowker, J. (1993). "Reporting Sexual Harassment: Reconciling Power, Knowledge, and Perspective." In *Sexual Harassment: Communication Implications*, ed. G. L. Kreps. Cresskill, N.J.: Hampton Press.

Boyer, E. L. (1990). *A Special Report. Campus Life: In Search of Community.* Princeton, N.J.: The Carnegie Foundation for the Advancement of Teaching.

Bradway, B. (1992). "Sexual Harassment: It's Not Hidden Anymore," *Survivor* 2: 2–4.

Bravo, E., and Cassedy, E. (1992). *The 9–5 Guide to Combatting Sexual Harassment.* New York: John Wiley and Sons.

Brooks, L., and Perot, A. R. (1991). "Reporting Sexual Harassment: Exploring a Predictive Model," *Psychology of Women Quarterly* 15: 31–47.

Brown, L. S. (1991). "Not Outside the Range: One Feminist Perspective on Psychic Trauma," *American Imago* 48: 119–33.

Bryson, C. B. (1990). "The Internal Sexual Harassment Investigation: Self-evaluation without Self-incrimination." *Employee Relations Law Journal* 15: 551–59.

Bureau of National Affairs (1992). *Affirmative Action Compliance Manual for Federal Contractors: News and Developments.* Washington, D.C.: The Bureau of National Affairs.

Burgess, A. W., and Holmstrom, L. L. (1979). "Adaptive Strategies and Recovery From Rape," *American Journal of Psychiatry* 136: 1, 278–89.

Calhoun, K. S., and Atkeson, B. M. (1991). *Treatment of Rape Victims.* New York: Pergamon Press.

Califa, A. J., Director for Litigation, Enforcement, Policy Service (August 31, 1981). Title IX and Sexual Harassment Complaints. *Memorandum to Regional Civil Rights Directors.*

Cammaert, L. (1985). "How Widespread is Sexual Harassment on Campus?" "Women in Groups and Aggression Against Women," *International Journal of Women's Studies* 8: 388–93.

Caudill, D. W., and Donaldson, R. (1986). "Is Your Climate Ripe for Sexual Harassment?" *Management World* 15: 26–27.

Charney, P. A., and Russell, R. C. (1994). "An Overview of Sexual Harassment," *American Journal of Psychiatry* 151(1): 10–17.

Charney, P. A., Russell, R. C., and Livingston, J. A. (1982). "Responses to Sexual Harassment on the Job: Legal, Organizational and Individual Actions." *Journal of Social Issues* 38: 5–22.

Charney, P. A., Russell, R. C., Robertson, C. E., and Campbell, D. (1988). "Campus Harassment: Sexual Harassment Policies and Procedures at Institutions of Higher Learning," *Signs: Journal of Women in Culture and Society* 13: 792–812.

Chickering, A. W. (1969). *Education and Identity.* San Francisco: Jossey Bass.

Clark, C. (1991). "Sexual Harassment." *Congressional Quarterly Researcher:* 539–55.

Cohen, M. D., and March, J. G. (1974). *Leadership and Ambiguity: The American College President*, 2nd ed. Boston: Harvard Business School Press.

Cole, E., ed. (1990). *Sexual Harassment on Campus: A Legal Compendium*, 2nd ed. Washington, D.C.: National Association of College and University Attorneys.

Coleman, M. (1987). *A Study of Sexual Harassment of Female Students in Academia. Dissertation Abstracts International* 47: 2815.

Coles, F. (1986). "Forced to Quit: Sexual Harassment Complaints and Agency Response," *Sex Roles* 14: 81–95.

Collins, E. G. C., and Blodgett, T. B. (1981). "Sexual Harassment: Some See It . . . Some Won't," *Harvard Business Review* 59(2): 76–95.

Connolly, W. B., Jr., and Marshall, A. B. (1989). "Sexual Harassment of University or College Students by Faculty Members," *Journal of College and University Law* 15: 381–403.

Conrad, J. (1990). *The Heart of Darkness.* In the *Norton Anthology of Short Fiction,* 4th ed., ed. R. V. Cassill. New York: W. W. Norton.

Cooperative Institutional Research Program of the Higher Education Institute of the University of California, Los Angeles (1996). *American Freshman: National Norms for 1996.* Los Angeles: University of California.

Coverdale, A., and Taylor, D. (1992). *Sexual Harassment: Women Speak Out.* Freedom, Calif.: The Crossing Press.

Crocker, P. (1983). "An Analysis of University Definitions of Sexual Harassment." *Signs* 8: 686–707.

Crocker, P. L., and Simon, A. E. (1981). "Sexual Harassment in Education." *Capital University Law Review* 10: 541–84.

Crull, P. (1979). *The Impact of Sexual Harassment on the Job: A Profile of the Experiences of 92 Women.* Working Women's Research Series, Report No. 3.

Crull, P. (1982). "Stress Effects of Sexual Harassment on the Job: Implications for Counseling," *American Journal of Orthopsychiatry* 52: 539, 544.

D'Ercole, A. (1988). "Sexual Harassment and Gender Issues in Community Psychology," *The Community Psychologist* 21: 22.

Deal, T. E., and Kennedy, A. A. (1983). *Corporate Cultures: The Rites and Rituals of Corporate Life.* Reading, Mass.: Addison-Wesley.

Deane, R. H. (1986). "Sexual Harassment: Is Your Company Protected?" *Business* 36: 42–45.

DeChiara, P. (1988). "The Need for Universities to Have Rules on Consensual Sexual Relationships Between Faculty Members and Students," *Columbia Journal of Law and Social Problems* 21: 137–62.

DeFour, D. C. (1996). "The Interface of Racism and Sexism on College Campuses." *Sexual Harassment on College Campuses: Abusing the Ivory Power.,* ed. M. Paludi. Albany: State University of New York Press.

Dey, E. L., Korn, J. S., and Sax, L. J. (1996). "Betrayed by the Acadamy: The Sexual Harassment of Women College Faculty," *Journal of Higher Education* 67: 149–73.

Dietz-Uhler, B., and Murrell, A. (1992). "College Students' Perceptions of Sexual Harassment: Are Gender Differences Decreasing?" *Journal of College Student Development* 33: 540–46.

Doyle, J., and Paludi, M. A. (1991). *Sex and Gender.* Dubuque, Ia.: W. C. Brown.

Dozier, J. (1990). "Sexual Harassment: It Can Happen Here." *AGB Reports* 32(1): 15–20.

Driscoll, J. B. (1981). "Sexual Attraction and Harassment: Management's New Problems," *Personnel Journal* 60: 33–36, 56.

Druck, K., and Simmons, J. C. (1985). *The Secrets Men Keep: Breaking the Silence Barrier.* Garden City, N.Y.: Doubleday.

Dziech, B. W. (1990). "Author's Note." In The *Lecherous Professor: Sexual Harassment on Campus,* 2nd ed., B. W. Dziech and L. Weiner. Boston: Beacon Press.

Dziech, B. W. (1991). "Colleges Must Help to Unravel the Bewildering Complexities of Sexual Harassment," *Chronicle of Higher Education* 38(12): B2-B3.

Dziech, B. W., and Weiner, L. (1990). *The Lecherous Professor: Sexual Harassment on Campus,* 2nd ed. Boston: Beacon Press.

EEOC Policy Guidance. N–915.050. March 19, 1990.

Eliot, T. S. (1967). *Little Gidding.* In *The New Oxford Book of English Verse, 1250–1950,* ed. H. Gardner. New York: Oxford University Press.

Equal Employment Opportunity Commission (1980). *Guidelines on Discrimination Because of Sex* [29 CFR Part 1604, Federal Register 45 (210)]. Washington, D.C.: U.S. Governmental Printing Office.

Equal Employment Opportunity Commission (1990). *Policy Guidance on Current Is-*

sues of Sexual Harassment, later published in part at 29 C.F.R. 1601 et al. (1991). Washington, D.C.: Equal Employment Opportunity Commission.

Equal Employment Opportunity Commission (1992). *Facts about Sexual Harassment.* Washington, D.C.: Equal Employment Opportunity Commission.

Eskenazi, M., and Gallen, D. (1992). *Sexual Harassment: Know Your Rights.* New York: Carroll & Graf Publishers, Inc.

Fain, T. C., and Anderton, D. L. (1987). "Sexual Harassment: Organizational Context and Diffuse Status," *Sex Roles* 17: 291–311.

Farber, G. (1967). "The Student as Nigger." *Daily Bruin Spectra.* Page cite unavailable.

Farley, L. (1978). *Sexual Shakedown: The Sexual Harassment of Women on the Job.* New York: McGraw-Hill.

Fasteau, M. F. (1974). *The Male Machine.* New York: McGraw-Hill.

Fasteau, M. F. (1975). "The High Price of Macho." *Psychology Today* 9(4): 60.

Finkel, J. J. (1985). "Stress, Traumas, and Trauma Resolution." *American Journal of Community Psychology* 3: 173–78.

Fitzgerald, L. F. (1990). "Sexual Harassment: The Definition and Measurement of a Construct." In *Ivory Power: Sexual Harassment on Campus,* ed. M. A. Paludi. Albany: State University of New York Press.

Fitzgerald, L. F. (1993). "Sexual Harassment: Violence Against Women in the Workplace," *American Psychologist* 48: 1073.

Fitzgerald, L. F., Gold, Y., Ormerod, M., and Weitzman, L. (1988). "Academic Harassment: Sex and Denial in Scholarly Garb," *Psychology of Women Quarterly* 12: 329–400

Fitzgerald, L. F., and Ormerod, A. J. (1991). "Perceptions of Sexual Harassment: The Influence of Gender and Academic Context," *Psychology of Women Quarterly* 15: 281–94.

Fitzgerald, L. F., Shullman, S., Bailey, N., Gold, Y., Ormerod, M., and Weitzman, L. (1988). "The Incidence and Dimensions of Sexual Harassment in Academia and the Workplace," *Journal of Vocational Behavior* 32: 152–75.

Fitzgerald, L. F., and Weitzman, L. (1990). "Men Who Harass: Speculation and Data." In *Ivory Power: Sexual Harassment on Campus,* ed. M. A. Paludi. Albany: State University of New York Press.

Franklin, P., Moglin, H., Zatling-Boring, P., and Angress, R. (1981). *Sexual and Gender Harassment in the Academy.* New York: Modern Language Association.

Franklin, P. A., and Cohen, B. B. (1992). "Research on the Sexual Victimization of Women," *Counseling Psychologist* 20: 151.

Freedman, M. B. (1967). *The College Experience.* San Francisco: Jossey-Bass.

Fuehrer, A., and Schilling, K. M. (1988). "Sexual Harassment of Women Graduate Students: The Impact of Institutional Factors," *The Community Psychologist* 21: 13–14.

Gallop, J. (1992). *Around 1981: Academic Feminist Literary Theory.* New York: Routledge.

Gallop, J. (1997). *Feminist Accused of Sexual Harassment.* Durham, N.C.: Duke University Press.

Gallop, J. (1994). "Sex and Sexism: Feminism and Harassment Policy," *Academe* 80: 16–23.

Gallop, J. (1988). *Thinking Through the Body.* New York: Columbia University Press.

Galvin, K.M. (1993). "Preventing the Problem: Preparing Faculty Members for Issues of Sexual Harassment." In *Sexual Harassment: Communication Implications,* ed. Gary L. Kreps. Cresskill, N.J.: Hampton Press.

Gartland, P., ed. (1983). "Sexual Harassment on Campus," *Journal of the National Association for Women Deans, Administrators, and Counselors* 46: 3–50.

Genesis 39:6 (1989). *Life Application Bible,* King James Version. Wheaton, Ill.: Tyndale House.

Gill, M. (1993). "Academic Sexual Harassment: Perceptions of Behaviors." In *Sexual Harassment: Communication Implications,* ed. G. L. Kreps. Cresskill, N.J.: Hampton Press.

Gillespie, D., and Leffer, A. (1987). "The Politics of Research Methodology in Claims-Making Activities: Social Science and Sexual Harassment," *Social Problems* 34: 490–508.

Gilligan, C. (1977). "In a Different Voice: Women's Conceptions of Self and Morality," *Harvard Educational Review* 47: 481–517.

Gilligan, C. (1982). *In a Different Voice.* Cambridge: Harvard University Press.

Glaser, R., and Thorpe, J. (1986). "Unethical Intimacy: A Survey of Contact and Advances Between Psychology Educators and Female Graduate Students," *American Psychologist* 41: 43–51.

Glass, B. (1988). "Workplace Harassment and the Victimization of Women," *Women's Studies International Forum* 11: 55–67.

Goodman, J. L. (1978). "Sexual Harassment on the Job," *American Civil Liberties Review* 4(6): 55–58.

Goodwin, M. P. (1989). "Sexual Harassment: Experiences of University Employees," *Journal of the National Association for Women Deans, Administrators, and Counselors* 52: 25–33.

Goodwin, M. P., Roscie, B., and Repp, S. E. (1989). "Sexual Harassment: Experiences of University Employees," *Initiatives* 52(3): 25–33.

Grauerholz, E. (1989). "Sexual Harassment of Women Professors by Students: Exploring the Dynamics of Power, Authority, and Gender in a University Setting," *Sex Roles* 21: 789–801.

Grisham, J. (1992). *The Pelican Brief.* New York: Doubleday.

Gruber, J., and Bjorn, L. (1986). "Women's Responses to Sexual Harassment: An Analysis of Sociocultural, Organizational, and Personal Resource Models," *Social Science Quarterly* 67: 814–26.

Gruber, J. E. (1990). "Methodological Problems and Policy Implications in Sexual Harassment Research," *Population Research and Policy Review* 9: 235–54.

Gruber, J. E. (1992). "A Typology of Personal and Environmental Sexual Harassment: Research and Policy Implications for the 1990's," *Sex Roles* 26: 447–63.

Gutek, B. A. (1985). *Sex and the Workplace: The Impact of Sexual Behavior and Harassment on Women, Men and Organizations.* San Francisco: Jossey-Bass.

Gutek, B. A., and Morasch, B. (1982). "Sex-ratios, Sex-role Spillover, and Sexual Harassment of Women at Work," *Journal of Social Issues* 38(4): 55–74.

Gutek, B. A., Nakamura, C. Y., Gahart, M., Handschumacher, I., and Russell, D. (1980). "Sexuality and the Workplace," *Basic and Applied Social Psychology* 1: 255–65.

Hall, R. M., and Sandler, B. R. (1982). *The Classroom Climate: A Chilly One for Women?* Washington, D.C.: Project on the Status and Education of Women, Association of American Colleges.

Hallinan, K. M. (1993). "Invasion of Privacy or Protection Against Sexual Harassment: Co-Employee Dating and Employer Liability," *Columbia Journal of Law and Social Problems* 26: 388–435.

Hamilton, J. A., Alagna, S. W., King, L. S., and Lloyd, C. (1987). "The Emotional Consequences of Gender-based Abuse in the Workplace: New Counseling Programs for Sex Discrimination," *Women and Therapy* 6: 155–82.

Helly, D. O. (1987). "Institutional Strategies: Creating a Sexual Harassment Panel." In *Ivory Power: Sexual Harassment on Campus,* ed. M. A. Paludi. Albany: State University of New York Press.

Henley, N. M. (1977). *Body Politics: Power, Sex and Nonverbal Communication.* Englewood Cliffs, N.J.: Prentice-Hall.

Henry, W. A., III (1994). *In Defense of Elitism.* New York: Doubleday.

Henzel, A. (1992). "Audit Slams UWM's Affirmative Action Office," *The UWM Post,* March 5: 1, 3.

Hesse, H. (1972). *Magister Ludi.* New York: Bantam.

Hindus, M. (1990). "Peer Counseling," *Journal of the National Association for Women Deans, Administrators, and Counselors* 52(4): 47.

Hoffman, F. L. (1986). "Sexual Harassment in Academia: Feminist Theory and Institutional Practice," *Harvard Educational Review* 56: 105–21.

Honstead, M. L. (1988). "Correlates of Coping Methods of Sexually Harassed College Students," *Dissertation Abstracts International* 48(8-A), 7512.

Hotelling, K. (1991). "Sexual Harassment: A Problem Shielded by Silence," *Journal of Counseling and Development* 69(6): 497–501.

Howard, S. (1991). "Organizational Resources for Addressing Sexual Harassment," *Journal of Counseling and Development* 69(6), 507–11.

Hughes, J. O., and Sandler, B. R. (1986). *In Case of Sexual Harassment: A Guide for Women Students. We Hope It Doesn't Happen to You, But If It Does.* Washington, D.C.: The Project on the Status of Women.

Hunter, C., and McClelland, K. (1991). "Honoring Accounts for Sexual Harassment: A Factorial Survey Analysis," *Sex Roles* 24: 725–752.

Ingulli, E. D. (1987). "Sexual Harassment in Education," *Rutgers Law Journal* 18: 281–342.

Israeli, D. N. (1983). "Sex Effects or Structural Effects? An Empirical Test of Kanter's Theory of Proportions," *Social Forces*, 153–65.

Jacklin, C. N. (1989). "Femininity and Masculinity: Issues of Gender," *American Psychologist* 44: 127–33.

Janoff-Bulman, R. (1992). *Shattered Assumptions: Towards a New Psychology of Trauma.* New York: Free Press.

Janoff-Bulman, R., and Frieze, I. H. (1983). "A Theoretical Perspective for Understanding Reactions to Victimization," *Journal of Social Issues* 39: 1–17.

Jaschik, M. L., and Frentz, B. R. (1991). "Women's Perceptions and Labeling of Sexual Harassment," *Sex Roles* 25: 19–23.

Jaschik, S. (1991). "U.S. Plans Policies to Fight Harassment and Bias at Colleges," *Chronicle of Higher Education* 371: 1, 26.

Jensen, I. W., and Gutek, B. (1982). "Attributions and Assignment of Responsibility for Sexual Harassment," *Journal of Social Issues* 38: 121–36.

Johnson, R., and Schulman, G. (1989). "Gender-Role Composition and Role Entrapment in Decision-making Groups," *Gender and Society* 3(3): 355–72.

Jossem, J. H. (1991). "Investigating Sexual Harassment Complaints," *Personnel* 68: 9–10.

Jost, K. (1994). "Questionable Conduct," *ABA Journal* 80: 71.

Jung, C. G. (1958). *The Undiscovered Self.* Boston: Little, Brown.

Kanter, R. M. (1977). "Some Effects of Proportions on Group Life: Skewed Sex Ratios and Responses to Token Women," *American Journal of Sociology*, 965–90.

Kanter, R. M. (1979). *Men and Women of the Corporation.* New York: Basic Books.

Kanter, R. M. (1983). *The Change Masters.* New York: Simon & Schuster.

Kaplan, W. A. (1985). *The Law of Higher Education.* San Francisco: Jossey-Bass.

Kaschak, E. (1992). *Engendered Lives: A New Psychology of Women's Experience.* New York: Basic Books.

Kazantzakis, N. (1952). *Zorba the Greek.* New York: Simon & Schuster.

Keller, E. A. (1988). "Consensual Amorous Relationships Between Faculty and Students: The Constitutional Right to Privacy," *Journal of College and University Law* 15: 21–42.

Keller, E. A. (1990). "Consensual Relationships and Institutional Policy," *Academe* 76: 29–32.

Keller, G. (1983). *Academic Strategy: The Management Revolution in Higher Education.* Baltimore: Johns Hopkins University Press.

Kenig, S., and Ryan, J. (1986). "Sex Differences in Levels of Tolerance and Attribution of Blame for Sexual Harassment on a University Campus," *Sex Roles* 15: 535–49.

Kerr, S. (1990). "UWM Sex Harassment Coverups Charged." *Shepherd Express*, November 8–15, 1: 17–18.

Kerr, S. (1993). "Bodies of Evidence," *Heterodoxy*. Page cite unavailable.

Kirby, D., Murrell, P., and Riggs, R. (1992). "Title IX: The Paper Tiger Gets Teeth," *AGB Reports* 34(8): 23–26.

Kirschman, L. (1994). "First Amendment: Do 'Hostile Environment' Charges Chill Academic Freedom?" *ABA Journal* 80: 41.

Kissinger, M. (1994). "She's No Plain Jane," *The Milwaukee Journal*, November 8, A2.

Koen, C. M., Jr. (1989). "Sexual Harassment: Criteria for Defining Hostile Environment," *Employee Responsibilities and Rights Journal* 2: 289–301.

Komaromy, M., Bindman, A. B., Maber, R. J., and Sande, M.A. (1993). "Sexual Harassment in Medical Training," *New England Journal of Medicine* 328: 322–26.

Konrad, A. M., and Gutek, B. A. (1986). "Impact of Work Experiences on Attitudes Toward Sexual Harassment," *Administrative Science Quarterly* 31: 42–48.

Koss, M. P. (1990). "Changed Lives: The Psychological Impact of Sexual Harassment." In *Ivory Power: Sexual Harassment on Campus,* ed. M. A. Paludi. Albany: State University of New York Press.

Kreps, G. (1993). "Promoting a Sociocultural Evolutionary Approach to Preventing Sexual Harassment: Metacommunication and Cultural Adaptation." In *Sexual Harassment: Communication Implications,* ed. G. L. Kreps. Cresskill, N.J.: Hampton Press.

Kronenberger, G. K., and Bourke, D. L. (1981). "Effective Training and the Elimination of Sexual Harassment," *Personnel Journal* 60: 879–83.

Leatherman, C. (1991). "Colleges Seek New Ways to Deal with Sexual Harassment as Victims on Campus Are Reluctant to File Complaints," *Chronicle of Higher Education*: 1.

Leo, J. (1992). "P.C. Follies: The Year in Review," *U.S. News and World Report* 112(3): 22.

Lester, D., Banta, B., Barton, J., Elian, N., Mackiewicz, L., and Winkelried, J. (1986). "Is Personality Related to Judgments about Sexual Harassment?" *Psychological Reports* 59: 1114.

Licata, B. J., and Popovich, P. M. (1987). "Preventing Sexual Harassment: A Proactive Approach," *Training and Development Journal* 41: 34–38.

Linenberger, P. (1983). "What Behavior Constitutes Sexual Harassment?" *Labor Law Journal* 34: 238–47.

Livingston, J. A. (1982). "Responses to Sexual Harassment on the Job: Legal, Organizational, and Individual Actions," *Journal of Social Issues* 38: 5–22.

Lloyd, K. L. (1992). *Sexual Harassment: How to Keep Your Company out of Court.* New York: Panel Publishers, Inc.

Lott, B., Reilly, M. E., and Howard, D. R. (1982). "Sexual Assault and Harassment: A Campus Community Case Study," *Signs* 8: 296–319.

Luthar, H. K. (1995–96). "The Neglect of Critical Issues in the Sexual Harassment Discussion: Implications for Organizational and Public Policies," *Journal of Individual Employment Rights* 4(4), 261–76.

Maccoby, E. E., and Jacklin, C. N. (1974). *The Psychology of Sex Differences.* Stanford: Stanford University Press.

MacKinnon, C. A. (1979). *Sexual Harassment of Working Women: A Case of Sex Discrimination.* New Haven: Yale University Press.

MacKinnon, C. A. (1992). "Sexual Harassment: The Experience." In *Sexual Harassment: Know Your Rights,* ed. M. Eskenazi and D. Gallen. New York: Carroll & Graf.

Maihoff, N., and Forrest, L. (1983). "Sexual Harassment in Higher Education: An Assessment Study," *Journal of the National Association for Women Deans, Administrators, and Counselors* 46: 3–8.

Malovich, N. J., and Stake, J. E. (1990). "Sexual Harassment on Campus: Individual Differences in Attitudes and Beliefs," *Psychology of Women Quarterly* 14: 63–81.

Marks, M. A. (1993). "Sexual Harassment on Campus: Effects of Professor Gender on Perception of Sexually Harassing Behaviors," *Sex Roles* 28: 207–17.

Markunas, P., and Joyce-Brady, J. (1987). "Underutilization of Sexual Harassment Grievance Procedures," *Journal of National Association for Women Deans, Administrators, and Counselors* 50: 27–32.

Mayo, C., and Henley, N. M., eds. (1981). *Gender and Nonverbal Behavior.* New York: Springer-Verlag.

Mazer, D. B., and Percival, E. F. (1989). "Ideology or Experience? The Relationships Among Perceptions, Attitudes, and Experiences of Sexual Harassment in University Students," *Sex Roles* 20: 135–47.

Mazer, D. B., and Percival, E. F. (1989). "Students' Experiences of Sexual Harassment at a Small University," *Sex Roles* 20: 1–22.

McCaghy, M. D. (1984). *Sexual Harassment: A Guide to Resources.* Boston: G. K. Hall.

McCormack, A. (1985). "The Sexual Harassment of Students by Teachers: The Case of Students in Science," *Sex Roles* 13: 21–32.

McCormick, N., Adams-Bohley, S., Peterson, S., and Gaeddert, W. (1989). "Sexual Harassment of Students at a Small College," *Journal of the National Association for Women Deans, Administrators, and Counselors* 52(3): 15–23.

McIntyre, P. I., and Renick, J. C. (1982). "Protecting Public Employees and Employers from Sexual Harassment," *Public Personnel Management Journal,* 282–92.

McKinney, K. (1990). "Sexual Harassment of University Faculty by Colleagues and Students," *Sex Roles* 23: 421–38.

McKinney, K., Olson, C., and Satterfield, A. (1988). "Graduate Students' Perception of and Reaction to Sexual Harassment." *Journal of Interpersonal Violence* 3: 319–25.

McMillen, L. (1986). "Council Offers Sexual Harassment Policy Guidelines," *Chronicle of Higher Education* 33: 16.

McMillen, L. (1986). "Many Colleges Taking a New Look at Policies on Sexual Harassment," *Chronicle of Higher Education* 33: 1.

McMillen, L. (1991). "A Mixed Message for Campuses Seen in Thomas Hearings," *Chronicle of Higher Education* 38: 1, 14.

Metha, A., and Nigg, J. (1982). "Sexual Harassment: Implications of a Study at Arizona State University," *Women's Studies Quarterly* 10: 24–26.

Metha, A., and Nigg, J. (1983). "Sexual Harassment on Campus: An Institutional Response," *Journal of the National Association for Women Deans, Administrators, and Counselors* 46: 9–15.

Meyers, M. C., Berchtold, I. M., Oestreich, J. L., and Collins, F. J. (1981). *Sexual Harassment.* New York: Petrocelli Books.

Milkman, R. (1987). *Gender at Work.* Urbana: University of Illinois Press.

Morgan, G. (1986). *Images of Organization.* Newbury Park, Calif.: Sage.

National Education Association (1992). *Sexual Harassment in Higher Education: Concepts and Issues.* Washington D.C.: National Education Association.

"New Rules about Sex on Campus" (1993). *Harper's* (September), 33–42.

Nieva, V. F., and Gutek, B. A. (1981). *Women and Work: A Psychological Perspective.* New York: Praeger.

Olswang, S. (1992). "Reassessing Effective Procedures in Cases of Sexual Harassment," *New Directions for Institutional Research,* No. 76. San Francisco: Jossey-Bass.

O'Neil, R. M. (1996). "Protecting Free Speech When the Issue Is Sexual Harassment," *Chronicle of Higher Education* 43(3): B4.

O'Neill, E. (1955). *Long Day's Journey into Night.* New Haven: Yale University Press.

Padgitt, S., and Padgitt, J. (1986). "Cognitive Structures of Sexual Harassment: Implications for University Policy," *Journal of College Student Personnel* 27: 34–39.

Paludi, M. A., ed. (1990). "The Student in the Back Row: Avoiding Sexual Harassment in the Classroom." In *Ivory Power: Sexual Harassment on Campus.* Albany: State University of New York Press.

Paludi, M. A., and Barickman, R., eds. (1991). "Definitions and Incidence of Academic and Workplace Sexual Harassment." In *Academic and Workplace Sexual Harassment: A Resource Manual.* Albany: State University of New York Press.

Paludi, M. A., and Barickman, R., eds. (1991). "In Their Own Voices: Responses from Individuals Who Have Experienced Sexual Harassment and Supportive Techniques for Dealing with Victims of Sexual Harassment." In *Academic and Work-*

place Sexual Harassment: A Resource Manual. Albany: State University of New York Press.

Paludi, M. A., and Barickman, R., eds. (1991). "Sexual Harassment of Students: Victims of the College Experience." In *Academic and Workplace Sexual Harassment: A Resource Manual.* Albany: State University of New York Press.

Payne, K. (1993). "The Power Game: Sexual Harassment on the College Campus." In *Sexual Harassment: Communication Implications,* ed. G. L. Kreps. Cresskill, N.J.: Hampton Press.

Pearson, J. C., Turner, L., and Todd-Mancillas, W. (1991). *Gender and Communication.* Dubuque, Ia.: W. C. Brown.

Perley, J. E. (1995). Reprint of speech presented at the University of Cincinnati. In *AAUP Works for You* (February): 1–3.

Peters, T. J., and Waterman, R. H. (1982). *In Search of Excellence: Lessons from America's Best-Run Companies.* New York: Harper & Row.

Petersen, D. J., and Massengill, D. (1982). "Sexual Harassment—A Growing Problem in the Workplace," *Personnel Administrator* 27: 79–89.

Pettigrew, A. M. (1990). "Organizational Climate and Culture: Two Constructs in Search of a Role." In *Organizational Climate and Culture,* ed. B. Schneider. San Francisco: Jossey- Bass.

Pope, K., Levenson, H., and Shover, L. R. (1979). "Sexual Intimacy in Psychology Training: Results and Implications of a National Survey," *American Psychologist* 34: 682–89.

Pope, K., Schover, L., and Levenson, L. (1980). "Sexual Behavior Between Clinical Supervisors and Trainees: Implications for Professional Standards," *Professional Psychology* 11: 157–62.

Popovich, P. M. (1988). "Sexual Harassment in Organizations," *Employee Responsibilities and Rights Journal* 1: 273–82.

Popovich, P. M., Licata, B. J., Nokovich, D., Martelli, T., and Zoloty, S. (1986). "Assessing the Incidence and Perceptions of Sexual Harassment Behaviors Among American Undergraduates," *Journal of Psychology* 120(4): 387–96.

Popovich, Paula M. (1992). "Perceptions of Sexual Harassment as a Function of Sex of Rater and Incident Form and Consequence," *Sex Roles* 27: 609–25.

Powell, G. N. (1983). "Definition of Sexual Harassment and Sexual Attention Experienced," *Journal of Psychology* 113: 113–17.

Powell, G. N. (1986). "Effects of Sex Role Identity and Sex on Definitions of Sexual Harassment," *Sex Roles* 14: 9–19.

Pryor, J. B. (1988). "Interpretation of Sexual Harassment: An Attributional Analysis," *Sex Roles* 18: 405–17.

Pryor, J. B. (1987). "Sexual Harassment Proclivities in Men," *Sex Roles* 17: 269–90.

Pryor, J. B., LaVite, C., and Stoller, L. (1993). "A Social Psychological Analysis of Sexual Harassment: The Person/Situation Interaction," *Journal of Vocational Behavior* 42: 68–83.

Pryor, J.B., Giedd, J. L., and Williams, K. B. (1995). "A Social Psychological Model for Predicting Sexual Harassment," *Journal of Social Issues* 51: 69–84.

Quina, K. (1990). "The Victimization of Women." In *Ivory Power: Sexual Harassment on Campus,* ed. M. A. Paludi. Albany: State University of New York Press.

Rabinowitz, V. C. (1990). "Coping with Sexual Harassment." In *Ivory Power: Sexual Harassment on Campus,* ed. M. A. Paludi. Albany: State University of New York Press.

Reilly, M. E., Lott, B., and Gallogly, S. M. (1986). "Sexual Harassment of University Students," *Sex Roles* 15: 333–58.

Reilly, T., Carpenter, S., Dull, V., and Barlett, K. (1982). "The Factorial Survey: An Approach to Defining Sexual Harassment on Campus," *Journal of Social Issues* 38: 99–110.

Renick, J. C. (1980). "Sexual Harassment at Work: Why It Happens, What to Do About It," *Personnel Journal* 59: 658–62.

Rhodes, A. L. (1983). "Effects of Religious Denomination of Sex Differences in Occupational Expectations," *Sex Roles* 9: 93–108.

Richman, J. A., Flaherty, J. A., Rospenda, K. M., and Christensen, M. L. (1992). "Mental Health Consequences and Correlates of Reported Medical Student Abuse," *JAMA* 267: 269–94.

Riger, S. (1991). "Gender Dilemmas in Sexual Harassment Policies and Procedures," *American Psychologist* 46: 497–505.

Riggs, R. O., Murrell, P. H., and Cutting, J. C. (1993). *Sexual Harassment in Higher Education: From Conflict to Community. (ASME-ERIC Higher Education Report No. 2)*. Washington, D.C., George Washington University, School of Education and Human Development.

Robertson, C., Dyer, C. E., and Campbell, D. (1988). "Campus Harassment: Sexual Harassment Policies and Procedures at Institutions of Higher Learning," *Signs* 13(4): 792–812.

Roiphe, K. (1993). *The Morning After: Sex, Fear and Feminism on Campus*. Boston: Little, Brown.

Rubin, L. J., and Borgers, S. B. (1990). "Sexual Harassment in Universities During the 1980s," *Sex Roles* 23: 397–411.

Saal, F. E., Johnson, C. B., and Weber, N. (1989). "Friendly or Sexy? It May Depend on Whom You Ask," *Psychology of Women Quarterly* 13: 263–76.

Safran, C. (1996). "What Men Do to Women on the Job: A Shocking Look at Sexual Harassment," *Redbook* (November), 217–24.

Salisbury, J., Ginorio, A. B., Remick, H., and Stringer, D. M. (1986). "Counseling Victims of Sexual Harassment," *Gender Issues in Psychotherapy* 23: 316–24.

Sandler, B. R. (1981). "Sexual Harassment: A Hidden Problem," *Educational Record* 62: 52–57.

Sandler, B. R. (1983). *Writing a Letter to the Sexual Harasser: Another Way of Dealing with the Problem*. Washington, D.C.: Project on the Status and Education of Women, American Association of Colleges.

Sandler, B. R. (1986). *The Campus Climate Revisited: Chilly for Women Faculty, Administrators, and Graduate Students*. Washington, D.C.: Project on the Status and Education of Women, Association of American Colleges.

Sandroff, R. (1988). "Sexual Harassment in the Fortune 500," *Working Women* 13: 69–73.

Sartre, J. P. (1956). *Being and Nothingness*. New York: Philosophical Library.

Schein, E. (1968). "Organizational Socialization," *Industrial Management Review* 2: 37–45.

Schneider, B. E. (1987). "Graduate Women, Sexual Harassment and University Policy," *Journal of Higher Education* 58: 46–65.

Schroeder, J. H. (June 13, 1991). Letter to Christine Ruh.

Segrave, K. (1994). *The Sexual Harassment of Women in the Workplace, 1600 to 1993*. Jefferson, N.C.: McFarland.

"Sexual Harassment: Suggested Policy and Procedures for Handling Complaints" (1983). *Academe* 69: 15a–16a.

"Sexual Harassment: Suggested Policy and Procedures for Handling Complaints" (1990). *Academe* 76: 42–43.

"Sexual Harassment: Suggested Policy and Procedures for Handling Complaints" (1995). *Academe* 81: 62–64.

Shotland, R. L., and Craig, J. M. (1988). "Can Men and Women Differentiate Between Friendly and Sexually Interested Behavior?" *Social Psychology Quarterly* 51: 66–73.

Silverman, D. (1976). "Sexual Harassment: Working Women's Dilemma," *Quest: A Feminist Quarterly* 3: 15–24.

Simon, A., and Forrest, L. (1983). "Implementing a Sexual Harassment Program at a Large University," *Journal of National Association for Women, Deans and Counselors* 46: 23–29.

Snyder, B. R. (1971). *The Hidden Curriculum.* New York: Alfred A. Knopf.

Somers, A. (1982). "Sexual Harassment in Academe: Legal Issues and Definitions," *Journal of Social Issues* 38: 23–32.

Stimson, C. R. (1989). "Over-Reaching: Sexual Harassment and Education," *Journal of the National Association for Women Deans, Administrators, and Counselors* 52: 1–5.

Stites, M. C. (1996). "University Consensual Relationship Policies." In *Sexual Harassment on College Campuses: Abusing the Ivory Power*, ed. M. A. Paludi. Albany: State University of New York Press.

Stites, M. C. (1996). "What's Wrong with Faculty-Student Consensual Sexual Relationships?" In *Sexual Harassment on College Campuses: Abusing the Ivory Power*, ed. M.A. Paludi. Albany: State University of New York Press.

Stokes, J. (1983). "Effective Training Programs: One Institutional Response to Sexual Harassment," *Journal of National Association for Women, Deans and Counselors* 46: 34–38.

Strauss, S. (1988). "Sexual Harassment in the School: Legal Implications for Principals," *NAASP Bulletin* 72: 93–97.

Stringer, D. M., Remick, H., Salisbury, J., and Ginorio, A. B. (1990). "The Power and Reasons Behind Sexual Harassment: An Employer's Guide to Solutions," *Public Personnel Management* 19: 43–52.

Strouse, Jeremiah S. (1994). "Correlates of Attitudes Toward Sexual Harassment Among Early Adolescents," *Sex Roles* 559–77, November 1994, v. 31 n. 9–10.

Struckman-Johnson, Cindy. (1993). "College Men's and Women's Reactions to Hypothetical Sexual Touch Varied by Initiator Gender and Coercion Level," *Sex Roles* 371–385, September 1993, v. 29 n. 5–6.

Sundt, M. (1992). "Effective Sexual Harassment Policies: Focus on the Harasser and the Campus Culture," *Synthesis: Law and Policy in Higher Education* 4: 333–34.

Susanna. (1965). *Oxford Annotated Apocrypha*, Revised Standard Version, ed. B. M. Metzger. New York: Oxford University Press.

Talmud. Attribution information unavailable.

Tangri, S., Burt, M., and Johnson, L. (1982). "Sexual Harassment at Work: Three Explanatory Models," *Journal of Social Issues* 38: 33–54.

Tangri, S., Burt, M., and Johnson, L. (1982). "Sexual Harassment in the University," *Journal of College Student Personnel* 24: 219–24.

Tannen, D. (1990). *You Just Don't Understand.* New York: William Morrow.

Taylor, S. E. (1983). "Adjustment to Threatening Events: A Theory of Cognitive Adaptation," *American Psychologist* 38: 161–73.

Terpstra, D. E., and Baker, D. D. (1986). "A Framework for the Study of Sexual Harassment," *Basic and Applied Social Psychology* 7: 17–34.

Terpstra, D. E., and Baker, D. D. (1987). "A Hierarchy of Sexual Harassment," *Journal of Psychology* 121: 599–605.

Terpstra, D. E., and Cook, S. E. (1985). "Compliant Characteristics and Reported Behaviors and Consequences Associated with Formal Sexual Harassment Charges," *Personnel Psychology* 38: 559–74.

Thomann, D. A., and Weiner, R. L. (1987). "Physical and Psychological Causality as Determinants of Culpability in Sexual Harassment Cases," *Sex Roles* 17: 573–91.

Thornton, A., Alwin, D. F., and Camburn, D. (1983). "Causes and Consequences of Sex-Role Attitudes and Attitude Change," *American Sociological Review* 48: 211–27.

Till, F. J. (1980). *Sexual Harassment: A Report on the Sexual Harassment of Students.* Washington, D.C.: National Advisory Council on Women's Educational Programs.

Tronto, J. C. (1987). "Beyond Gender Differences to a Theory of Care," *Signs* 12: 644–63.

U.S. Department of Health, Education, and Welfare. (1975). *Final Title IX Regulation Implementing Education Amendments of 1972 Prohibiting Sex Discrimination in Education.* Washington, D.C.: U.S. Department of Health, Education, and Welfare, Office for Civil Rights.

U.S. Merit System Protection Board. (1981). *Sexual Harassment in the Federal Work-place: Is It a Problem?* Washington, D.C.: Office of Merit Systems Review and Studies: U.S. Government Printing Office.

U.S. Merit System Protection Board. (1988). *Sexual Harassment in the Federal Work-place: An Update*. Washington, D.C. Office of Merit Systems Review and Studies: U.S. Government Printing Office.

University of Wisconsin-Milwaukee Office of Equal Opportunity Programs. (1993). EOP Case No. 44. Beckelman, Dana, versus Gallop, Jane. 1–5, 13.

Valentine-French, S., and Radtke, H. L. (1989). "Attributions of Responsibility for an Incident of Sexual Harassment in a University Setting," *Sex Roles* 21: 545–55.

Wagner, E. N. (1993). "Fantasies of True Love in Academe," *Chronicle of Higher Education*, 26: B1–3.

Wagner, K. (1990). "Prevention and Intervention: Developing Campus Policy and Procedures," *Journal of the National Association for Women Deans, Administrators, and Counselors* 52: 37–45.

Waxman, M. (1990). "Institutional Strategies for Dealing with Sexual Harassment," *Employee Responsibilities and Rights Journal* 3: 73–75.

Webb, S. L. (1991). "Step Forward: Sexual Harassment in the Workplace—What You Need to Know," *Master Media Limited*.

Weber-Burden, E., and Rossi, P. H. (1982). "Defining Sexual Harassment on Campus: A Replication and Extension," *Journal of Social Issues* 38: 111–20.

Weddle, C. J. (1992). "The Case for 'Structured Negotiation' in Sexual Misconduct Cases," *Synthesis Law and Policy in Higher Education* 4: 291–92.

Williams, E. A., Lam, J. A., and Shively, M. (1992). "The Impact of a University Policy on the Sexual Harassment of Female Students," *Journal of Higher Education* 63: 50–64.

Wilson, K. R., and Kraus, L. A. (1983). "Sexual Harassment in the University," *Journal of College Student Personnel* 24: 219–14.

Winks, P. L. (1982). "Legal Implications of Sexual Contact Between Teacher and Student," *Journal of Law and Education* 11: 437–78.

Wood, J. T. (1993). *Gendered Lives: Communication, Gender and Culture*. Belmont, Calif.: Wadsworth Publishing.

Wood, J. T. (1993). "Naming and Interpreting Sexual Harassment: A Conceptual Framework for Scholarship." In *Sexual Harassment: Communication Implications*, ed. G. L. Kreps. Cresskill, N.J.: Hampton Press.

Wood, J. T., and Lenze, L. F. (1991). "Strategies to Enhance Gender Sensitivity in Communication Education," *Communication Education* 40: 16–21.

York, K. M. (1989). "Defining Sexual Harassment in Workplaces: A Policy Capturing Approach," *Academy of Management Journal* 32: 830–50.

Zalk, R., Dedrich, J., and Paludi, M. A. (1991). "Women Students' Assessment of Consensual Relationships with Their Professors: Ivory Power Reconsidered." In *Academic and Workplace Sexual Harassment: A Resource Manual*, ed. M. A. Paludi and R. B. Barickman. Albany: State University of New York Press.

Zalk, S. R. (1990). "The Lecherous Professor: Psychological Profiles of Professors Who Harass Their Women Students." In *Ivory Power: Sexual Harassment on Campus*, ed. M. A. Paludi. Albany: State University of New York Press.

Index

Garland Studies in Higher Education

Philip G. Altbach, Series Editor

This series is published in cooperation with the
Program in Higher Education, School of Education,
Boston College, Chestnut Hill, Massachusetts.